REFLECTIVE HISTORY SERIES

Barbara Finkelstein and William J. Reese, Series Editors

Access to Success in the Urban High School:
The Middle College Movement
HAROLD S. WECHSLER

The Irony of School Reform:
Educational Innovation in Mid-Nineteenth
Century Massachusetts
MICHAEL B. KATZ

Curriculum & Consequence:
Herbert M. Kliebard and the Promise of Schooling
BARRY FRANKLIN, EDITOR

Schooled to Work:
Vocationalism and the American Curriculum,
1876–1946
HERBERT M. KLIEBARD

Moral Education in America:
Schools and the Shaping of Character
from Colonial Times to the Present
B. EDWARD MCCLELLAN

The Failed Promise of the
American High School, 1890–1995
DAVID L. ANGUS & JEFFREY E. MIREL

Access to Success in the Urban High School

THE MIDDLE COLLEGE MOVEMENT

HAROLD S. WECHSLER

Foreword by William J. Reese

TEACHERS COLLEGE PRESS

Teachers College, Columbia University
New York and London

Grateful acknowledgment is made to the Ford Foundation for support of this research.

Published by Teachers College Press, 1234 Amsterdam Avenue, New York, NY 10027

Library of Congress Cataloging-in-Publication Data

Wechsler, Harold S., 1946–
    Access to success in the urban high school : the middle college movement /
Harold S. Wechsler ; foreword by William J. Reese.
        p. cm. — (Reflective history series)
    Includes bibliographical references and index.
    ISBN 0-8077-4052-7 (cloth)
        1. College-school cooperation—United States—Case studies.   2. Urban
schools—United States—Case studies.   3. Alternative education—United
States—Case studies.   I. Title.   II. Series.
    LB2331.53 .W43 2001
    378.1'61—dc21   2001027494

ISBN 0-8077-4052-7 (cloth)

Printed on acid-free paper
Manufactured in the United States of America

08   07   06   05   04   03   02   01   8   7   6   5   4   3   2   1

For
Abigail Gordon Wechsler
and
Samuel Benjamin Wechsler

Contents

Foreword *by William J. Reese*   ix

Preface   xiii

Acknowledgments   xvii

1. Precedents and Influences   1

    Background: High School–College Relations   *1*
    The Rationales for Reorganization   *4*
    The 11–14 Idea in Practice   *12*
    Resurrecting the Vision   *16*
    Conclusion   *18*

2. Coming Together: Open Admissions and
    Philanthropy   20

    Access to Public Higher Education in New York City   *21*
    LaGuardia Community College   *23*
    The Designer and the Design   *27*
    An Elite School for At-Risk Students: The Components   *33*
    Who'll Run the School?   *44*
    Approval   *49*
    Conclusion   *51*

3. Living at the Border: Design and Implementation   53

    Middle College High School: The First Years   *54*
    The Greenberg Years: Academic Reform   *66*
    "Cece's" Era: "School Membership and Academic
        Engagement   *77*
    Conclusion   *89*

4. Replications   94

    The New York City Sites   *95*
    The Ford Foundation and the Reform of Urban Education   *98*
    Selecting the Inner Circle   *105*
    Five Successes   *108*
    Two Failures   *132*
    Conclusion   *135*

5. The Sum of the Parts   139

    Did It Work? Tales of the (Data)tape   *140*
    Adept Adaptation?   *142*
    Collaboration, Leveraging, and Normative Congruence   *149*
    Facilitating Transition   *158*
    Conclusion   *165*

    Notes   169
    References   173
    Index   193
    About the Author   206

Foreword

At the dawn of the 21st century, education remains a potent symbol of America's deepest fears and soaring aspirations. Despite a roaring economy, the collapse of the Soviet Union, and relative good times, complaints about the quality of education in the nation's schools have not dissipated since the early 1980s. In *A Nation at Risk* (National Commission on Excellence in Education, 1983), the most influential educational manifesto of the late 20th century, the Reagan administration blamed public schools for a declining economy, moral collapse, and overall weakening of the social order. In the post-Columbine era, other Jeremiahs have bemoaned the random outbreak of school violence, mediocre classroom performance, bureaucratic mindlessness, and related embarrassments in America's beleaguered schools. As markets have boomed and stock portfolios fattened, faith in private alternatives to the "public school monopoly" has rapidly accelerated.

Beneath the doom and gloom exists another America, more hopeful about public education and its promise. A substantial majority of Americans rate their own children's schools as very good—if imperfect and in need of various improvements. Many realize that schools even in impoverished areas are safer than the surrounding neighborhoods. Numerous citizens also think that doing well on standardized tests, however important, is not the sole purpose of attending school. Virtually everyone agrees that big-city schools need to do much better, that the good life otherwise will be unattainable for the inner-city poor. While their labors do not capture headlines, as does a bomb blast or a report on standardized test scores, many parents, educators, and reform-minded citizens continue to strive to make public schools more serviceable and effective.

Harold S. Wechsler's fascinating history of one such school innovation offers a particularly vivid reminder of the idealism that continues to inspire many contemporary school reformers. *Access to Success in the Urban High School* recounts the painstaking labors of those who have tried to educate a troubled segment of American youth: potential high school dropouts in the nation's largest cities. These reformers have largely rejected the usual explanations of school failure: that the poor suffer from a "culture of poverty," or are genetically inferior, or some combination of the two. Rather, they have tried to create new institutional spaces for those who reach late adolescence yet appear destined to leave school prematurely, cutting them off from access to opportunity and further education. Instead of simply blaming traditional high schools and higher education for this problem, these educators have worked positively to find a way to reach and serve those currently falling through several institutional cracks.

Concern with "at-risk" students has been commonplace among the nation's educators during the past generation. By the late 1960s, many citizens realized that comprehensive high schools—first created in the early 20th century—were ineffective in the lives of many urban youth. Educators earlier might have complained about high dropout rates, but the military and blue-collar jobs absorbed those who failed to receive a sheepskin, either at high school or college. The fading of the Industrial Revolution in America, however, meant that the personal and social costs of low educational attainment became much higher after mid-century. Once college attendance became the norm for White middle-class families, high dropout rates for African-American, Hispanic, and other poor students increasingly gained national attention.

As Wechsler makes clear, by the late 1960s youth who approached late adolescence and appeared on the verge of leaving school often had few places to turn, educationally speaking. High schools soon were expected to hold all students accountable for higher levels of academic achievement, even those who traditionally left early to work or fight for their country, as the working classes, notably still, did in Vietnam. Community colleges, growing by leaps and bounds by the 1960s, worked to differentiate themselves from high schools, which in turn were understandably sensitive to mounting criticisms of their failure to educate the poor well.

Several times in the 20th century, reformers urged the nation's educators to shorten the length of high school and to accelerate the path to college. Few school or college administrators listened, and most experiments in those directions were short-lived. So it was noteworthy when something special happened in New York City, then in the throes of major debates about the quality of its public schools and Open Admissions policies in its public universities. The year was 1974. Middle College High School opened at the relatively new Fiorello H. LaGuardia Community College in Queens. Its clientele were "at-risk," poor students, in late adolescence, fitting the profile of the countless who came before them and dropped out of school. Compared with other alternative high schools in New York, the new place of learning would yield much more academic success for those otherwise likely to leave school. Graduation rates were relatively high, and educators demonstrated new ways to make education effective.

Wechsler's compelling narrative of the rise of the middle college at LaGuardia, and attempts to replicate it in many urban areas across the nation, rests upon the author's unparalleled knowledge of high school and college relations since the 19th century. His impressive mastery of the history of admission practices adds a perspective rare in modern policy analyses. In addition, *Access to Success in the Urban High School: The Middle College Movement* is unusually clear in explaining how institutions work, and especially how certain individuals can seize the right opportunity to bend them for good ends. In a fundamental way, this volume reflects the author's deep moral passion and sense of fair play about who gains access to and benefits from America's schools and colleges. Without new institutional arrangements, he warns, the nation's highest democratic aspirations will be trampled and placed at risk in the coming generation.

William J. Reese
Madison, Wisconsin

Preface

Access to Success in the Urban High School: The Middle College Movement picks up where my book, *The Qualified Student* (1977), left off. That study pondered the ironies in the process of admitting students to college, especially to "selective" colleges—a term whose meaning expanded substantially during the 20th century to include social class, racial, ethnic, as well as academic criteria.

The final chapter of *The Qualified Student* discussed the late 1960s controversy over using admissions criteria designed to increase the number of racial and ethnic minority students at the City University of New York (CUNY), New York City's system of public two- and four-year colleges. CUNY's exclusive reliance on high school grades and SAT scores had produced entering classes of able, largely White, working- and middle-class students. But educating the next generation of New York City students—given the city's changed demographics and weakened public high school system—led CUNY officials to increase the use of "nontraditional" admissions criteria favoring minority students. Confronted with an April 1969 sit-in at Manhattan's City College by minority students demanding widened access, and by counterprotests reaffirming admissions criteria favoring the university's traditional constituency, CUNY staff decided to offer admission to all New York City high school graduates.

Open Admissions—a political solution to a political problem—required a formerly selective public college system to change the ways it educated its students. Could CUNY, observers asked, effectively educate a racially and ethnically heterogeneous population, including many students whose "general" diplomas suggested inadequate preparation? The answer depended heavily on CUNY's nine two-year colleges, including Fiorello H. LaGuardia Community College, opened in 1971, a year after the first Open Admissions class matriculated. Situated in a commercial section of Long Island City, in western Queens, and surrounded by ethnic neighborhoods, LaGuardia admitted and educated many White, African-American, and Hispanic working-class students who would not have gained admission to CUNY before Open Admissions.

LaGuardia's teaching and administrative staff attested to a spirit of commitment and excitement at the outset; a quarter century later the community college retained its reputation as an academic innovator. But, CUNY officials argued, the university's commitment to Open Admissions required commensurate innovation on the precollegiate level. Could LaGuardia help to prepare New York City secondary school students to take advantage of increased higher education opportunity? Staff at the community college responded by proposing a "middle college" that integrated at-risk high school students with college students from similar backgrounds. *Access to Success in the Urban High School* tells the story of Middle College High School—its design, growth, and replication.

Chapter 1 relates the history of moves to integrate high school and college; the rationales for this reform offered by administrators, curriculum reformers, and psychologists; and the reasons why prior to the 1970s the movement was confined to a handful of two-year and independent colleges.

Chapter 2 shows how LaGuardia staff attempted to realize the goals of Open Admissions by adapting an innovation heretofore aimed at able students to the needs of their at-risk peers. At-risk high school students, designers agreed, would profit from a less-restricted collegiate environment, access to LaGuardia's curriculum and extracurriculum, and the influence of older students who overcame similar obstacles. Secondary-level students could accelerate their postsecondary studies by enrolling in—and receiving college credit for—LaGuardia's college courses. Conversely, student success at the secondary level would reduce the need for postsecondary-level developmental courses.

But location, environment, and integration were not enough; the school would directly address the academic, vocational, and affective needs of its students. The curriculum would feature interdisciplinary courses, extend LaGuardia's signature cooperative education program—with alternating periods of work and classroom attendance—to the secondary level, and keep small groups of students together in a "house" for counseling and guidance throughout their tenure at the school. Teacher-counselors—subject teachers selected for their commitment to at-risk students and specially trained to cultivate their affective development—would guide their houses across several years. Collaboration between middle college and LaGuardia faculty and staff would sustain and enrich students' education and development.

Chapter 2 then traces the process by which LaGuardia staff obtained city and state approvals for a grade-integrated school located at a community college with no prior administrative relationship with the city's public schools. No small task; it took almost a year, for example, to determine whether a unit of CUNY could even run a secondary school. The two-year approval process forced a year's postponement in opening the school and required LaGuardia to agree to open the school as an "alternative" high school under the jurisdiction of the New York City Board of Education.

Chapter 3 tells how LaGuardia and Middle College High School (MCHS)—the school's official name after its 1974 opening—grew up together, overcoming internal resistance, jurisdictional questions, and opposition by local high school principals. The design took time to implement, and not all components were successfully realized. But the school adopted most key elements; each of the four principals who nurtured its growth during the first quarter century emphasized different components. MCHS and LaGuardia faculty and staff gave the school time to learn how to "live at the border." Two physical moves and several curricular revisions later, MCHS showed a substantial graduation rate, often accompanied by the accumulation of college credits, among students who likely would never have finished 10th grade in a comprehensive New York City high school.

Chapter 4 discusses attempts at replicating the school. By the late 1980s, concepts developed at MCHS entered the national discourse on school reform, a visitor influx often disrupted the school's routine, and replications appeared in New York City and at other community colleges. These schools were located at older community colleges with less available space, less administrative flexibility, more resistance from community college faculty members, and more scrutiny from school districts having to pay heed but reluctant to ask why a replication succeeded where traditional high schools failed. Success depended on the proficiency of faculty and administrators committed to the design—and on political acumen.

Chapter 5 places the middle college movement in the context of current attempts by educators and policy-makers to rethink, yet again, the transition between high school and college. Growing cohorts of late adolescents, growth in the number of advanced placement (AP) exams administered and in high school–college dual enrollment plans, and the prospect of a 14-year educational norm—a goal that looked attainable as two-year college enrollments topped 5 million in the 1990s—portended further changes in high school–college relations.

Community colleges, often pressured to reduce or terminate developmental education, may want to—or have to—help prepare an academically at-risk to average, socially diverse high school student population. *Access to Success in the Urban High School: The Middle College Movement* shows the problems and opportunities attendant on adapting innovations aimed at academically and socially elite students to this population.

Acknowledgments

Ford Foundation's L. Steven Zwerling commissioned this study, although neither of us anticipated a book-length manuscript. I'm grateful to Steve for his strong support and for his patience. Thanks also to Alison Bernstein, director of Ford's Education and Culture division, and to Hedy Rema and Kathy Donovan.

I first met Janet Lieberman, the designer of Middle College High School at LaGuardia, at a 1988 conference on *Exploring Transfer*, another Lieberman-designed, Ford-sponsored initiative, aimed at facilitating minority student transfer between two- and four-year colleges. Janet later invited me to participate in the activities of the Pew Center for At-Risk Students and to evaluate the replications of *Exploring Transfer*. She provided me full access to her files and spent many hours discussing the grand design and subtle nuances of Middle College High School at LaGuardia and the educational and political aspects of replicating the innovation. Janet has remained a supportive friend and astute critic. Thanks also to Janet's assistants for their support.

Arthur Greenberg and Cecilia Cunningham, principals of MCHS at LaGuardia, sat for lengthy interviews, responded to many research requests, and provided many leads and insights.[1] Students, faculty, and staff at LaGuardia's MCHS and at its replications provided access and enthusiasm. Natalee Battersbee and Myra Silverman, principals of replications in Los Angeles and Richmond, California, respectively, indulged me in requests for follow-up interviews.

Julie Y. Hungar and I engaged in an extended dialogue on the politics of coalition building throughout the writing of this book. The commitment of Sonny Byers, my host at Seattle Central Community College, to his students and colleagues symbolizes the best of the middle college movement. Special thanks to the students at the school who permitted me to attend a group counseling meeting, the first visitor granted this privilege.

Sandra Ingram and Ingrid Overacker, former students at the University of Rochester, were painstaking research assistants and archivists for this project. Special thanks to Robert Pedersen, a friend and colleague for 30 years and an authority on community colleges, for his good-humored encouragement and critiques. Thanks also to Elizabeth Demarest, Richard Donovan, Kevin Dougherty, Linda Eisenmann, Deborah Gardner, Floyd Hammack, Elizabeth Hawthorne, David Lavin, Howard London, Amaury Nora, James Palmer, Laura Rendon, James Rosenbaum, Carol Schneider, Carol Stoel, and James R. Valadez; to colleagues in the Ford Foundation's Urban Partnerships Program; and to community college faculty and staff members of the National Education Association for many discussions and suggestions. The special collections librarians at City University of New York, Columbia University, and LaGuardia Community College provided me with important archival materials.

In Rochester, thanks to Carol Adams, Floyd Amann (now president of Corning Community College), Christopher Belle-Isle, and Peter Spina, former president of Monroe Community College, and to Ruth Danis, Manuel Fernandez, and Jean Slattery of the Rochester City School District for their insights and for access to their deliberations. Also thanks to my faculty colleagues at the Margaret S. Warner Graduate School of Education and Human Development, and to students in EDU 494, *The American Community College*, whose academic and professional insights into the politics of collaboration strengthened many sections of this book.

Access to Success in the Urban High School: The Middle College Movement appears in the *Reflective History Series*, published by Teachers College Press. Thanks to series editors Barbara Finkelstein and William J. Reese for adding this book to that fine series. Thanks also to Brian Ellerbeck, Carole Saltz, Karl Nyberg, Myra Cleary, and Wendy Schwartz of Teachers College Press for their professionalism and encouragement, and for allowing me to continue a cherished relationship with Teachers College that started when I was a Columbia College undergraduate.

By coincidence, I was an adjunct faculty member at LaGuardia just as Middle College High School opened in 1974. My class included immigrant, African-American, and Hispanic students, veterans, unemployed workers, working mothers, and vocational and liberal arts majors. I did not know about the high school located across the street, but, like its faculty, I enjoyed teaching a heterogeneous class at a new community college located in a converted factory building two blocks from the IRT subway Flushing line.

Most authors reserve the end of their acknowledgments for their families; this expression of thanks to Lynn, Abby, and Sam comes as we emerge from a difficult period. I hope they enjoy this book and see that writing it was an important part of my dealing with the past few years.

Rochester, New York
September 22, 2000

Precedents and Influences

*Like the Basques, a minority in two different lands whose
common border they straddle, late adolescents in America
have no homeland of their own, no institutions with edges,
staffs, and missions congruent to their needs.*
                    —Four-School Study Committee (1970, p. 16)

Could a "middle college"—a school that integrated grades 10–14—
increase the college-going rate for an at-risk population? Could it transcend
the many academic and administrative boundaries between compulsory
secondary education and volitional higher education? Believing the historical moment was ripe, the designers of Middle College High School at
Fiorello H. LaGuardia Community College, in Long Island City, Queens,
New York, said yes.

The design for this school rejected the conventional wisdom of the
1960s—reliance on compensatory education programs targeting resources
into elementary schools with large numbers of at-risk students (Cohen,
1972). This strategy, concluded Janet Lieberman, the school's chief archi-
tect, and LaGuardia Community College founding president Joseph
Shenker, did not address the critical problem: changing the structure and
organization of public schooling to serve the academic and developmental
needs of *late adolescent* at-risk students. Instead, Lieberman and her colleagues proposed to increase the rate of college attendance for at-risk students by adapting practices established for other groups: college work
while in high school, affective support, and cooperative education—alternating periods of academic studies and supervised on-the-job experience.
The soil nurturing Lieberman's design contained deep roots.

BACKGROUND: HIGH SCHOOL–COLLEGE RELATIONS

Middle College designers cited a history of proposals—some implemented,
some not; some successful, some less so—to bridge the academic divide at

the point where education ceased to be compulsory. Many students did not enter college, asserted critics of early 20th-century college admissions policies, because of poor articulation—ensuring that the college picked up a subject where the high school left off. Observers attributed this condition to the development of high schools *after* elementary *and* collegiate education (Hampel, 1993; Krug, 1969; Wechsler, 1977).

Nineteenth-century educational institutions saw little need for articulation. Tuition-dependent private academies, offering most secondary education, often competed with neighboring public grammar schools and with colleges. In turn, many colleges, in lieu of feeder schools, established campus-based preparatory departments—often larger than their collegiate departments—to ensure a flow of students with acceptable entrance credentials. Public high schools, when they existed, provided terminal education for most students. Articulation with the entrance requirements of nearby colleges had a lower priority than articulation with their grammar school feeders, and articulation with remote colleges had little priority at all. Until the 1890s, few states had "systems" by which students might undertake a four-year public high school course, continue sequential work in a four-year college, and receive a baccalaureate.

Sustained growth of secondary education, beginning in the late 19th-century, led college reformers to question continued reliance on preparatory departments. Communities and states would amply reward colleges with aspirations to growth, reformers argued, if they closed these departments and articulated their entrance requirements with the courses offered by public high schools. Colleges also would recruit students from a larger area, free their faculty members to teach college—not preparatory—courses, and admit an older, presumably more mature student body. Late 19th-century changes in entrance requirements at Harvard, for example, raised the average age of entrance by a year. Greater maturity, the reformers added, would reduce a major academic preoccupation: the need to supervise and discipline students (Krug, 1969; Reese, 1995).

Strengthening high schools—and colleges—via collaboration on entrance requirements, reformers claimed, required colleges to demonstrate flexibility when discussing articulation and to reduce the number of students admitted conditionally—without completing all high school subjects required for admission. Reformers found an audience—most colleges, for example, had preparatory departments in 1870; few did in 1920, although colleges for African-Americans, Catholics, and women often delayed closure, citing the lack of alternatives.

Discussions of entrance requirement articulation focused on the lack of uniformity among colleges. High schools, principals argued, had to allocate most of their resources to terminal students, the majority. Preparing the college-bound minority for idiosyncratic, although often similar, entrance requirements was not feasible. Obtaining cooperation from high schools, the principals added, required that colleges cease to specify their own entrance requirements and recognize more subjects in the high school curriculum as acceptable for admission.

Beginning in the 1880s, secondary school and college officials met often to identify respective responsibilities for instruction in many subjects. Successful delineation, reformers believed, might lead to uniform college entrance requirements and examinations. The reformers succeeded; the report of the so-called Committee of Ten (National Education Association, 1893) promoted a national dialogue on the contents of the high school curriculum; seven years later the College Entrance Examination Board was founded to offer uniform exams based on negotiated requirements. After 1905, the Carnegie Foundation for the Advancement of Teaching used the institutional eligibility criteria for awarding faculty pensions to specify minimal academic criteria for high schools and colleges; future generations saw the Carnegie units, and accreditation policies based on these units, as helping to set academic boundaries.

Considerable standardization resulted from several decades of work, and entrusting college preparation to high schools helped to increase higher education enrollments. But by World War I mutual dissatisfaction ended most collaboration. Secondary school educators focused on the rapidly increasing numbers of terminal students—public high school enrollments doubled each decade between 1900 and 1940. These educators objected to offering college preparatory courses to proportionately fewer students. Some college officials responded by adding vocational courses to the list of acceptable entrance subjects, usually by increasing the permissible number of "electives." But complaints about "oppressive" college entrance requirements continued; the *Cardinal Principles of Education*, issued by the National Education Association in 1918, gave no primacy to the high school's academic mission, much less to college preparation (Duffus, 1936; Learned & Wood, 1938; Wechsler, 1977). The Eight-Year Study—an ambitious secondary school curricular experiment conducted during the 1930s—promoted a "democratic way of life" over subject mastery; participating colleges accepted high school certification in lieu of all entrance subjects (Aikin, 1942; Krug, 1972; Tyack & Cuban, 1995).

By the 1920s, some college representatives concluded that entrance requirement liberalization had gone too far and that too many socially and academically undesirable students had enrolled in college. Declaring key articulation issues resolved, these administrators concluded that, when possible, colleges must place their own interests first. "Selective" colleges used internally established criteria to choose a class from the pool of students with the appropriate high school credentials. Admissions tests that predicted future academic performance by measuring "intelligence" or "aptitude" enabled colleges to reduce emphasis on assessing knowledge acquired in high school. These colleges also required candidates to provide information about social background, including race and religion (Wechsler, 1977).

As high schools and colleges went their separate ways, colleges offered more basic instruction. Articulation meant little if a student did not study a subject in high school—a frequent occurrence as prescribed work declined—or if students repeated high school work in college. A 1925 study, for example, estimated a 14.9% rate of repetition between high school and college work (Koos, 1925). Further, many colleges continued to admit "on condition" students who failed one or more subjects or came from high schools that offered inadequate college preparation. These students made up missing work at a local high school or on campus. Selective colleges reduced or eliminated conditional admission, but other colleges continued the practice under different names, thereby reconciling the desirable and the possible.

Communication and cooperation between high schools and colleges became sporadic and formal between the world wars. Fixing a boundary between high school and college appeared elusive, impractical, or undesirable given the academic heterogeneity of the student population. But, asked some reformers, instead of conceding defeat, why not remove the boundary and group late adolescents in the same institution?

THE RATIONALES FOR REORGANIZATION

Little noticed among the growing number of terminal students, some early 20th-century high schools began to offer college-grade courses and "joint enrollment postgraduate programs." These programs—growing to enroll about 70,000 students by 1930—permitted students to begin college work in a familiar setting, thus delaying or avoiding enrollment at remote institutions. Observers could not generalize about the number, quality, or level of courses, tuition charges, or postgraduate extracurricular participation. But these programs often evolved into public junior colleges when enrollments attained a critical mass and when the sponsoring community made the necessary financial commitment. Between 1900 and 1940, notes one estimate, 278 public junior colleges opened; 75 were discontinued (Pedersen, 2000).

Beginning in the 1920s, some jurisdictions—including districts with postgraduate programs and junior colleges—moved to integrate 11th and

12th grades with the first years of college (Eby, 1928, 1932; Wilson, 1939). Pasadena Junior College (PJC) received the nod as the first combined *public* institution to demonstrate long-term survival. Sharing a plant and principal with Pasadena High School from its 1924 founding, the junior college and the high school merged in 1928 into a single institution covering grades 11–14; the district's junior high schools covered grades 7–10 (Harbeson, 1928, 1931, 1940; Sexton & Harbeson, 1946).

PJC offered "integrated," four-year college preparatory, terminal, and vocational courses, including engineering and business. But consistent with its self-image as a capstone unit of secondary education, the college classified at least half the 11th- and 12th-grade courses taken by all students as "general" or nonvocational. This classification, argued advocates for four-year junior colleges, freed up the 13th and 14th years for vocational education. Two-year junior colleges, in contrast, were forced to emphasize general education, sometimes pushing vocational studies into an undesirable third year (Harbeson, 1940).

Guidance counselors closely supervised 11th-grade students and remained close to these students in subsequent years. Guidance, argued advocates of the "6-4-4 plan," was more effective when a counselor got to know a student over a sustained period, permitting the formulation and attainment of educational and vocational objectives. PJC 11th graders received *more* supervision than high school peers. "It is a big leap from the tenth grade to a college situation," wrote the school's principal. Control mechanisms included study halls, calling home when a student was absent, prohibiting fraternity membership, and immediate counselor appointments when academic problems arose (Harbeson, 1940). Successful 11th graders received "the full freedom of a college situation" in 12th grade, including membership in sanctioned "clubs" that substituted for fraternities and sororities. "His classes are organized on a college schedule, his time is his own, he joins the college organizations, he may play on varsity teams and enroll in college courses for which on transfer to the university he is granted degree credit" (Harbeson, 1940, p. 99; see also Harbeson, 1931).

The Pasadena experiment set off a debate among observers of junior colleges on the merits of integrating high school and college. Advocates— deeming academically able 16- to 20-year-olds educationally homogeneous—argued that the "artificial" division between high school and college at the end of 12th grade denied many students an opportunity for postsecondary education and permitted unnecessary duplication in high school and college offerings. Agreeing that schools covering grades 11–14 would increase student access to college-level work, proponents offered structural, curricular, and developmental rationales for realignment.

Structural Justifications

Perhaps the majority of advocates offered a structural rationale. Grade realignment, reformers argued, would attract students who otherwise might bypass the liberal arts college to enter a professional program directly from high school. Normal schools remained at the high school level for up to two decades into the 20th century. Many early-20th-century law and theological schools directly competed with liberal arts colleges, and few medical schools required two years of college for admission before 1915.

Advocates saw a grades 11–14 school as a viable link between secondary and professional (and graduate) education. The growth of the high school and the move to standardize college work, wrote Leonard Koos, a University of Chicago professor of education and a proponent of a 6-4-4 public education system, had raised the age of college entrance by perhaps two years, thereby arbitrarily forcing apart the satisfactory grouping of 16- to 20-year-olds in college. Standardizing college entrance requirements and examinations, he added, neither achieved administrative coordination nor reversed the (undesirable) trend toward a prolonged education. The normative gap between secondary schools and four-year colleges, he insisted, had become virtually unbridgeable (Koos, 1949).

In contrast, a grades 11–14 school that bridged the shorter academic and social distance between high school and junior college would produce curricular and administrative unity. Students, Koos wrote, could obtain a general or liberal education and then proceed directly to the many professional schools that had raised their entrance requirements to the equivalent of two years of college. Such a school might move some articulation questions to the divide between 10th and 11th grades, but coordination on that level, Koos argued, could build upon many years of secondary-level curricular reform efforts.

The writings of Koos influenced members of the President's Commission on Higher Education (1947), advocates of expanded postsecondary education opportunities and proponents of plans to eliminate curricular gaps and overlaps. "The academic work of the last 2 years of the high school and that of the first 2 years of the typical liberal arts college are essentially identical in purpose," asserted the commission's report. "Therefore, to have half of this 4-year period administered by the high schools, under one system of controls, and the other half administered by the colleges, under another system of controls, constantly raises many serious questions" (vol. 3, pp. 12–13).

Inadequate planning for students who terminated their education after 14th grade, the report argued, resulted in curricular waste. The report cited the research of Koos, suggesting that attending four-year junior colleges resulted in more curricular flexibility, reduced duplication of coursework, fewer sign-ups for questionable course sequences, and more enrollments in commendable sequences—the President's Commission (1947) lauded courses that transmitted "a common cultural heritage toward a common citizenship" prior to specialization (p. 1:49; see also Blanchard, 1971; Koos, 1949).

Integration, added advocates, also would yield substantial time savings, especially in a general education sequence. Koos urged junior colleges to award the baccalaureate—the recognized symbol for completing a general education—since recipients then could move to three-year graduate and professional programs requiring two years of college. The advantages, he added, outweighed the admitted problems: confusion, a threat to weak independent colleges, and the lack of an accepted general education curriculum (Koos, 1949). Other advocates emphasized educational enrichment; eliminating duplication permitted students to enroll in additional courses.

Structural reformers also advanced an economic rationale: Four-year, grades 11–14 schools permitted savings in capital construction and housing, and in maintenance and operation. The cost per student, Koos conceded, depended more on school size than on organization. But unified administrative and supervisory responsibility and integrated use of plant and facilities, he argued, meant fewer administrators and fewer sites, giving the four-year junior college a strong economic advantage over separate schools (Koos, 1949). An integrated unit, Koos added, gave students in grades 13–14 access to specialized facilities, including laboratories, that many separate junior colleges lacked, and reduced redundancy in library book collections. The success of the movement, Koos noted, depended on these "substantial" financial advantages, which would exert more influence on school board and public officials than would the academic advantages.

Last, advocates argued, the 6-4-4 plan would ensure the success of the junior high school. Four-year junior high schools, argued Koos, were more respected than schools with shorter curricula and were far superior to the traditional 8-4 plan. These schools, he added, displayed greater program breadth, student maturity, and staff preparation and ability, and superior facilities (Koos, 1949).

Advocates of the 6-4-4 plan supplied a string of endorsements. "I am looking forward," wrote Stanford University president David Starr Jordan, "to the time when the large high schools of the state in conjunction with the small colleges will relieve the two great universities from the expense and from the necessity of giving instruction of the first two university years." Jordan added: "The instruction of these two years is of necessity elementary and of the same general nature as the work of the high school itself" (quoted in McLane, 1913, pp. 166–167).

George A. Merrill, a California vocational educator often considered the first 6-4-4 advocate, based his views on dropout patterns—large cohorts of students in the state left school after 6th and 10th grades. Ending grammar school after 6th grade freed up the next four grades for general education; grades 11–14—which covered the same age range as typical apprenticeship programs outside schools—were ideal for vocational courses (Cooke, 1931). Most discussions of the 6-4-4 plan did not single out vocational education, but some argued that the plan would facilitate education for the "semi-professions" (Cooper, 1929; Leonard, 1925; National Education Association, 1929).

Curricular Justifications

Other advocates of integration offered curricular justifications (Cooper, 1929). A curricular rationale appeared most prominently in the plan for undergraduate education proposed by University of Chicago president Robert M. Hutchins in the 1930s. Arguing that the university's feeders failed to prepare students for Chicago-style higher education, faculty members had devised a required general education college-level curriculum during the late 1920s and early 1930s. This curriculum included three-year courses in the humanities, natural sciences, and social sciences, and in reading, writing, and criticism; a one-year integrative course; and two elective departmental courses. A later modification permitted substitution of additional electives for some required coursework.

Building on these reforms, Hutchins (1936) pushed for opening the undergraduate college to students completing the sophomore year of high school and awarding the baccalaureate after completion of the general education program four years later. This proposal met resistance from faculty members who did not wish to teach on the "secondary" level or who did not agree with the content of the curriculum. Its approval in principle (1932) therefore came years before its implementation (1937). Even then, the grades 11–14 unit did not replace the existing college; it remained a special program comprising largely students at the affiliated University High School. Only in 1942, when the pressures of war forced educators to accelerate postsecondary education, could Hutchins merge the two undergraduate programs and obtain faculty permission to award the baccalaureate upon completion of the general education course (Dzuback, 1991; Wechsler, 1977). Seniors could enroll simultaneously in the college and in the university's upper divisions. Not all proponents of an integrated grades 11–14 school advocated awarding a bachelor's degree upon completion of the sophomore year of college. But those, like Koos, who did, often seconded Hutchins's belief in a liberal education as the best preparation for all students, not only those continuing to university studies (Koos, 1949).

But this belief came at a price. Reformers were united in denouncing curricular duplication, but difficulties in obtaining consensus on the content of the general education curriculum made the concept vulnerable. The Chicago college reverted to admitting high school graduates after 1953, two years after Hutchins moved to the Ford Foundation. The general education courses gave way to a more conventional array of core courses, followed (in 1957) by a departmental major. But the experiment left a dual legacy. First, Hutchins brought Clarence Faust and F. Champion Ward, two former deans of the college, to the Fund for the Advancement of Education (FAE), Ford's subsidiary for educational reform. While at FAE, these officers continued to promote shortened programs of study and reformed undergraduate liberal education. The Chicago experiment was also a concrete, frequently discussed, if not always understood, challenge to the academic disciplines and to the structure of secondary and higher education. The ethos created by these curricular experimenters stimulated designers and funders of the middle college movement a generation later.

Developmental Justifications

The developmental rationale for grouping the latter years of high school and the first years of college is traceable to late-19th-century theorists, such as Clark University president and psychologist G. Stanley Hall. Hall posited "a real and not a merely theoretical break or transition in the intellectual development of a youth and in his appropriate studies at about the time which is marked in the United States by the completion of the second or sophomore year of college work" (Butler, 1939, p. 1:146). At that point, argued developmental theorists, students became more capable of abstract (university) work.

James Rowland Angell, dean of the college of the University of Chicago during the 1910s, and later president of Yale, saw age 20 as an upper limit for a collegiate education. Attempts to break down boundaries between secondary education and college, he argued, were motivated by a conviction that the move between high school and college marked no real educational transition and that "most of our Freshman work and much of our Sophomore work is purely secondary in character, whereas there is a period some time toward the end of the second college year where a genuine transition does occur in the case of a very large proportion of the students in all stronger colleges and universities." American practice, he added, "is widely at variance with continental usages" (Angell, 1915, p. 84).

Later justifications for a four-year intermediate institution also drew upon psychological theory. "Middle adolescence," wrote a reformer in 1929, "is the age of great decisions." "The deepest decisions of life are confronted at this era," he added, "and permanent choices are made which determine the future and affect every feature of the rapidly congealing personality." Nearly all youth, he wrote, "settle at this stage their life-attitude in regard to religious beliefs and practices." During middle adolescence youth evinced the highest ideals, formed the deepest, most enduring friendships, and developed their intelligence. "For all normal individuals," he noted, "the mating instinct with its secondary and associated phenomena begins to dominate the mind and will." During this period, "above all others . . . the main feature of personality, the lifelong habits of thought and action, are determined." "A final decision of vocation is made, and the life career motive becomes the impelling force" (Eby, 1929, p. 36). "If a single school unit with a trained staff could deal with this period of life," echoed U.S. Commissioner of Education William J. Cooper (1929), lending the weight of his office to the 6-4-4 plan, "most beneficial results might be expected" (p. 340).

A generation later, Ralph Tyler, chair of the Department of Education at the University of Chicago in the early 1940s, wrote, "So far as the biological and mental equipment is concerned, there is considerable evidence that a degree of maturity is reached somewhere between age 14 and 16 that should make successful college work quite possible" (Koos, 1949, p. 83; see also National Society for the Study of Education, 1944).[1] Allied with the plans of Hutchins to reform general education, Tyler added: "Although mental growth is not stopped even at 24, the growth curves flatten out typically between age 15 and 16, so that most young people of this age have 90 percent of the mental abilities characteristic of adults." Mental growth, Tyler noted, then depended largely on the degree of intellectual stimulation experienced by the student (quoted in Koos, 1949, p. 84).

During the 1950s and 1960s, Nevitt Sanford and Erik H. Erikson analyzed academically able college students who often demanded curricular "relevance." These students, the psychologists noted, often showed mental maturation, but neither their egos—in the Freudian sense—nor their life plans showed similar development (Blos, 1966; Erikson, 1963; Group for the Advancement of Psychiatry, 1968). Late adolescents, they added, therefore required four years of emotional nurture—a need for "a sense of personal identity, of achievement, and of self-esteem, and their thirst for tentative, yet real, engagements in the adult world" (Four-School Study Committee, 1970, p. 10).

Sanford identified a "late adolescent" stage, associated with ages 17–18, and characteristic of freshman-year college students. "High school students and college sophomores as well as freshmen may be in this stage," he noted, "and it may be that not all juniors and seniors have passed beyond it." But, he added, "the freshman seems more likely to be in this stage than do the other categories of older and younger people" (Sanford, 1962, p. 260). College recognition of this stage, Sanford added, would help students to resolve related developmental issues.

The headmasters of four elite, residential preparatory schools, collectively known as the Four-School Study Committee (1970), invoked Sanford and Erikson in calling for a more activist—"touching real life"—less discipline-oriented, general education program emphasizing personal growth.[2] Students, concurred these authors, "no longer come to college to become socialites or scholars but rather to discover 'a viable relationship between knowledge and action, between the questions asked in the classroom and the lives they lead outside it'" (pp. 10, 16).

The Middle College proposal frequently cited *16–20: The Liberal Education of an Age Group* (1970), the report of the Four-School Study Committee—especially the committee's call for a single institution for late adolescents, offering a multidisciplinary, liberal curriculum leading to the baccalaureate degree. Bringing students "to a more direct confrontation with their world than traditional training in the disciplines can provide," the school would prepare students to enter "more focused, action-oriented master's programs aimed at preparing them for their first careers" (Four-School Study Committee, 1970, pp. 99, 101; see also Jencks & Riesman, 1962, 1968). Adherents of the developmental rationale for an intermediate school failed to agree on a designation: Angell, for example, called for a secondary institution; Tyler, for a college.

The Hall-inspired "saltatory" theory—that "there are certain periods when sudden and profound mental, physical, and social changes occur"— had its early detractors (Eells, 1931b, p. 311; see also Eells, 1931a). E. L. Thorndike's contrasting theory of gradual development, wrote one critic in 1930, "shows that these periods are not radically different and distinctly separable from those immediately preceding or immediately following." Seeing the junior college as a "completion unit of secondary education, designed to fit the period of later adolescence," this critic added, "involves more than the mere mechanical readjustment of administrative machinery" (Campbell, 1930, p. 74). Walter Crosby Eells (1931b), a Stanford professor of education, dismissed Hall's theory "as having little if any bearing on the question of the relative merits of the two-year or four-year junior college" (p. 313). Administrators as easily might use a stage theory to justify the ascendant pattern: a distribution requirement completed in the first two years of college, followed by a major—both completed in the same institution (Veysey, 1973).

Ignoring the existence of stages was perilous, advocates replied. Nevitt Sanford (1962) called for cultural acceptance of "the concepts of the developer and of stages of development" and for social acceptance of the role of student. This acceptance, he added, would allow students to "comfortably and more profitably *be* what they are—developing persons." But this role, Sanford concluded, "goes against a strong trend in American culture, which is to smudge the boundaries between developmental stages and permit younger people to define themselves as miniatures of older people—for example, social dancing at age 10, beer and a high-powered car at 16" (p. 282).

Sanford did not challenge existing organizational arrangements. The traditional four years of college, he wrote, could nurture the transition to adulthood. College permitted a student to turn from the internal issues of late adolescence to the issues of defining a role in the larger world: "The maximum crisis of adolescence is over, and controlling mechanisms are again in ascendancy." The controls, he added, "are likely to operate in a rigid manner . . . nevertheless impulses are now inhibited or contained with sufficient effectiveness so that the young person can turn his attention to . . . his relations with the external world—to improve his understanding of that world and find a place within it" (Sanford, 1962, p. 260).

"The problem for the student," Sanford noted, "is how to wait; how to tolerate ambiguity and open-endedness in himself while he is preparing for adult roles." He continued: "He is constantly tempted . . . to take shortcuts to maturity, neglecting the paths to full development by imitating adult behavior and prematurely defining himself in terms of future social roles." Colleges, Sanford suggested, should be guided by developmental theory and should make extra efforts "to make the concept of person-in-transition available to the student as a meaningful self-conception." They should help students find their places in the world, instead of isolating students within a stage. A stage, he concluded, "should include a clear statement about its termination" lest students remain indefinitely in a "socially acceptable and personally satisfying" stage. Student success in facing "the realities of poststudent life" depended more "on the education they acquired in the student stage than their ability to adapt to student life" (Sanford, 1962, pp. 281–282).

THE 11–14 IDEA IN PRACTICE

The 11–14 debate rarely got to the point of empirical validation; few colleges accepted students without a high school diploma or based their curricula on a developmental theory. Arguments for "early colleges" based on contested psychological stage theories fell victim to organizational imperatives. Many developers of two-year colleges, wrote J. B. Lillard (1930), gave primacy to internal, not structural, issues, such as developing a curriculum, a counseling program, and support services, and recruiting "types of teachers who understand young men and women" (p. 264).

The movement converted only a few two-year districts and independent colleges. A generation after Pasadena Junior College opened, Koos (1949) identified only 32 viable grades 11–14 schools: 22 independent four-year junior colleges—most students, Koos noted, enrolled in the third (college-freshman) year—and ten public, four-year junior colleges, spread over five states (Diener, 1986). This minimal rate of growth failed to convince skeptics that the obstacles to a 6-4-4 system could or should be overcome.

Despite a nod to the 6-4-4 system, the President's Commission saw the two-year college as the preferred mode of educational expansion; it did not recommend the substantial restructuring necessary to bring grades 11–14 under one jurisdiction. Robert M. Hutchins (1936) may have believed that public junior colleges were destined to "become the characteristic educational institution of the United States" and would "find it easy to take over the last two years of high school and develop a four-year unit devoted to general education" (p. 16). But the commissioners knew that administrative control of community colleges was more important than their location in high school buildings. States vesting administrative control of community colleges in a state board, noted the President's Commission (1947) had, for all practical purposes, opted for a 12-2 configuration since "the State will hesitate to disturb the organization of the local high schools" (p. 3:12).

Most educational associations opposed the reform. Favorable North Central Association (NCA) and National Education Association (NEA) committee reports (1915 and 1938, respectively) generated little enthusiasm among the general memberships. A 1920 NCA resolution, defining ages 12–20 as the normal years for secondary and collegiate education, failed, argued historian Edward C. Krug, mainly because of opposition from advocates of the junior high school, a group Koos relied on for support. "The preservation of the junior high school," Krug (1972) wrote, "had become more important than the saving of two years in the student's program" (p. 50). Many association activists had worked to strengthen colleges and secondary schools by identifying their distinctive missions and *separating* their educational work. High school partisans tried to weaken the influence of college entrance requirements on the secondary school curriculum; extending secondary education upward would reopen many resolved issues. The NCA reflected the consensus when it defined the junior or community college as an institution with a jurisdiction and faculty clearly separate from those of local high schools (Geiger, 1970).

Many reformers looked to other ways to shorten the time to the bachelor's degree. A late-19th-century proposal by Harvard president Charles W.

Eliot to establish a three-year baccalaureate went nowhere; the Carnegie Commission on Higher Education (1970a) unsuccessfully renewed the call 75 years later. But Columbia University professor—later president— Nicholas Murray Butler, an influential late-19th-century educational re- former who nurtured the Committee of Ten, advocated a "professional option"—conferring "the baccalaureate as a university degree after a four years' course of study, the last year of which is the first year of a three years' university course." The traditional four-year college, Butler rea- soned, was too ingrained, and shifting the undergraduate years to include 11th and 12th grades would harm the development of the high schools. Double-counting professional option years was a better strategy than losing students to professional schools that did not yet require the baccalaureate for admission. The many students at Columbia and elsewhere who exer- cised a professional option, Butler (1939) argued, would "be led to look upon . . . [their] education not as completed, but as only begun" (p. 1:139; see also Wechsler, 1977).

Structural and curricular reformers and stage theorists thus failed to change the organization of American education. Timing helps to explain the failure. America had approximately 14,000 high schools by the end of World War I, but a majority of the country's students did not complete a 12th-grade, much less a 14th-grade, education. Expanding the high school system to include noncompulsory 13th and 14th grades, concluded many local school boards, could require *additional* academic and administrative expenditures (Pedersen, 1993). Conversely, most four-year colleges would not give up freshman- and sophomore-year instruction, which cost less to offer than did subsequent years.

Arguments for articulated curricula, reduced time, and saved costs did not persuade defenders of free-standing, two-year colleges who invoked precedent and practice. Course duplication, argued Eells (1931b), might even be desirable, since the same subject "may be handled with profit by different methods and with different levels" (p. 313). Some time savings was possible, Eells conceded, although he believed only a small proportion of students would avail themselves of the opportunity. For most students, he added, enrichment was more important than acceleration. Capital out- lays, amortized over an "extra" building's expected life-span, would be minimal; administrative savings might be illusory, and faculty salaries, the main item in school and college operating budgets, would be largely unaf- fected.

Most junior college advocates did not love four-year junior colleges less; they loved free-standing, two-year colleges more. School boards were attracted to the purported virtues of separate two-year junior colleges, es- pecially their flexibility. Coordination *within* a four-year junior college, argued a two-year partisan, came at the cost of articulation with multiple feeders, a real cost since students from other districts often paid tuition. What, asked one interwar observer, did four-year partisans recommend for communities that could not afford a junior college (Lillard, 1930)?

Critics of four-year junior colleges also noted the advantages of having students work with new instructors and students in new schools—a tendency that, Eells claimed, also facilitated transfer between levels. "In many instances," wrote another early advocate of two-year junior colleges, "it is desirable that a student have a new environment—a new setting, so to speak—to vie new zest and an added stimulus to his efforts." "Even though a local institution offers equal advantages," this observer concluded, "it is often advisable to throw the young high-school graduate on his own responsibility for a time by severing home relationships" (McLane, 1913, p. 165). Others disagreed about the virtues of leaving home, but most saw virtue in separating older from younger students in age-homogeneous, two-year junior colleges.

In 1931, the Chaffey Junior College principal asked students about the advantages of separation. Many students, he noted, "reported a heightened 'college atmosphere'"; others cited a greater work incentive, a *narrower* student age range, more student–faculty interaction, more freedom of expression, and a smoother transition from high school to university (Hill, 1931, p. 10). A collegiate atmosphere, others argued, allowed student leadership to develop earlier and more rapidly than in four-year colleges. In contrast, these observers noted, school spirit appeared low among students entering a four-year junior college at an advanced level after attending a rival high school (Eby, 1928).

Most schemes envisioned that students would commute to high schools or local junior colleges. Students who saw these plans as delaying access to residential colleges until the junior year stayed away. But even nonresidential junior colleges, Eells concluded, permitted more Americans to feel they derived the benefits of attending college. "It is difficult enough to get the notion into the public consciousness that the two-year junior college is real college," he wrote, and "it will be far more difficult for it to feel that 'college' is a centaur-like hybrid—half high school and half college" (Eells, 1931b, p. 321). Koos (1949) considered this objection the key deterrent to the 6-4-4 plan; critics of the middle college movement often resurrected the argument.

Moving from school board to junior college district governance compounded status considerations since districts often competed for local and state funding (Breneman & Nelson, 1981; Garms, 1977). Moreover, the geographic boundaries of junior college and K-12 school districts often were not coterminous—junior college districts were typically larger—

although jurisdictions and funding practices varied widely. State systems of junior colleges, argued one four-year junior college advocate, might overcome parochialism and status considerations, thus promoting greater high school–college curricular coordination (Reynolds, 1965). But these systems were a long way off in most states.

The 6-4-4 movement waned after World War II. Many observers seconded the recommendation made by the President's Commission on Higher Education for expansion to 14th grade. But few reformers asked whether the extra years would be compulsory and, if so, who would pay, and who would opt for grades 11–14 schools over traditional public or independent two- or four-year colleges (Educational Policies Commission, 1964). Only high school–college collaborations requiring no structural changes—such as advanced placement—grew substantially in the 1950s.

Any remaining hopes faded as schools and community colleges independently prepared for the arrival of the baby boomers during the 1960s; the growth of public two-year colleges preempted the middle ground. Their two-per-week growth rate, sustained in the late 1960s and early 1970s, was not quite the "school-a-day" pace shown by high schools earlier in the century. But two-year college enrollments increased from under 1 million to over 5 million students in less than 30 years; these schools emphasized horizontal expansion into new curricula, not vertical expansion into grades covered by other schools. The few early 1970s moves toward systemic realignment failed. California and Florida officials, for example, abandoned early-exit plans for high school students when they could not resolve the issue of parental involvement in choosing to leave early (Schmidt, 1993).

RESURRECTING THE VISION

Some reformers continued to experiment. In 1964, Elizabeth B. Hall established Simon's Rock Early College—a rural, residential, independent liberal arts institution straddling grades 11–14. Hall, former headmistress of Concord Academy, a private girl's school, funded the college through family philanthropy—her father owned the Chicklet Gum Company, the Long Island City neighbor of LaGuardia Community College. Simon's Rock awarded the associate of arts degree to students completing the 14th year, confining recruitment to women until 1970. The college continued to appeal mainly to women even after its move to coeducation (Grant & Riesman, 1978; Levine, 1978; Martorana & Kuhns, 1975; Riesman, 1980; Whitlock, 1978).

Many observers viewed Simon's Rock as an isolated experiment, but Hall saw the school as a model for public education. "The community college, as a logical extension of the high school, could better be related to the needs of some youth," she wrote, "by providing an unfractured four-year sequence in the liberal arts to students who have completed tenth grade instead of the two-year miscellany that comprises so many junior college programs" (Hall, n.d., p. 10). Like most advocates of a four-year junior college, Hall envisioned a clientele of average or above-average students who would benefit from accelerated or enriched education.

Hall soon encountered an old objection: Rapid growth among two- and four-year colleges reduced the likelihood that students would remain in a "secondary school" for another two years. In 1972, Baird Whitlock, Hall's successor at Simon's Rock (1972–1977), announced a new baccalaureate program that admitted students after 10th grade. That program, wrote one observer, was essential. "Without it, the college was an expensive private liberal arts junior college at a time when such colleges were closing for lack of students" (Levine, 1978, p. 384). But enrollment problems persisted. Some parents preferred to defer high tuition charges; students hesitated to leave high school after finding their social niche, school administrators feared "creaming," and Simon's Rock confronted high attrition rates associated with transfers to other colleges (Levine, 1978). In 1979 Simon's Rock became a unit of Bard College, Annandale-on-Hudson, New York, and Bard president Leon Botstein—who began studies at the College of the University of Chicago at 16—became its president. Simon's Rock retained its identity and continued to admit students who completed 10th grade.

The ferment surrounding the 1960s student movement inspired many plans for "restructuring" higher education. *Continuity and Discontinuity,* a report of the Carnegie Commission on Higher Education (1973), echoed the ideas of Hutchins, Koos, and the President's Commission on Higher Education. The commission—sponsored by the Carnegie Corporation, which also would seed LaGuardia's Middle College High School—proposed eliminating duplication and discontinuity via a liberal education curriculum spanning the last two years of high school and the first two years of college, a shortened time for the B.A., early admissions, concurrent enrollment, and college credit for work completed in the senior year of high school.

The commission recommended "middle colleges"—mentioning the plans of LaGuardia—among ideas for improved school–college collaboration. These schools, the commission suggested, "might well appeal to a sizable number of students and institutions today," and "provide an excellent answer to curriculum overlap and discontinuity between school and college." "*This middle college concept should be seriously explored by large numbers of private liberal arts colleges,*" the commission added, since it opened these colleges to a new pool of students while giving liberal education "a new lease on life." With liberal or general education moved into one institution, "universities might then feel free to concentrate upon what they can do best, which is advancing knowledge through research and providing professional training" (Carnegie Commission, 1973, p. 80, emphasis in original).

Skeptics asked whether the divergent histories of schools and colleges had led to incompatible normative and reward structures. Was cooperation fated to be at best situational, sporadic, and perhaps forced (Overacker, 1994; Rogers, 1968)? Foundations periodically attempted to support, nurture, and even inspire collaborations between schools, colleges, and community-based organizations—the Eight-Year Study, science curriculum revision during the 1960s, and the academic alliance movement of the 1980s, for example. But project directors often failed to take practicalities into account, to render costs against benefits, and to plan for sustaining the project past a grant's expiration date or the departure of the original coalition members (Rogers, 1968). Demonstrated successes, even if maintained and replicated, were more likely to remain on the periphery than to affect the core functions of secondary or higher education systems.

The Carnegie Commission, too, questioned the feasibility of ambitious collaborations between levels of education that responded to different norms, missions, prestige hierarchies, and reward structures. "But why the slow progress, the resistance to improvement, the continuing tension between school and college?" asked the commissioners. All collaborations, noted the commission, face tensions "stemming from personal fears of exposure and scrutiny, practical problems inherent in developing new procedures and programs, reluctance to change old ways, and misunderstanding and disagreement about respective institutional purposes, language, style, and operating procedures." The level of threat and tension increased, the commission added, with the significance of the collaboration. Moreover, schools and colleges lived in different worlds. Activist, problem-solving school teachers "distrust the academic elitism of the college"; college teachers, in contrast, take the long view and "are often disdainful of anti-intellectualism in the schools." "In oversimplified terms," wrote the commissioners, "these differences reflect the teaching emphasis of the schools and the theoretical and research interests of the universities" (Carnegie Commission, 1973, p. 101).

CONCLUSION

Combining the last two years of high school and the first two years of college—a key to the design of LaGuardia's Middle College High School—

usually fell before academic and bureaucratic imperatives. Late in the 19th century, the American public high school found its place between grammar schools and colleges; a few generations later, the community college became a formidable sector of public higher education. But the strength of these victories made moves toward integration difficult to implement. Who, for example, would be responsible for the proposed intermediate unit? And who would pay for it?

There the idea stood—often-debated, rarely adopted—until Janet Lieberman and her colleagues at LaGuardia Community College took up the challenge. But instead of designing a four-year middle college for students with other options, she asked if a deft adaptation of the idea might increase the aspirations and abilities of students with little chance for postsecondary education, or who even were "at-risk" of dropping out of high school. Adapting any elite model to nonelite schools—general education as liberal education for nonelites, for example—was more easily advocated than accomplished. Many elite models were "doomed to success" by the persistence or charisma of the innovator or by freedom from market pressures. A transplant benefitting at-risk adolescents appeared especially problematic (Greenberg, 1987; President's Commission, 1947).

If the experiment had any chance, a community college in New York City would be a logical sponsor. Administrators at the City University of New York had changed what they considered an overly selective system of public higher education into an open access university (Gordon, 1975; Lavin, Alba, & Silberstein, 1981; Lavin & Hyllegard, 1996; Rossman, Astin, Astin, & El-Khawas, 1975; Wechsler, 1977). Along with this change came a resolve to improve relations with New York City's high schools—the university's main source of students. Janet Lieberman and Joseph Shenker, the forces behind LaGuardia's initiative, hoped to use this transformation and resolve to advantage. Designers would capitalize on the college's newness, its commitment to educating nontraditional students, and its relative indifference to status concerns to create a school that "worked" and that overcame the concept's spotty history.

No key feature of LaGuardia's Middle College proposal was *sui generis*; several other contemporary institutions were contemplating or opening "middle colleges" (Doxey, 1980). But no other design targeted at-risk students, or offered comparable pedagogical, developmental, and structural features. And if not now, mused Lieberman and Shenker, when?

2

Coming Together: Open Admissions and Philanthropy

The major failure of American education has been the inability to develop a constructive and satisfying program of education in the broad sense (including work and community service) for the least successful 30 per cent of adolescents in the academic school. This will be the main problem in the decade 1970–1980.

—Robert Havighurst, Professor of Education,
University of Chicago (Kopan, 1972, p. 323)

The colleges rather than the schools will be the first to break up the system in order to meet the needs of black and Puerto Rican students.

—E. Alden Dunham,
Carnegie Corporation (1969, p. 144)

In Spring 1969, officials at the City University of New York announced they would find places for all New York City high school graduates somewhere in the university, beginning in Fall 1970. That decision put an end to several years of racial and ethnic confrontation in New York City over access to higher education. But it also began several years of debate about the preparation for higher education of "nontraditional" students. Successful implementation of Open Admissions, some CUNY officials concluded, meant that preparation could no longer be entrusted solely to others.

ACCESS TO PUBLIC HIGHER EDUCATION IN NEW YORK CITY

Founded in 1847 as the Free Academy, the City College of New York (CCNY), the city's first municipal college, celebrated its free tuition policy and its accelerated curricula. City College, its leaders argued, provided higher education to first- and second-generation Americans who could not remove themselves from the workforce long enough to satisfy the requirements of "elite" colleges and universities. Many students enrolled in Townsend Harris Hall, CCNY's preparatory division, whose three-year program led directly to a two-year preprofessional course offered by the college. Students completing this course could enroll in local professional schools admitting students after the sophomore year of college.

Rival presidents scorned the education provided by City College. Frederick A. P. Barnard, president of neighboring Columbia College from 1864 to 1889, charged in 1872 that City College offered

> a sham education at a low price in labor and time. . . . [I]t gives the academic degree for which other colleges demand a patient toil of seven or eight years in consideration of the amount of hurried work which can be compressed into five years. [Worse,] it holds out to young men the most seductive of all allurements which could be invented to entice them to give it their preference, viz., exemption from some years of distasteful though salutary preliminary drill in the secondary schools, and free and cordial welcome directly from the primaries. (p. 10)

But by 1910, Columbia and other colleges aspiring to academic or social selectivity saw City College not as a competitor, but as an alternative for the increasing numbers of high school graduates who were not "their material." CCNY administrators, reluctant to accept a second-rank position in the city's academic pecking order, contemplated eliminating Townsend Harris Hall. But the school survived as a yardstick that could help evaluate conventional public high schools until it finally succumbed to economic and academic pressures in 1942. Hunter College High School, a laboratory school associated with Hunter College, the city's college for teachers, remained as the only precollegiate unit affiliated with a municipal college (Grunfeld, 1991).

Meanwhile, academic admissions requirements increased at City College and at the three other municipal colleges founded before World War II. The influx of returning veterans after that war led some observers to ask whether these colleges were confining educational opportunity to a smaller-than-desirable academic stratum. But the founding of New York Community College (now New York City Technical College) in 1946, and of additional community colleges in each borough by the mid-1960s, reduced immediate concerns. These colleges enrolled students whose cumulative high school averages were too low for admission to a senior college with capped enrollments (Community College Planning Center, 1964). Creation in 1957 of the City University of New York, composed of all municipal senior and community colleges, and soon to include a graduate school, facilitated coordination of admissions requirements of the constituent units.

A cascade of applications to CUNY from baby boomers, including growing numbers of non-White students, reopened the access issue during the mid-1960s. Soon after assuming office in 1963, Chancellor Alfred H. Bowker skirmished over future growth with the Board of Higher Education (BHE), CUNY's governing board, and with its chair, Gustave Rosenberg. The following year, Bowker implemented "Operation Shoehorn," overutilizing all space in existing CUNY units to accommodate the first baby boomers to reach college. Wishing to avoid future space shortages, and to educate a growing and changing population, Bowker called for major capital expenditures to expand existing CUNY units, and for new units for students living at a distance from the nearest college. His calls for long-range planning and for ensuring adequate financing led to a major public confrontation with the more status quo-oriented BHE in late 1965.

Bowker won the battle; within a year Rosenberg left the board for a judgeship, and a revamped BHE adopted a goal of 100% admission of public New York City high school graduates to CUNY by 1975. But this goal appeared distant in a city with years of intense racial and ethnic confrontation, brought to a head by a 1968 New York City public school teacher strike. Suburbanization of the city's White population, Bowker argued, necessitated revamped admissions mechanisms to ensure minority student access to CUNY, although not at the cost of the political support of the city's remaining White ethnic residents.

During the late 1960s, the city's ethnic and racial groups charted their gains and losses under Bowker's policy of gradual expansion. But his initiatives for increasing CUNY's minority enrollments heightened racial tension; White students, parents, and politicians viewed targeted admissions programs as coming at the cost of—rather than in addition to—more advantageous "regular" admissions programs. The issue came to a head during the South Campus seizure at City College in Spring 1969, when minority students occupied several buildings and demanded increased access. Wishing to avoid further polarization in a city already divided that academic year by a teachers' union strike protesting public school decentralization, CUNY leaders announced that the university would offer admission to all New York City high school graduates by Fall 1970.

LAGUARDIA COMMUNITY COLLEGE

By the early 1970s, community colleges, growing nationally at the rate of one or two a week, provided the main entryway to higher education for urban minority students. In New York, construction began on several new CUNY units listed in its 1968 master plan, including the system's ninth and last community college, Fiorello H. LaGuardia Community College. When it opened in 1971, LaGuardia served about 450–500 full-time day students from northern and western Queens who otherwise would have had to complete lengthy commutes to Borough of Manhattan Community College or Queensborough Community College. Available space—mostly rented—limited growth, but within a decade the college offered liberal arts, education, business, human services, and occupational therapy programs to 6,000 full-time equivalent students (Hyland, 1981). A LaGuardia student profile, compiled two months after its opening, found that 56% of the students taking the California Achievement Test in reading scored below the 12th-grade level; 72% scored below that level on the writing test (Lieberman, 1971).

LaGuardia's "Signature"

LaGuardia distinguished itself from other CUNY units by mandating cooperative education—alternating periods of academic studies and supervised on-the-job experience (McCabe, 1980; Williams, 1979). "Co-op" originated in engineering schools in the early 20th century and expanded to business and other professional schools after World War I and into the liberal arts curriculum at Arthur Morgan's Antioch College during the 1920s (Grant & Riesman, 1978; Newman, 1987; Sealander, 1988). During the 1950s, several foundations saw co-op—dismissed by mainstreamers as a financing mechanism for poorer students—as a way to expand higher education to the working class, increase collaboration between business and education, deepen the educator pool at a time of faculty shortage, *and* make higher education more affordable (Frederick, 1982; Woodring, 1970). Cooperative education, said a 1961 Ford Foundation-sponsored study, also would break down strong, often anti-academic adolescent peer group cultures and improve intergenerational social skills (President's Science Advisory Committee, 1974; Tyler, 1961; Tyler & Mills, 1961; Wilson & Lyons, 1961).

    Ford's interest spurred federal government action during the 1960s. The Economic Opportunities Act (1964), a response to President Johnson's declaration of a war on poverty, encouraged colleges to establish "work/ study" programs, including co-op, for needy students. Title III of the 1965

Higher Education Act authorized spending for cooperative education at "developing institutions"; the program gained its own provision (Title VIII) in the 1976 amendments to the act (Adams & Stephens, 1970; Cohen et al., 1976; "Cooperative Education," 1971; Frederick, 1982; Grant, 1972; Henderson, 1970, 1971; Knowles, 1971; Ryder, 1987; Ryder, Wilson, et al., 1987; Wilson, 1978).

Blessed with federal endorsement—"one of the few times the federal government put its stamp of approval on a particular type of education" (Knowles, 1971, p. 334)—and promoted by many reformers, cooperative education expanded from 35 colleges in 1961 to 225 in 1971, and to almost 1,000 in 1975 (American Academy of Arts and Sciences, 1971; Carnegie Commission on Higher Education, 1970a; Knowles, 1971; Newman, 1971). Co-op, contemporaries argued, responded to student demands for greater "relevance," to political pushes for self-help programs, and to corporate interest in professional education that integrated theory and practice. Cooperative education, wrote a key booster, "is relevant, it is innovative, and it is student-oriented, not only through its built-in financial aid feature but through its individualization of the educational process as a whole. No other type of higher education in the world can make these claims" (Knowles, 1971, p. 335).

By the late 1960s, some community colleges experimented with the practice. Northeastern University, the movement's flagship institution, helped several local two-year colleges with student counseling, placement, and financial assistance, and explored joint registration and transfer. New York City's community colleges, believed CUNY administrators, could benefit from similar collaborations. "Cooperative education," noted CUNY's 1968 master plan, "has been confined in the past to the business area. New programs of study may enhance this concept within other specializations, such as the technologies and the human services field" (Board of Higher Education, 1968, p. 110).

While at Kingsborough Community College, Joseph Shenker noted the value of clinical placements for nursing students. Could this arrangement, he asked during the planning for LaGuardia, be applied across the board? Shenker listed co-op among contemplated "signatures" for the new community college—a list that also included large interdisciplinary divisions (which quickly folded) and community service. Several traditional White ethnic groups and a conservative African-American population, he noted, resided in western Queens. A college combining academic and vocational programming, parents and community leaders told him, would have community support since students customarily worked after high school (Shenker, 1992). Cooperative education, Shenker concluded, would demonstrate the relevance of higher education for the children of unionized workers in trades requiring only high school diplomas. The program also would raise the aspirations of its students, encourage an understanding of the world of work, and facilitate vocational choice.

LaGuardia accommodated the views of a conservative Nixon administration as well as a conservative section of Queens. Sidney Marland, Assistant Secretary for Education, called teaching "every student about occupations and economic enterprise, a system that would markedly increase career options open to each individual and enable schools to do a better job than we have been doing of meeting the manpower needs of the country" (speech of May 4, 1971, as quoted in *Middle College Proposal*, 1973, p. 4). According to its mission statement, LaGuardia would create "a total learning experience through which students will gain not only specific skills and a broad range of knowledge, but also a sense of professional, financial, and personal responsibility" (Fiorello H. LaGuardia Community College, *Objectives and Programs*, p. 3, as quoted in *Middle College Proposal*, 1973, p. 5).

Most LaGuardia students liked cooperative education, Shenker later noted, but a small number of liberal arts students held a one-day demonstration, asking for an optional plan. Shenker did not back down; students wishing to opt out could attend Queensborough Community College. No one raised the issue again after that demonstration, and LaGuardia officials took pride in calling their school the "first community college and the first public institution in the country to offer a 'cooperative education' program to all its students" (*LaGuardia Community College: Profile*, c. 1980, p. 1; see also Shenker, 1992). Only a few four-year college divisions—mainly engineering and business—had *required* cooperative education. Co-op elicited community support, while differentiating the fledgling school from CUNY's eight other community colleges. The Board of Higher Education readily accepted co-op; its public relations value helped when Shenker needed assistance from the chancellor with the Middle College proposal. To ensure its efficiency and high status, Shenker centralized co-op in a separate division—a decision that later permitted Middle College High School to avail itself of knowledgeable staff.

The Responsibility and the Blame

Cooperative education, asserted LaGuardia's officials, was a commitment to the community. But Open Admissions and community involvement, they added, implied more than curricular innovation. During the 1970s, critics charged that community colleges more often provided a terminal education than a bridge over the widening chasm between urban high schools and four-year colleges (Carnegie Commission, 1970b). LaGuardia, like all other units of CUNY, relied on the questionable academic preparation offered by the city's public high schools. "If we look at areas of poverty in New York City," Bowker wrote, "we find major erosion of the schools. We find high schools with only twenty or thirty graduates with academic diplomas, and other factors which could lead us to say that higher education is an unrealizable aspiration for many" (Board of Higher Education, 1964, pp. 198–199). Ensuring that Open Admissions would not become a revolving door, decided Bowker and Shenker, required LaGuardia to venture into secondary education.

Beginning in the 1950s, some educators called upon urban community colleges to share responsibility for preparing high school students for higher education.[1] By 1970, CUNY had complemented nearly a decade of implementing alternative admissions procedures with some precollegiate interventions (Eaton, 1994; Pedersen, 1994). College Discovery in 1963 admitted students to community colleges on the basis of the principal's recommendation; another component sent identified 9th graders to high school development centers for intensive college preparation (Dispenzieri & Giniger, 1969). SEEK (1966)—authorized by the New York State Legislature at the behest of some African-American legislators from New York City with the covert support of CUNY officials—placed students from impoverished areas into special programs in CUNY's senior colleges. In 1968, the BHE recommended that CUNY assume administrative responsibility for five New York City public high schools, one in each borough, as an alternative to increasing remediation at CUNY. But possible jurisdictional strife with the Board of Education (BOE) led CUNY officials to drop these plans; the BOE would accept help only on its own terms.

High school preparation became a more pressing issue with implementation of Open Admissions. "[I]f the colleges can no longer rely on [adequate] preparation," stated a report drafted during the height of CUNY's admissions controversies, "then any educational process based on the traditional premise is bound to be ineffective. . . . [A] private university is largely free to select students from the population of all American high schools and the most prestigious colleges do just that." CUNY, the report concluded, "however, is tied to one set of high schools; it is not free to sample the secondary school universe" (City University of New York, 1969, pp. 1.6–1.7).

Open Admissions implied a proactive role for CUNY in preparing its future students; finger pointing was no longer permissible (Lavin, Alba, & Silberstein, 1981). Critics might lament a "decline in standards" brought about by Open Admissions, but, CUNY and LaGuardia staff countered, ignoring potential students solved nothing. "The senior colleges blamed the community colleges; the community colleges blamed the high schools,"

Shenker noted in an interview. "We said publicly, 'Let's stop blaming the high schools—either we do it better or shut up.'" Addressing the secondary education of working-class New Yorkers, he added, might further cement LaGuardia's relationship to the western Queens community, improve the quality of the community college student body, and reinvigorate the acceleration and yardstick functions performed by New York's municipal colleges earlier in the century (Shenker, 1992).

Targeted public school interventions made sense even if CUNY's programs incurred the ire of a territorial New York City Board of Education. The 1972 CUNY master plan contemplated multiple initiatives for improved articulation of K–12 and higher education; the initiatives aimed at reducing the basic skills deficiencies of potential CUNY students at a time of growing financial stringency. Locating a combined high school and college for the at-risk students of New York on CUNY premises and drawing on LaGuardia's cooperative education signature were among the bolder proposals (Board of Higher Education, 1972).

Janet Lieberman, the school's chief designer, LaGuardia president Joseph Shenker, and their colleagues spent almost three years developing the plan, obtaining the myriad needed approvals, and preparing the school to greet its first students. Agreeing quickly on the key idea—a unified educational experience for late adolescents—designers needed time and money to identify and design the key components—including the curriculum, the house, the teacher-counselor—and to work out the physical logistics. Selling the idea then proved a time-consuming process made more complex by difficulties in identifying all concerned constituencies. Last, the school had to complete many practical steps, including staff and student recruitment, between approval and opening. These delays frustrated LaGuardia's staff, but in retrospect the wonder was that, given the academic, jurisdictional, political, and financial obstacles, the school opened at all. But open it did in Fall 1974.

THE DESIGNER AND THE DESIGN

Janet Lieberman's biography suggests reasons for her interest in a school for at-risk adolescents. Born in 1921 and graduating from the Berkeley Institute, a New York City independent school, Lieberman attended Vassar College for a year before transferring to Barnard, where she completed an accelerated program of college studies. Transferring and acceleration, she suggested, led her to question the "givenness" of a standard academic day, year, and career, and of existing relationships between educational structures. Lieberman appreciated Vassar's tradition of community involvement and its emphasis on a residential experience (Gordon, 1990; Herman, 1979). She contrasted Vassar favorably to Barnard, which she saw as too much like high school—more traditional pedagogy, a less challenging curriculum, and fewer opportunities for individual expression.

Lieberman earned a masters degree in school psychology at City College and, becoming interested in reading as a manifestation of intelligence and cognitive ability, trained to become a clinical diagnostician while working in the New York City public schools. By the late 1950s, Lieberman had become a full-time psychologist for the Bureau of Child Guidance of the New York City schools, determining whether referred students should go to special classes. At about this time, concern about school violence prompted the New York City BOE to create the first "600 school" for girls—now the Livingston School for Girls—who posed disciplinary problems in their home schools. City school administrators recruited Lieberman as the school psychologist. Unable to do therapy directly with the students, Lieberman instead worked through the teachers. She watched how a strong faculty could reach a highly at-risk population by creating a nurturing environment.

Lieberman left the school after four years to pursue a Ph.D. in educational psychology at New York University, where she renewed her interest in reading. She offered to teach at the Dalton School, an independent school on Manhattan's east side, in exchange for permission to study the school's 5th-grade population for her dissertation research. Recognizing that many Dalton students had reading problems, but that their parents would object to their placement in remedial classes, Lieberman devised a class in spelling, reading, and comprehension, calling it "English W(onderful)." Her dissertation compared the relationships among knowledge of vocabulary, intelligence, and reading comprehension in English W(onderful) students and in a group of low-income public school students (Lieberman, 1965).

Lieberman taught at Hunter College during the late 1960s, a period of student activism that affected much of CUNY. She noted the affinity between students and many younger faculty members who expressed sympathy with the demonstrations and building occupations that halted regular academic activities. Knowing that Hunter students had to graduate to take teacher licensing exams, these faculty members taught in their homes, in parks and schools, or in Hunter's stairwells and cafeteria. The physical arrangement of teaching, Lieberman observed, affected its vitality. Freed from facing each other across a desk, students and faculty turned any available physical space into a stimulating seminar.

Soon after coming to LaGuardia in 1971, Lieberman met with CUNY Acting Chancellor Timothy Healy, who noted that the significant and persistent New York City high school dropout rate limited the potential benefits of CUNY's new Open Admissions policy (Shenker, 1992). He asked Lieberman to design a program to increase LaGuardia's enrollments. After reading the works of G. Stanley Hall, Leonard Koos, Ralph Tyler, and the Four-Schools Committee on reconfiguring secondary and higher education, Lieberman proposed that LaGuardia sponsor a middle college aimed at at-risk students (*Summary of Activity*, 1972). CUNY, agreed an impressed Healy, would pick up the cost of its students as regular allocations if LaGuardia opened the school. Shenker agreed to continue planning and officially assigned Lieberman to the project.

Knowing that neither the BHE nor the BOE was likely to fund a planning year, Shenker and Lieberman sought outside support. Applications to a half dozen foundations and government agencies produced only one response—from E. Alden Dunham, higher education program officer at the Carnegie Corporation. Dunham came to Carnegie after service as Princeton's admissions director and as assistant to James B. Conant, secondary school reformer and former Harvard president. For Conant, he coined the phrase "social dynamite" to refer to tensions confronting inner-city education. While at the corporation, he was also secretary of the Carnegie Foundation for the Advancement of Teaching (CFAT) and liaison to the Carnegie Commission on Higher Education, a CFAT creation. "Really for the first time in our national history," Dunham wrote, a group [the commission] would "set forth a blueprint of what higher education in the U.S. *should* look like ten to twenty years from now" (Lagemann, 1989, p. 228, emphasis in original).

Colleges of the Forgotten Americans: A Profile of State Colleges and Regional Universities (1969), Dunham's contribution to the commission, identified the community college as the postsecondary institution most likely to collaborate with secondary schools to ensure increased access of minority groups to higher education. The research interests of faculty, and a preference for specialized over introductory work, he argued, led regional, four-year colleges to emulate doctoral universities, making it unlikely they would focus on beginning students.

CUNY's former emphasis on "rigorous standards"—which Dunham attributed to "the importance that the heavy Jewish population in New York has traditionally paid to education as a means of upward mobility"—was "not relevant to the new population found in the city's schools" (1969, p. 144). But Open Admissions would change the *gestalt* of postsecondary education, he added, thereby leveraging needed reform in the New York City public schools.

Dunham shared Lieberman's optimism that the smaller academic and status distances between community colleges and high schools boded well for "school–college" collaboration at LaGuardia. Reformers often needed external support, Lieberman noted, but a college would exert no salutary influence if the academic distance were excessive.[2] Emphasizing their common origins and their current similarities as comprehensive institutions, she counted on two factors to overcome any conflicts: targeting secondary school students from the same socioeconomic backgrounds and neighborhoods as those served by LaGuardia, and sharing LaGuardia's cooperative education signature. If necessary, she added, the strong presidents more typical of two-year than of four-year colleges could support the collaboration. Years later, noting several failed attempts to create similar schools at four-year colleges, Lieberman questioned whether any four-year college could nurture a replication.

Seeing the Middle College proposal as part of CUNY's transformation, and as means of ending the grasp of the Ph.D. octopus over regional and local institutions, Dunham requested information on student demographics, project leaders, and the proposed student selection process. He also asked CUNY officials to signify willingness to assume the costs of the school after the planning year. Last, cognizant of Sidney Marland's strong interest in career education, he asked Lieberman to assess the interest of officials in the U.S. Office of Education (USOE). His last words to Lieberman—"Make sure you come back and let me know what happens"—were an implicit commitment to help if USOE did not fund the project (Lieberman, 1991; *Record of Interview*, February 10, 1972). Dunham agreed to visit LaGuardia when Lieberman reported that federal officials were preoccupied with securing legislation creating the National Institute of Education and that projects requiring funding would take at least a year to approve.

During his visit, Dunham learned that the long-range plan for LaGuardia had hinted at an intermediate college, that the current master plan made an explicit commitment, that Shenker foresaw no conflicts between the existing Queens public high schools and the proposed school, and that Middle College would be certified as a high school or require its students to take the high school equivalency examination. A CUNY dean emphasized potential coordination of remediation efforts among a diverse student body (James J. McGrath to Karen Peterson, August 17, 1972, CCP, "New York City University—LaGuardia C. C. Middle College" file). Shenker told Dunham that he considered asking Lieberman to run the school, but that he would object to joint "CC–LaGuardia" approval of a director, since the community college would have sole long-term responsibility for the success of the school.[3]

Dunham met other concerned constituencies. LaGuardia faculty members, he learned, believed the school would save remediation time and encourage students who otherwise would not have been prepared to enter college. The faculty as a whole had not fully discussed the idea, but key faculty members announced their support. The designers were confident of faculty approval: "[T]he entire LaGuardia faculty was recruited after open admissions so that all have students, innovation, and change at heart" (*Record of interview*, June 26, 1972, p. 3).

The reality was more complex. Some members of the LaGuardia faculty were incensed, recalled Raymond Bowen, then LaGuardia associate dean of faculty with responsibility for creating academic programs: "We're trying to become a college and you're trying to turn us back into a high school." Lieberman, Bowen added, "had her work cut out for herself." LaGuardia had never been a high school, yet some faculty members expressed the status concerns that thwarted most attempts at creating an intermediate-level school. Bowen ran interference with suspicious or hostile faculty members, a story later repeated at many replications. His efforts paid off: LaGuardia's faculty members, Bowen noted, were recruited for student-centered outlooks as well as for their academic credentials. The infighting, he asserted, was within the context of how best to accomplish agreed-upon goals (Bowen, 1991).

Supportive faculty members, meanwhile, sketched out an academic program for the school. Curricular work already completed for grades 13–14, where "remediation is so much a part of the current curriculum," could shape the curriculum for grades 10–12. Dunham noted extensive interdepartmental curricular cooperation at LaGuardia. Mathematics courses, for example, were listed under "Symbolic Communication"; English courses under "Interpersonal Communication." He expected similar nontraditional courses to evolve from collaboration on the secondary school level, since "the faculty does not want to get hung up with bureaucratic tradition." "This is a faculty with an experimental attitude," he concluded, "which will be applying new notions to high school curriculum development." The approach of the college "is for students to enlarge themselves as thinking people" (*Record of interview*, June 26, 1972, p. 3).

Meetings with three "articulate and concerned" LaGuardia students left Dunham impressed. They "agreed that attending a NYC high school is a living death, and that anything would be preferable." Endorsing LaGuardia's venture into secondary education, the students nonetheless cautioned that its current college-level course offerings were fewer and less innovative than advertised. About 95% of surveyed high school students, Dunham recounted, favored the new school, since "any program is better than the present one" (AD and KP to DZR and AP, August 11, 1972, CCP, "New York City University—LaGuardia C. C. Middle College" file).

LaGuardia, reported Sheila Gordon, director of cooperative education, found internships for all its students, including the 40% enrolled in liberal

studies. The positions, she added, were not "make-work"; employer interest and creativity arose from the recruitment potential of the jobs. In contrast to other co-op programs for at-risk New York high school students,
LaGuardia aimed for a "much closer mesh between school and work,
thinking and doing" (*Record of Interview*, June 26, 1972; Lieberman to
"All Involved," June 19, 1972, MCA; AD and KP to DZR and AP, August
11, 1972, CCP, "New York City University—LaGuardia C. C. Middle
College" file).

The Carnegie Corporation subsequently approved a $95,116 grant
that covered the planning-year salaries of the director, two faculty-curricu-
lum developers, and a recruiter-counselor (FA to Shenker, October 13,
1972, CCP, "New York City University—LaGuardia Middle College"
file). Echoing the themes of *Colleges of the Forgotten Americans*—earlier
student maturation, student interest in vocational studies—and noting a
1% per year increase in the New York City public high school dropout
rate, Dunham concluded that a middle college promised greater freedom
for students. This freedom, he wrote, would help to ensure graduation
from high school, and "break down the traditional departmentalized curriculum to provide the liberal education referred to in the *Four-School
Study* [16–20]," another Carnegie-funded project.

LaGuardia's multidisciplinary remedial courses, Dunham noted, provided models for the middle college curriculum. Successful implementation
of this curriculum, he added, in turn would reduce the need for college-
level remediation. Again citing *16–20*, Dunham said that a grades 10–14
grouping made curricular and psychological sense. He lauded the attempt
to apply this grouping, designed for middle- and upper-class students, to a
mostly blue-collar student body with a growing minority population. "As
a model for expanding options and aiding victims of the New York city
school system," Dunham concluded, "this could be a significant grant"
(AD and KP to DZR and AP, August 11, 1972, CCP, "New York City
University—LaGuardia C. C. Middle College" file). Dunham also helped
create contacts between Lieberman and officials of the Fund for the Improvement for Postsecondary Education (FIPSE), established under the
1972 Higher Education Amendments in response to yet another Carnegie
Commission recommendation. FIPSE supported staff expansion beyond the
levels permitted by the BOE for alternative high schools, including funds
for a full-time guidance counselor (*Summary and Clarification*, 1973).

The grants permitted Lieberman's team to plan the school's academic
program and funding plans during 1972–1973 and gave Shenker and Lieberman leverage to obtain approval of the design from the BOE, CUNY,
and myriad state agencies. Lieberman targeted a Fall 1973 opening, but
the time needed to work the system resulted in delays in opening the

school, while conforming to administrative mandates and budgetary realities resulted in a constricted educational design. It would take several years for Middle College High School at LaGuardia to realize its potential.

AN ELITE SCHOOL FOR AT-RISK STUDENTS: THE COMPONENTS

A middle college at LaGuardia had to relate key curricular and organizational features to the world of the host community college and to the structure of public education (Houle, 1996). Dealing with LaGuardia was relatively easy since Lieberman, Shenker, and other LaGuardia staff played key roles in conceiving and designing the school. LaGuardia's newness meant that few traditions and routines inhibited collaboration, and an atmosphere of enthusiasm and experimentation made all problems appear solvable. But dealing with the New York City BOE, unfettered by the need for external collaboration and set in its ways, was another matter.

The school would offer a flexible, multidisciplinary, "relevant" program of studies designed to heighten student interest in education and to permit close articulation between the school's secondary and collegiate components. It also would use the city as a resource for reducing student parochialism and for examining "the meaning of individuality in a metropolitan setting" (Lieberman, 1973, p. 17).

The designers held exploratory meetings with BOE officials, students, parents, and religious leaders to develop an agenda of activities. In early 1973, Lieberman contacted state education officials in Albany to determine state certification and high school requirements. CUNY and College Board officials helped develop plans for the cooperative education component—in 1977 co-op incorporated a version of the College Board's career decision curriculum. The Carnegie grant permitted visits to schools with cooperative education programs and to alternative schools for at-risk students. These preliminary discussions led to a June 1973 proposal detailing the school's key features. No feature was unprecedented, but the mix—and the target clientele—were unique.

The 16–20 Age Grouping

The designers expressed affinity with the thinking behind the College of the University of Chicago and Simon's Rock College. Hutchins, Koos, and Hall were onto something—16-year-olds had more in common with 20-year-olds than with younger adolescents. Students matured two years earlier than they used to, Lieberman claimed, making the grouping of grades

10–14 sensible. An appealing, enriched, relevant curriculum would overcome any initial reluctance among college sophomores to associate with
high school students. Younger students, Lieberman added, would hold
their own; stereotypes and barriers would break down rapidly (Lieberman,
1975).

Students completing the equivalent of the college sophomore year
would receive the associate of arts degree—not the baccalaureate. Tenth
graders would proceed to the A.A. at their own pace without an admissions
hurdle at the end of the 12th year. The designers "expected" all students
to take the five-year sequence. "To realize the full benefits of the five year
program," stated one document, "candidates should seriously consider admission to LaGuardia as their immediate college goal" (*Agenda*, 1973, attachment 2, p. 1). But the school would award the high school diploma at
the end of the 12th year, thereby permitting students to remain at LaGuardia or to apply to other colleges, including any other CUNY unit. Students
completing the 14th year could transfer to a senior college within CUNY;
students wishing to leave before completing 12th grade could move to a
regular city high school.

The proposal assigned remedial instruction—anticipated as necessary
for two-thirds of entering 10th graders—to the secondary level. Many students, designers assumed, "will achieve college levels in reading and mathematics by the time they complete the third year of the program (12th
grade)" (*Middle College Proposal*, 1973, pp. 10–11). The resulting de-
crease in the budget for remediating students in grades 13–14 would free
funds to be used for more college courses. To facilitate "a longitudinal
view of the learning process which will aid in development of improved
course content and sequences," Middle College instructors would teach on
the college level, and LaGuardia faculty would teach part-time at the Middle College (*Middle College Proposal*, 1973, p. 7). When would students
begin to take college courses? The proposal stated only, "College courses
would be offered at the high school level." The school initially placed many
10th-grade students—the only grade admitted the first year—in college
courses, but later retreated from that practice.

Designers used cautious language when discussing academic acceleration. "The program is not primarily designed for acceleration, but to open
the plan of education in content and format" (*Middle College Proposal*,
1973, p. 16). Finishing on time probably would require summer study and
college coursework during the first three years, since many regular LaGuardia students did not complete their programs in two years. Individualized
pacing, in any case, was more important than acceleration; some students
might take *more* time to finish their high school education. "It's OK to

have a mustache," counselors asserted; little stigma would accompany slower pacing since students blended in among the older LaGuardia students.

Would a five-year school—planned to break down undesirable age isolation among late teens—simply isolate a slightly younger age cohort (President's Science Advisory Committee, 1974)? Designers offered three responses. First, the school would produce more age heterogeneity than did traditional high schools, which isolated one-year cohorts. Enrolling high school-age students in college courses would ensure salutary academic and social mixing. Second, community colleges, including LaGuardia, attracted many adults along with late adolescents. The median age of matriculated students at some community colleges rose to upward of 27 years during the 1970s. The objections of some older LaGuardia students to a high school on their campus was perhaps a sign of *too much* mixing. Last, the designers deemed cooperative education a proven method of ensuring exposure to the adult world.

Recruitment

The school's designers wished to recruit underachievers, "defined as a level of achievement significantly below their potential, as evaluated by the school staff." But the New York City Board of Education objected to the vague operative definition—"poor attendance, cutting, high rate of scholastic failure, sometimes combined with talent or interest in one area, or dissatisfaction with some aspect of the current or anticipated program"—and to the proposal to leave admissions decisions to school staff. The BOE tried to discourage "creaming"—recruiting academically able students into alternative high schools. But the "dissatisfaction" criterion set off bells, especially since the proposal continued: "The last item will identify youngsters who appear academically successful but feel that the flexibility and individualization of an alternative educational setting will free their potential" (*Middle College Proposal*, 1973, p. 14). A decade later, Queens principals similarly would attribute the school's success to creaming.

Designers expected a 125-student entering class, with equal numbers of young men and women drawn from the Astoria, Long Island City, and Queensbridge sections of Queens. LaGuardia would host a "neighborhood school," encouraging parental and community support and involvement, and reflecting the ethnic composition of the community college. Students would be selected randomly if applicants exceeded available places, but the proposal did not specify how designers reconciled this principle with the goal of ethnic distribution. The first class would include only 10th graders—most New York City students spent 7th–9th grades in a junior high school—and the school would grow through successive recruitment of two additional 10th-grade classes.

"Delicate" negotiations with the BOE forced the school to satisfy some stringent conditions. Generally, both sides agreed, "all components of the students' reading and mathematics score shall be at or above sixth grade level." But the BOE, wishing to assuage the local Queens high schools, mandated that "to provide a cross-section of a tenth grade population, approximately 15% of the students selected will have reading and/or math scores between the fourth and sixth grade-levels," that is, more than four years below grade level (Academy for Educational Development, 1974, p. 12). The Board also required the school to accept three-fourths of its students from applicants functioning below grade level in reading and mathematics; planners had targeted two-thirds.

A clarification of the plan, negotiated with high-level city school officials, identified the target population as "disaffected high risk students who have already been identified as potential dropouts." The school—viewed as "another in a series of experiments to provide a route to achievement for the non-achieving student"—would "not recruit those students who are benefiting from the present high school setting" (*Summary and Clarification*, 1973, p. 1).

These severe conditions, evaluators later noted, reduced the probability that the BHE would save enough money from cuts in community college remediation to fund its promised contribution (Academy for Educational Development, 1974). But the designers believed northern Queens contained enough "disaffected" 9th graders to open a school that addressed the affective, academic, and vocational development of its students.

The Plant

The proposal noted

> The common physical setting of a high school/college program offers a positive ambience for the new student, in which successful academic and social peers outnumber failures. . . . The halo effect of the college upon a small group of younger students integrated into some college classes and activities is regarded by many junior high and high school educators as a major innovation of great impact. (*Middle College Proposal*, 1973, p. 7)

The common, familiar setting, along with continuous instructional and guidance services, also facilitated a gradual transfer to college.

The school would be located in seven rooms in LaGuardia's "Sony Annex," directly across (wide) Thompson Avenue from the main building.

The main building housed the library; business, communication, and skill laboratories; lounges; cafeterias; and recreation areas. These shared spaces, Shenker (1992) noted, helped to ensure the presence of role models to encourage students to stay in school: "I see my neighbors at LaGuardia. If they can be there, I can be there too."

The school moved several times over the next two decades; discussions about the relative virtues of integrated and dedicated academic, social, and administrative space accompanied the moves. Similar conversations occurred in the late 1980s when Lieberman attempted to identify replication sites. Planners, she noted, often had to accept any available space at well-established, two-year colleges.

The Curriculum

Should schools put the marginal dollar into structural reform—the five-year program, for example—or into curricular reform? The proposed school could do both, and could integrate structure and content (Ford Foundation, 1972). But while the school could freely borrow structural features, it could not, planners argued, borrow a curriculum. "Usually," added a memorandum, "curriculum is imposed on a learning institution. Middle College curriculum planning will be done in advance on a continuing basis, with knowledge of the specific needs of entering students who will have been selected before the beginning of the staff training period" (*Summary and Clarification*, 1973). Designing the curriculum from scratch also would build teacher professionalism—a response to 1960s "teacher-proof" curricula.

What would be studied? Curricular goals included broadening "analytic skills and general comprehension," and enabling students "to make the multiple connections that are the essence of learning." "Concepts," the proposal added, "will be made relevant when related to urban problems, careers, and current experience." *Macbeth*, for example "will be taught in terms of political power and recent assassinations."

LaGuardia intended to develop "the largest possible number of multidisciplinary core courses" in each division. For example, "a Division of Human Services would stress Sociology and Psychology courses and might encompass career options of Education; Child Care; Social Service; Rehabilitation and Geriatrics" (quoted in *Middle College Proposal*, 1973, p. 8). Middle college courses, likewise, would "minimize . . . compartmentalization" by combining traditional high school subjects. The designers envisioned six interdisciplinary concentrations—art, business, communications, environmental control, health and human services, and humanities. The school would integrate social science "with the mathematical, scientific, and language skills needed for a specific career area," in courses such as "Environmental Awareness" and "Human Behavior" (*Middle College Proposal*, 1973, p. 18).

Along the way, students would complete the state's requirement for high school graduation by completing 16 units—subjects requiring four or five 40-minute periods per week for a year, the traditional Carnegie unit. Required courses included four units of English, three units of social studies, a unit of science, a half unit of health education, and a three-unit sequence chosen from math, science, language, music, art, business, or a vocational subject. Students would fill out their program with electives and could earn units through field work and testing (*Middle College Proposal*, 1973).[4]

How would a day, week, and year be organized to synthesize academic and cooperative education? The proposal called for 20-minute modules, permitting short periods for reading, math, counseling, and electives, and combined modules—40, 60, or 80-minute periods—for laboratories, tutoring, field activities, and articulation with community college classes. The school, agreed the BOE, could conform with LaGuardia's academic schedule and—reflecting the designers' emphasis on student independence— include a full day per week for student trips, apprenticeships, internships, and conferences.

Cooperative Education

LaGuardia was only a few months old when planning for the new school began, and only three years old when Middle College High School opened in Fall 1974. Cooperative education at the school, while not "inevitable," would build on the community support and business contacts cultivated by LaGuardia officials. The school, stated its planners, would present academic work, such as mathematics, in the context of career and life situations; stimulate the exploration of work settings while orienting students to the demands of a career, not only of a first job; and counsel them to an awareness of "the many possibilities which they have in careers, styles of life, and decision-making," while reducing "the effect of pure chance," and increasing "that of informed choice, as a determinant in each student's life" (*Middle College Proposal*, 1973, p. 5).

Planners differentiated cooperative education from the part-time jobs held by many potential students—jobs that often provided income to blue-collar families at the price of lowered academic aspirations—by proposing to select work activities "for the greatest possible yield in skills, role identification, and personal satisfaction." Each job, stated the proposal, "will be a source of learning about labor unions, economics, sociology, and group dynamics. Students will have opportunities to evaluate and integrate academic and work experience in terms of their own interests and capacities" (*Middle College Proposal*, 1973, p. 5).

The design called for "pre-job experiences" for 10th and 11th graders, emphasizing field trips; internships and apprenticeships in for-profit and not-for-profit institutions would begin in 11th grade. The school would coordinate these experiences with practica that instilled desirable social skills, including "tact, understanding of job hierarchies, and dealing with associates of all ages"—to "provide a closed loop between the job and the classroom" (*Middle College Proposal*, 1973, pp. 19–20). Classroom work and counseling would enhance these activities.

A middle college would *not*, its planners insisted, be a "narrow" vocational school. It would "develop independent, self-actualizing human beings"; graduates would "know how to raise the right questions, gather data, sift, hypothesize, test their hypotheses, and evaluate their conclusions." The school would not teach specific skills for entry-level jobs that might soon become outmoded. "Modern technology," the proposal noted, "is generating data so rapidly that half of our knowledge becomes obsolete in eleven years. Education must shift its focus from learning of information to learning how-to-learn." Instead, the school would provide "lifelong learning" skills by liberalizing cooperative education.

The proposal specified generic business-related competencies—advanced business concepts relating to "the economic environment, government functions, and to general survival as a citizen"—and specific college-level skills, including accounting, secretarial science, and data processing. Students are not going to be "tracked" into one or another field, a CUNY official told the *New York Times* ("City U. Planning Middle College" 1973; see also *Middle College Proposal*, 1973, pp. 10, 12).

In any case, cooperative education, requiring an elaborate curriculum and agreements with many employers, was not in place when the school opened. Proponents cited this absence as evidence against viewing the school as an exercise in vocational education. But, when internships were added several years later, the school provided college preparation, work skills, *and employment*. "It is expected," added the proposal, "that all students will have been placed in jobs by the 12th grade" (*Middle College Proposal*, 1973, p. 19). The planners did not see preparing students for the rigors of college work as incompatible with job placement.

The House

It is clichéd to note the search for community underlying the myriad undergraduate reforms of the 1960s and 1970s. "Community," to reformers, was antithetical to impersonal, specialized universities and multicampus systems. Many college students sacrificed the depth of knowledge and anonymity associated with universities for a sense of intellectual and social belonging provided by small educational units.

But even small schools could be subdivided; the "house" was a long-standing, replicable model. Harvard president Abbott Lawrence Lowell had advocated a house system in the 1920s to reintroduce homogeneity in the student body while reducing ostentation (Levine, 1986; Lowell, 1934; Morison, 1936). But wealthy and poor students avoided the houses, and similar experiments met with indifferent fates.

During the late 1960s, many reformers—perhaps unknowingly invoking an idealized image of the 19th-century college, where students and faculty resided together—advocated experimentation with smaller units. Colleges, said the authors of *16-20*, should complement "the undergraduate's professionalized formal curriculum with an ad hoc environment that offers him a complicating, enriching reflection of his maturing self" (p. 22). Adolescents in a residential college could not depend on the family or other social institutions to nurture their social and affective development. Peer groups might help or hinder, but they were insufficient. The authors of *16-20* cited Montieth College of Wayne State University; the separate colleges at Santa Cruz, the University of Michigan, and Yale; and the Old Westbury campus of the State University of New York (SUNY) as environments that aimed to facilitate the cognitive *and* affective development of students (Four-School Study Committee, 1970).

High school enrollments grew rapidly during the postwar years—the result of population growth, increased academic and social demands, and school district consolidation. Small school districts and high schools became anachronistic; the number of districts declined from 120,000 in 1930 to 20,000 in 1970, while the number of high schools grew incrementally. "Small high schools can be satisfactory only at exorbitant expense," wrote James B. Conant. "In many states the number one problem is the elimination of the small high school by district organization" (Conant, 1959, pp. 37, 38, 40).

But beginning in the 1920s and intensifying in the 1960s, some secondary school reformers echoed the call of their college-level colleagues for smaller, more manageable educational units (Bremer & von Moschzisker, 1971; Duke, 1995; Eriksen & Gantz, 1974; Labaree, 1988; Meier, 1995; Trickett, 1991). "Home room"—an established component of high schools by the 1920s—could serve a developmental purpose; enthusiasts quickly seized upon a familial analogy. "[T]he home room becomes a family. It acquires family characteristics, family loyalties, and family unity," wrote the principal of a Chicago junior high school in 1930. "A poor record in

conduct for an individual pupil or group of pupils," the principal continued, "becomes a matter of group consideration, group diagnosis, and
group insistence upon reform as an essential to the maintenance of high
standards for the home room." The principal offered an example: "Phyllis
likes to dawdle along to school, but her tardiness is a disgrace to the home
room, so public opinion requires her to get to school on time" (quoted in
Krug, 1972, pp. 138–139). Some high schools devised intermediate-sized
units with similar aims—the "school within a school" at Evanston Township High School in Illinois, for example (Stocking, 1926).

New York's Dalton School took the concept a step further. Dalton
aimed to break the high school "lockstep" by permitting students to proceed through the curriculum at their own pace, not with their entire grade.
Like a social caseworker, a Dalton teacher was responsible for, and became
the advocate of, a "house" of cross-graded students (Semel, 1992; Semel &
Sadovnik, 1999; Tyack & Cuban, 1995). In contrast, argued some advocates, the administrative requirements of the large high school could divert
teachers from, or, worse, might become an incentive for teachers to avoid,
working toward the developmental goals of home rooms or of intermediate-sized units.[5]

Lieberman's "house" was designed to realize the potential of the
smaller entities. Traditional home rooms, she wrote, provided neither engagement nor academic support. Bored, many students arrived at school
only after home room was over. In 10th grade, stated the proposal, "the
fifteen students will be housed together with the designated faculty member
in an integrated group"—a "'house,' modeled after the Dalton, Harvard,
Yale plan"—that "will be the primary unit in student government"; and
"will be the first level of group identification in the Middle College."
Within the house, "cooperative learning will be the major emphasis, and
members of the house will be encouraged to teach each other. The 'house'
can be the basic structure for understanding group dynamics" (*Information
for New York State*, n.d., p. 17; see also *Middle College Proposal*, 1973,
p. 25).

Lieberman, drawing upon her experience as a house head at Dalton,
saw the house as ensuring student visibility and individuality. Its small size
counteracted the danger of lost identity on a large, anonymous campus
(Freedman, 1990; Morisseau, 1975). Links to the house head would give
students the sense of belonging. A *gemeinschaft*, she concluded along with
the authors of *16-20*, was essential at a middle college, whether for elite or
at-risk students (Four-School Study Committee, 1970).

The house, Lieberman added, also could insulate students from detri-
mental elements in the community, although this rationale was not mentioned in most documents.[6] Underlying the concept was an ambivalent

attitude toward the family life of minority students. "[T]he fabric of conventional social relationships," contended the report of the U. S. Department of Labor, commonly referred to as the controversial "Moynihan Report," "had disappeared for many inner city, working class African Americans." Broken homes, the report noted, "provided weak or non-existent support for educational persistence." Moreover, "the academic attendance and performance of African-American students from homes with one or no parents was worse than the record of counterparts from two-parent families." The absence of alternative role models, Moynihan added, had an unfortunate effect on the economic chances of African-American youth. "Negroes," noted a 1960 report quoted by Moynihan, "are not apt to have relatives, friends, or neighbors in skilled occupations. Nor are they likely to be in secondary schools where they receive encouragement and direction from alternate role models" (U.S. Department of Labor, 1965, p. 37).

Planning documents recognized the need for parental and community involvement, and the difficulties faced by working-class and minority parents and community members in finding time to participate. But Lieberman gave great weight to the community college—a "home away from home" that was open and populated from early morning to late evening—and to the house and its teacher-counselor heads for nurturing the cognitive *and* affective development of at-risk students.

Teacher-counselors

Lieberman called for expanding the role of teachers to include responsibility for the affective development of at-risk students. The teacher, stated a contemporary essay quoted in the proposal, "serves as consultant, friend, facilitator of learning, director of learning strategies, and hopefully, arouser of latent enthusiasm." Frequent, one-to-one personal contact with advisees strengthens their relationships and "enables each to recognize the others as real identities" (Trump & Georgiades, 1972, p. 116). Proposals for professorial involvement in the affective development of college students also emerged in the 1960s, but professionalized student development roles and faculty reluctance to go beyond teaching and research confined reforms to short-lived experiments.

The concept's defenders argued that the role required—and in turn would nurture—a high degree of teacher professionalism. Teacher-counselors also would produce better academic results than curriculum specialists enamored of "teacher-proofing" instruction, or psychologists focused exclusively on the cognitive development of at-risk students. The holistic tone of Lieberman's plan implied complex roles for teachers and staff; teacher-proof curricula would not do. Each teacher-counselor would stay with a house of 15 students over several years as an advocate and stabilizing influence, as a subject teacher when possible, and as an assistant with internship placements and with career education coordination (*Summary and Clarification*, 1973).

To jump ahead, subject teachers, despite their dedication, were unable to master these complexities. The problem at the high school level, contended sociologist Morris Janowitz, was not with the staff, but with student transience that thwarted long-term development of the one-on-one relationships. Leaving aside the difficulty of training teacher-counselors, he argued, developing intense relationships might socialize the student to the school, not the larger society, just as model prisoners did not adjust to society upon their release from jail.

The concept, noted sympathetic critics, correctly identified the centrality of the teacher of at-risk students. However, an organization cannot function on the basis of the sheer energy of its constituent elements, but requires a division of labor and a system of effective supports" (Janowitz, 1969, p. 39). A teacher, in short, cannot do it all. Realistically, teachers could at most coordinate delivery of needed specialist services.

Recognizing the difficulties in fulfilling the role, Lieberman proposed that teacher-counselors have three to five years of service and a master's degree or equivalent. She inserted the education requirement to address "the job requirements of guidance training and skill in teaching at the college level" (*Budget and Funding Rationale*, c. 1973, p. 23). But the teacher's union opposed the designation. One could teach or counsel, but not both. Adding a new title to the roster of positions in union contracts, some union leaders feared, might lead to eliminating counselor positions.

Principals therefore looked to other mechanisms, such as peer counseling, to ease the pressure on teachers in promoting affective growth. But subject mastery, although necessary, was never sufficient for faculty membership.[7]

Student Governance

An elected Faculty–Student Governance Committee would address "curriculum, discipline, community regulation, and student affairs." Students would learn governance skills and procedures through the academic program. "The experience of governing their own community," designers noted, "will be valuable for personal development and for understanding of social science" (*Middle College Proposal*, n.d., p. 23).

Relying at first upon successful implementation of the house, the governance took considerable time to implement. The delay probably reduced the influence of the school, since one study of social integration into college suggests that the importance of participation in formal governance and in associations is greater for minority than for White students (Pascarella, 1985; Tinto, 1993).

Evaluation

"Anything that is worth evaluating," stated an alternative school director, "cannot be evaluated; anything that can be evaluated is not worth evaluating" (Center for New Schools, 1972, p. 339). The director—reversing a famous aphorism—voiced the skepticism expressed by many participants in the alternative school movement about evaluative research. But middle college proponents disagreed—in any case neither CUNY, the BOE, nor the philanthropic foundations would have had it otherwise. Lieberman's proposal to the Carnegie Corporation included a strong evaluation component, and the Academy for Educational Development (AED), a private, nonprofit agency, closely scrutinized the school's first year of operations— the first of many evaluations.

During the 1950s and 1960s, colleges and universities, supported by increased state appropriations, responded positively to calls for a substantial increase in the proportion of American youth attending college, especially the 13th and 14th years (President's Commission, 1947). LaGuardia's proposal took these calls a step further: At-risk urban students, no less than their suburban middle-class peers, were entitled to preparation for college. But such preparation required attention to affective, cognitive, and vocational growth; the vehicle was a school straddling traditional institutional divides. Open Admissions thus permitted educators to raise fundamental questions about "who should go to college" and whether "the schools can do it alone."

WHO'LL RUN THE SCHOOL?

The proposal in place, Shenker and Lieberman set out to obtain approval for the new venture. But approval from whom? By the time Shenker and Lieberman answered this question, they had negotiated a bureaucratic labyrinth that forced significant changes to the school's design.

This much was clear: All public and independent colleges and universities in New York State were part of the University of the State of New York, an entity governed by the state's Board of Regents and administered by the New York State Education Department (NYSED). SUNY and CUNY, the state's two public university systems, although nominally part of this "university," had independent governing boards. In part because SUNY was established in 1948, some jurisdictional issues remained unclear. Which actions of SUNY and CUNY trustees, for example, required approval by the Regents? To complicate matters, all community colleges in New York State, including CUNY-operated schools, were considered part of the SUNY system and received SUNY funds. SUNY had limited jurisdiction in New York City, but CUNY officials expressed concern each time they needed—or thought they needed—SUNY approval, as they would in this instance.

The infrequency of collaboration between K–12 and postsecondary officials at the state and city levels further blurred the approval process. In 1972, the relationship between the New York City schools and CUNY was emerging from a period of flux. Activists charged the BOE with a history of indifference to higher education initiatives. New York University professor David Rogers, for example, documented "habitually negative experiences with board officials." "We have had so much trouble with Livingston Street [BOE headquarters]," a CCNY professor told Rogers. "There was a guy down there who would always say when we brought some new programs 'get it cleared,' and he would run from office to office until he got a no." "You talk with the board, and nothing happens," related another interviewee. "It's a bureaucracy par excellence. There's such inertia in that kind of structure" (Rogers, 1968, p. 496).

Communication between CUNY and city school staff, and between the BHE and the BOE, improved under Schools Chancellor Harvey Scribner (1972). BHE bylaws reserved ex-officio membership for the Schools Chancellor—previously known as the Superintendent of Schools. Scribner was the first schools chief executive to attend BHE meetings in almost 20 years—one of his many attempts to improve relationships with CUNY. Scribner's support permitted serious discussion of thorny questions related to Lieberman's proposal. Were the school's students to receive a high school diploma? Shenker and Scribner said yes, but that meant approval by New York State secondary school officials. Would the school award the associate of arts degree? Again yes, but that required approval by another NYSED office and an amendment to the SUNY master plan.

Scribner's resignation in 1973 complicated LaGuardia's constant, multiple, and often simultaneous negotiations with city and state agencies, accreditors, private funders, and federal officials. "I remember," wrote Lieberman, "sitting in my apartment at breakfast, opening the *New York Times*, seeing the announcement of his resignation and in a dream sequence, watching all the papers relating to Middle College fall out of the window from the 18th floor to the ground, taken away by the wind" (Lieberman, personal communication, November 19, 1991, MCA). Obtaining the myriad necessary approvals, Lieberman concluded, would require substantial alterations to the school's design.

The governing agencies repeatedly raised two key issues: the legal precedents for CUNY and LaGuardia to operate a high school free of BOE jurisdiction, and the funding mechanisms for the new school.

Legal Precedents

It took a year to determine whether the BHE could operate a high school. City College had offered most classes at the secondary school level in the 19th century, and it continued to operate Townsend Harris High School—despite opposition from New York City school authorities—until 1943. Hunter College High School, an autonomous unit of Hunter College, had operated continuously since 1869 (Rogers, 1968; Stone, 1992). But could a CUNY unit operate a *new* high school? After receiving an initial favorable opinion in 1972, Shenker elicited three more judgments. The first, from a CUNY counsel, noted that Hunter College High School, the obvious precedent, was founded before the 1926 establishment of the BHE, and that the enabling legislation for the BHE provided for continuing the educational work of Hunter College. But, this counsel ruled, CUNY had to seek legislative authority to *establish* a new precollegiate school (Shenker to Arthur Kahn, September 24, 1973; Kahn to Shenker, October 4, 1973, MCA, "Middle College History" file).

Another CUNY counsel reversed this ruling, noting a 1942 New York State Court of Appeals decision permitting the BHE to discontinue Townsend Harris High School by resolution. Discontinuance, the high school's partisans had argued, required legislation, but the court decided that the BHE had the right, although not the obligation, to operate preparatory schools (*Wasmund* v. *LaGuardia*, 1942).

A New York State Education Department counsel concurred that the proposal did not require the approval of the New York State Legislature. Section 6209, the counsel said, authorized the BHE to operate educational institutions below the collegiate level and to award high school diplomas to graduates. But the significance of the proposal, the counsel ruled, required amendments to the CUNY and SUNY master plans (Shenker to T. Edward Hollander, September 24, 1973; Hollander to Shenker, October 9, 1973, MCA, "Middle College History" file).

Funding Mechanisms

Determining funding arrangements for the new school proved even more complex. The new school, by targeting a population on the verge of dropping out, appeared able to recoup average daily attendance funds lost once at-risk students were on the streets. Carnegie's Dunham noted the absence of concrete plans for funding the school, but remained optimistic that the BOE and BHE would come to a viable arrangement (Dunham and Peterson to "DZR and AP," August 11, 1972, CCP, "New York City University—LaGuardia Middle College" file). Lieberman expected joint funding—the BHE would pay for the higher education and remediation components; the BOE would fund the high school component, an estimated 45% of total funding (*Record of Interview*, February 10, 1972).

But who would pay how much, and which jurisdiction would take the lead? A liberal reading of the state's education law, combined with leverage accorded by the Carnegie grant, gave planners two options. The first option—BOE funding as an alternative high school—meant funding by strict formula based mainly on the total number of students enrolled and their average daily number of subjects. A school with significant numbers of skills-deficient students was entitled to extra funding for reading, speech correction, and non-English speakers. A 100-student enrollment, estimated LaGuardia officials, would bring enough revenue to cover the salaries of 4.5 to 5.0 teachers ("including the teacher-in-charge"), a part-time guidance counselor, and some support staff. Teachers would receive regular salaries and benefits and would need a New York City BOE license, although the school's administrators would have considerable latitude in selecting staff members. The Long Island City location made the school eligible for federal Title I and New York State Urban Education funds. These revenues permitted hiring a reading or other corrective teacher, and some paraprofessionals; other federal monies were considered "chancy at best."

Strict formulas also covered BOE funding for supplies and books—about $25 per student from tax levies and $10 per student from the New York State Textbook Law. The board's high school division required schools to confine expenditures to approved categories and required administrators to obtain approval of all transfers of funds between categories. The BOE agreed to place an item in its capital budget to ensure that the school opened fully equipped (Frey, 1973). BOE sponsorship meant accreditation by board resolution; planners saw little problem obtaining this accreditation as long as Harvey Scribner was schools chancellor.

As an alternative high school with BOE jurisdiction and funding, stated an optimistic memo, "the school would have almost free rein to develop its own program using its own approach," by requesting waivers from BOE regulations—a time-consuming, although potentially effective, way of promoting creativity. The BOE also would waive traditional graduation requirements. Lieberman noted the possibility of obtaining a similar waiver of requirements from the Regents, "although these are minimal to begin with" (Funding for the Proposed Middle College, 1972). The consistency of BOE policies, and the high funding level, tempted the planners, as did the promises of curricular and logistical support, a long-term commitment, the ability to request waivers, and an assurance of cooperation by the BOE's Alternative High Schools Committee. The school would be the first alternative high school approved through this route.

But Lieberman noted disadvantages to this designation: Board and union contract restrictions on staffing could "inhibit creative programming"; restrictions on curriculum might produce a course of study that "may not match its own aims and philosophies"; over-regulation of equipment acquisition "precludes the making of independent decisions in some instances." The school, noted a consultant, "would come under every by-law and regulation laid down by central. It would be responsible for every report asked for by headquarters and would have to adhere to the demands of general circulars, special circulars, division circulars, and bureau circulars." In any given year, the consultant concluded, "these come in by the hundreds" (Frey, 1973, p. 8).

Lieberman therefore leaned to the second funding model—the Hunter College High School approach, providing for BHE supervision. Instead of a strict formula, the Hunter principal requested a number of positions from the BHE; once the positions were approved, the principal had discretion over internal allocations. Hunter teachers—chosen by peer committees—needed a bachelor's degree. These teachers received tenure after five years; by then, they would have earned a master's degree. State, not city, teacher certification was "generally" required. Teachers, under section 6209, received the same wages and worked the same number of hours as other New York City high school teachers ("Budget and Funding Rationale," c. 1973, p. 23).

Under this model, the school would go it alone on support items, including meals and monitoring attendance. The supply allocation was smaller than the per-student BOE rate, but the principal would have discretion over this allocation. BHE supervision would permit staffing and curricular flexibility, bypassing the BOE in favor of regulation by more-lenient state school officials, hiring of part-time teachers, and exchange teaching between school and LaGuardia instructors. Most important, noted Lieberman, this model provided a better chance for the school to "gear its program toward giving the students the kind of preparation needed for success in the college." LaGuardia officials therefore opted for BHE regulation, despite the fewer dollars.

By March 1973, Lieberman thought the difficult decisions were behind the planners, and assumed that the BHE would sponsor the school. But she and Shenker had not obtained assurances about *state* funding. The state, they learned, would not send financial support for secondary education to a college-level governing body. State funding for the school must go to the city's Board of Education, which would pay the salaries of the teachers and make the required reports to the state. Hunter was an exception permitted under state law: Funds could go to a *senior* college sponsoring a laboratory school for elementary and secondary school teacher training. The dean of Hunter's school of education could then allocate these funds to the high school. But community colleges in New York State could not offer teacher education in any substantial way; LaGuardia, even if it wanted to, could not modify the school's design to conform to this exception.

Only one choice remained—alternative high school status and funding under the aegis of the BOE. The board would employ faculty members licensed as high school teachers to meet union requirements and would award the New York City high school diploma. The BHE would provide a $45,000 contribution for the first year only; thereafter, it would pay for space, salaries of LaGuardia faculty teaching high school courses, and some support (*Summary of Middle College Activity*, 1974; see also "How New York City's High Schools Spend Their Money," 1996; Klohmann, 1987).

Opting for BOE funding raised key policy questions—how, for example, would the school recruit the "right" faculty and administrators? But Lieberman and Shenker had to complete the cumbersome approval process before addressing those issues.

APPROVAL

The change in funding schemes meant a one-year delay in the school's scheduled Fall 1973 opening. By Fall 1973, a working relationship with BOE officials and staff—developed during meetings to clarify the proposal—translated into approval from Irving Anker, the new schools chancellor, and from the BOE. LaGuardia's department chairs, cabinet, and academic program committee approved the plan; so did the staff of CUNY's dean of community colleges, and the university's committee on academic programs.

Shenker noted little enthusiasm from the BHE, despite the school's inclusion in its 1972 master plan. Some opponents, he recalled, cited its "goofiness." One board member said he voted for the proposal because he liked Shenker, but, opposing CUNY's involvement with secondary education, he hoped the Regents would reject the idea. The American Jewish Congress noted the clause in the proposal calling for the school's ethnic distribution to reflect LaGuardia's. Shenker removed the clause, seeing no need for a battle with the city's Jewish leadership over a sentence that he considered an example, not a call for a quota. The BHE approved the proposal on November 26, 1973 amid considerable publicity and without controversy (Board of Higher Education, 1973; "City U. Planning 'Middle College,'" 1973; Healy, personal communication, February 5, 1992, MCA).

Lieberman took the proposal to SUNY and the Regents in January 1974 (James J. McGrath to Bruce Dearing, December 6, 1973; Dearing to McGrath, December 12, 1973; Hollander to Robert Kibbee, December 17, 1973, MCA, "Middle College History" file). Shenker noted some opposition from NYSED, whose K–12 and postsecondary education divisions rarely dealt with issues crossing bureaucratic boundaries (Shenker, 1992). Fortunately, Theodore Hollander, a CUNY Vice Chancellor during the planning for LaGuardia, worked at NYSED and helped shepherd the plan through the Albany labyrinth.

All governing bodies, including the Regents, eventually approved the proposal, subject to negotiating the financial details. SUNY amended its master plan in February 1974. Governor Malcolm Wilson objected, stating that colleges should not operate public schools. But he approved the amendment in October 1974, a month after the school opened. Wilson added two provisos—termination after five years and no replications—that stemmed from jurisdictional concerns expressed by officials at upstate community colleges that had fought for separation from local school districts. But Wilson soon departed from office, and Shenker ignored the provisos. The five-year mark would come and go unnoticed, and several state-supported replications would open in New York City during the 1980s (Harry Charton to Bob McVeigh, February 27, 1974; Ernest L. Boyer to Board of Trustees, State University of New York, February 27, 1974; Martha Downey to Boyer et al., February 28, 1974; Shenker to Hollander, March 6, 1974; Boyer to Ewald Nyquist, March 14, 1974; Hollander to Boyer, October 2, 1974, MCA, "Middle College History" file).

The switch to BOE funding, noted Lieberman, slowed the planning, forced design alterations, and produced implementation problems. Perhaps most important, it changed a school for grades 10–14 into a high school. New York City high schools accepted students into 9th or 10th grade at ages 14 or 15; Middle College High School (MCHS) at LaGuardia would accept referred 9th graders for admission into the 10th year. The resulting 15- to 17-year-old cohort would study in close proximity to the older students at LaGuardia, and the modified design retained considerable community college participation in the life of the high school. But high school status meant fewer formal interactions between MCHS and LaGuardia students (although MCHS students would still enroll in college courses); three- (not five-) year age-heterogeneous activities, including house; and admission to LaGuardia as regular students, not as students in the last two years of an identifiable school.

CONCLUSION

The success of MCHS at LaGuardia depended on attaining flexibility in the midst of a bureaucratized urban school system, obtaining cooperation between jurisdictions that barely communicated with each other, and implementing a comprehensive plan within a community college that simultaneously pursued multiple functions. The short time span between the founding of LaGuardia and MCHS—even with the year's delay—made attaining the last goal easier. Reformers later wishing to replicate the innovation found that the maturity of the parent institution yielded advantages—willingness to take a long view, for example—and disadvantages—inertia, battles over space and other resources, and greater social distance between college and high school students, faculty, and staff.

Strings attached to funding threatened to offset LaGuardia's support and to compromise the design. But despite the change to the five-year sequence, MCHS officials could think creatively about the future of their students. Patience and support proved crucial; it took four MCHS principals and more than a decade to realize—or find substitutes for—lost or compromised features.

Were the design compromises fatal? In the early 1990s, with about 20 replications scattered throughout the country, Joseph Shenker saw the changes as advantageous. If the school were to prove anything, he contended, it had to be a model; that is, it had to work within the parameters specified for other New York City alternative high schools. Recruiting principals and teachers in the usual way, using the same budgetary formulas as other alternative high schools, and conforming to BOE rules tested the limits of innovation, and ultimately permitted replications as other urban school districts came to accept new modes of educating at-risk students. Lieberman and Shenker may not have made decisions on governance and finance with replications in mind, but they believed that the problems of urban education were too widespread to permit a solution that others considered *sui generis* (Shenker, 1992).

MCHS would still be multifaceted—sole reliance on smallness, college instruction, or cooperative education would not work. The planners overcame the first hurdles—designing and obtaining approval for an urban, nonresidential, intermediate-level public institution for low-achieving students out of precedents designed for students in other socioeconomic strata.

They could now turn to the next challenge—opening the school in a manner acceptable to themselves and to the school's governing bodies.

"The planning is over; the rigidities in the system have been confronted" stated an optimistic mid-1974 report. "A new model is ready for operation" (*Summary of Middle College Grant Activity*, n.d., p. 10).

3

Living at the Border:
Design and Implementation

*The director's responsibility as liaison between the Board of
Education and the college is crucial and demanding. He/she
must be aware of the procedures and policies of both institutions and be able to effectively draw upon the resources of both.*
                                                    —Carol M. Poteat (1975b)

The 1970s were, wrote two observers, "as volatile a period of educational
reform as America has ever experienced" (Grant & Riesman, 1978, p. 1;
see also Levine, 1980; Tussman, 1969). Alternative forms of higher education abounded, including colleges within colleges and "communiversities."
Many reforms went awry or were ephemeral, but some reforms carried
into mainstream higher education (Kerr, 1995). Colleges, for example, during the 1980s retailored experiments in experiential learning aimed at
adults for traditional-age undergraduates. Similarly, 1970s high school–
college articulation experiments foreshadowed the broader "academic alliance" movement. If LaGuardia's Middle College High School (MCHS)—
this book will use the school's official name; others continued to use
Middle College—were to model a new approach to educating at-risk adolescents, it had to reconcile an ambitious, if compromised, design with academic folkways, mores, laws, and regulations.

Improved school–college collaboration—distinguished by many observers from less-demanding "cooperation"—required strong commitments (Greenberg, 1991). Late-19th-century reformers could more easily
establish informal, voluntary mechanisms, such as the Committee of Ten,
to advocate reform of the secondary school curriculum and of college entrance requirements. Secondary schools were less set in their ways; both
sides saw advantage to reform and could build on personal relationships,
and all were free to ignore the committee's recommendations (Krug, 1969).
But in the 20th century, jurisdictions often became entrenched, and
strengthening school–college relationships required brokering between au-

tonomous, isolated, even insular entities. Few reforms could survive the daunting approval process encountered by backers of the Middle College proposal.

During the early 1960s, the baby-boomer influx and concerns about education generated by the Cold War helped to produce the first wave of computer-aided instruction and "teacher-proof" secondary school curricula, often designed by college professors. Teacher-initiated innovations, more common by the end of the decade, confronted layers of bureaucracy. On the postsecondary side, statewide coordination of public higher education—required under Section 1202 of the 1972 Higher Education Amendments—became the norm by the early 1970s, and the coordinated units often were growing multicampus systems. Internal imperatives—not a holistic view of the student's academic career—dominated planning.

Calls for collaboration intensified as increasing proportions of high school graduates continued to college. MCHS was, to some extent, a response to such calls. But the bureaucracies governing MCHS and LaGuardia had little experience in collaboration, and the resultant normative conflicts were not easy to broker when manifested daily at one site. MCHS students, for example, were subject to compulsory, although free, education and to the curricular structure and disciplinary rules demanded by the BOE. In contrast, LaGuardia students enrolled voluntarily, enjoyed greater freedom of curricular choice and schedule, and were subject to fewer behavioral strictures. But their textbooks were not free—and neither was their tuition after CUNY, reeling from major budget reductions after the 1975 New York City budget crisis, imposed tuition for the first time in 1976. Recovery from the compromises imposed by the rules of multiple, entrenched jurisdictions, each with its own values and practices, hindered implementation of key components of the design and forced further changes after the school's opening.

MCHS staff eventually attained substantial autonomy and realized more elements of the design by learning how to "play off" governing bodies and constituencies and by invoking the school's status as an alternative high school. But at the outset, the headaches were obvious, and freedom appeared elusive. MCHS staff, needing to get students through a day in someone else's home, shortened their sights.

MIDDLE COLLEGE HIGH SCHOOL: THE FIRST YEARS

A School Is Launched

During the school's first year, MCHS staff had to resolve many start-up issues—a difficult task given the lack of precedents and compounded by the delay in obtaining program approval. The success of the school, contemporaries believed, required the rapid resolution of these issues; there might be no "long run" without evidence of progress. But the first years of an innovation may not be predictive of what is to come. A bad start might suggest a bad design *or* hasty or poor implementation. A poor design might be fatal, but questionable implementation could be corrected as students, faculty, and staff created or learned and refined their roles. MCHS fell into this latter category; faculty and administrators solved many problems only after several years of experience. In any case, the first years, the good and the bad, became part of the school's "organizational saga"—a term coined by sociologist Burton R. Clark (1972)—relating how enthusiasm and energy sustained an embryonic innovation until a "great event"—a top-to-bottom reassessment of the school during its third year—ensured long-term success.

Did the year's delay in opening MCHS ensure quality in staff selection, curriculum design, and physical plant adaptation? An optimistic timetable envisioning a year's lead time for these activities evaporated as designers pursued the required approvals (*Summary and Clarification of Middle College Plan*, 1973). Shenker and Lieberman, who chose not to run the school herself, began the search for a director—alternative schools did not have principals—only after securing BHE approval in November 1973. Eight newspaper advertisements elicited over 200 resumes; a committee of LaGuardia deans reduced the pool to 20 interviewees. Lieberman and this committee eventually selected Fillmore K. Peltz. Two more staff members were hired to work with local guidance counselors on student recruitment (*Summary of Middle College Grant Activity*, n.d.).

The design envisioned six months of training to orient MCHS faculty members to the needs of high-risk students, develop the teacher-counselor role, use the house structure effectively, and ensure familiarity with LaGuardia's facilities. But recruiting faculty took longer than anticipated. Advertisements placed in January 1974 produced over 400 resumes, but MCHS recruited only one teacher-counselor from this pool. The next recruitment cycle began in May, and the school was still hiring faculty six weeks later (*Agenda: Middle College Advisory Committee*, 1973). These delays, combined with inadequate BOE funding for summer activities, resulted in a truncated (ten-day) orientation held shortly before the school opened. Evaluators singled out this shortened orientation period as primarily responsible for a "thin" curriculum (Poteat, 1975a).

Designers targeted a February 1994 date for completing student selection. The approved design listed five admissions criteria—residence in western Queens, interest in a five-year academic program featuring career education, parental permission, an inappropriate current academic setting, and the maturity to cope with the demands (and freedoms) of the school.

Students would come from feeder public, parochial, and "young mother" schools, including ten junior and senior high schools. MCHS staff would first meet with the guidance counselors and administrators at each school, and then with 9th graders and their parents. LaGuardia staff would interview all applicants and their parents before making the final selections (Lieberman, c. 1974).

But the delays in obtaining program approval and in staff hiring hindered student recruitment. MCHS postponed student briefings and recruitment visits until the winter, extended the application deadline to mid-April, and continued the admissions process until June. The delays limited student orientation and curricular design targeted to the needs of specific students.

The proposal called for admitting 125 10th-grade students; MCHS would grow to full size by admitting a similar-sized 10th-grade cohort in each of the two subsequent years. But, anticipating an 80% retention rate, the staff admitted 144 students, of whom 135 appeared when the school opened (*Agenda: Middle College Advisory Committee*, 1973). The proposal called for two-thirds of the students to be at or below a 10th-grade reading level, but reading and math scores for entering MCHS students conformed to the BOE's expectation of 75%. About 66% read at two or more years below 10th-grade level, and nearly three-fourths needed remediation in writing at the sentence or paragraph level. Composite reading scores ranged from 2.2 to 13.6 (mean = 7.3).[1]

In mathematics, 64% of the applicants computed at two or more years below grade level, and 35% at four or more years; math scores ranged from 2.5 to 11.7 (mean = 6.6). Over half the entering MCHS students enrolled in the math survey—essentially a remedial class (Academy for Educational Development, 1974). The entering class, in short, needed extensive academic and personal support. "The intake procedure," director Carol Poteat (1975b) later recommended, "should be so constructed that maximum information can be gathered on each student in an effort to provide needed supportive services" (p. 7).

The delays in obtaining approval and completing faculty and student recruitment gave staff too little time to anticipate the many small problems that arose once the school opened. Worse, extensive student orientation and school closures for the Jewish holidays meant that MCHS needed nearly four weeks to settle into a "normal" routine. And, no sooner did the staff attain some equilibrium than Peltz resigned to administer Alternatives, College Cooperation, Experimental, and Special Schools, a BOE office that oversaw about 50 programs, including MCHS and 11 other alternative high schools. Peltz advocated for MCHS within the BOE, obtaining approval for hiring a teacher who served as a career education trainer and for funding an MCHS basketball team (Poteat, 1975a).

Carol M. Poteat, assistant director under Peltz, became acting director, and later director. Poteat, an English teacher who had taught in the New York City schools since 1960, authored a "Human Relations Course for Teachers and Students" used in the city schools and simultaneously taught a composition course at LaGuardia. Opening an urban high school was never an easy matter; hastily orienting—and then reorienting—a new staff and student body to a complex program that took two years to design was extra burdensome.

Normative problems, also requiring the immediate attention of MCHS staff, compounded the start-up issues. These problems—often manifested in mundane areas of school life, such as brokering time and space—arose from the need to broker between K–12 and college systems with lengthy but differing histories and traditions. Coordinating an academic year, day, and period, for example, forced compromises. This problem was familiar to college and university administrators: Schools of education and cooperating elementary and secondary schools accepting student teachers, for example, had to adjust to each other's schedules. But the relative independence of professional schools from other university divisions and their physical separation from the cooperating institutions facilitated compromise. In contrast, MCHS, with a mandated 182-day-per-year schedule and with compulsory attendance from 9:00 a.m. to 2:40 p.m., was located on the campus of an operational college that functioned on 12-week quarters; had different holidays, recess schedules, academic days, and periods; and did not confine its students to the site, except for the need to attend classes.

Differences in the length of a classroom period required immediate resolution. The proposal envisioned combinable 20-minute periods, but MCHS staff found that course and activity coordination with LaGuardia meant basing its day on the college's 70-minute periods. But these periods, some staff argued, were too long for a typical MCHS student to remain fully attentive. So MCHS established 35-minute periods that conformed with the LaGuardia schedule while addressing the perceived needs of its students.

And so on. After years in the public schools, MCHS students routinely marked the beginning and end of a period by a gong or bell. "Since LaGuardia has no gongs or bells," stated one report, "students have difficulty getting to class on time. We have requested that wall clocks be installed in the lounges and MCHS classrooms" (Poteat, 1975a, p. 5). Two decades later, there were still no bells; nor did students need hall passes.

Space, a problem from the outset, became a preoccupation as the year progressed. The buildings used by a rapidly growing parent college—originally factories—were undergoing renovation. MCHS had dedicated space, but growth and renovation affected the efficiency of its use. The student lounge was reserved for day care; recreational areas were closed for renovation; assemblies became impractical when a lecture hall was assigned for class instruction; the math, reading, and science labs were reserved for LaGuardia students, and faculty had no private space (Poteat, 1975b).

The location of MCHS across a wide street from the rest of the community college may have dissuaded its students from utilizing the support services located in LaGuardia's main building. The physical arrangements remained less than ideal after a subsequent move into the main community college buildings. MCHS moved into a more spacious, although less central, site in the late 1980s. Many replications had even greater difficulty securing a physical presence on an established, often space-starved, college campus.

Normative issues affected plans for enrolling MCHS students in college courses. The designers envisioned placing 11th-grade MCHS students in regular LaGuardia classes. Instead, about a hundred 10th-grade students registered in special MCHS sections of college-level art and typing classes. Enthusiastic LaGuardia faculty members voluntarily taught these sections, beginning ten days before the start of the college academic year. Another 20 students enrolled in LaGuardia classes—mainly Italian and computer— with regular community college students. Cross-over enrollments provided another reason for MCHS to accept LaGuardia's 70-minute periods, although the special sections permitted all MCHS students to begin their academic year at the same time.

Still, this component got off to a wobbly start. By opting for special sections, MCHS staff chose independence over integration, thereby losing the chance for direct contact with college students from similar backgrounds. Worse, inadequate orientation may have given MCHS students the wrong idea about college courses. High school courses met daily; college courses met two or three times per week. MCHS students tended to equate the number of meetings per week with the significance of the course. Offering college courses in skills areas—college typing, speedwriting, French, and Italian—compounded the misperception.

MCHS student enrollments in LaGuardia courses rapidly decreased during the fall. Only a few students remained enrolled by winter, and virtually no new students enrolled in college courses later that year. "The taking of college level courses," Poteat (1975b, p.7) later suggested, "should be deferred until the 11th grade when there can be a better understanding of each student's abilities." MCHS, under Arthur Greenberg, subsequently would prohibit 10th graders from enrolling in college courses and require successful completion of the CUNY freshman skills exam before permitting 11th and 12th graders to enroll. Recognizing the need for assessment before placing MCHS students in college courses, the staff adopted a "pre-course" strategy that "enables the student in a protected atmosphere to learn enough about a subject to decide whether or not he is really interested in studying it in a college setting" (Poteat, 1975a, p. 1) An affirmative answer led to enrollment in regular LaGuardia classes instead of special sections of college courses.

Resolving each normative conflict involved questions of mission and self-definition. How would MCHS determine, attain, and maintain an optimal degree of independence, given the legitimate concerns of the community, the educational systems, and the student clientele? If the need to conform to LaGuardia's routine practices and procedures was vexatious, daunting, and reminiscent of early-20th-century fears of "college domination," could MCHS and LaGuardia collaborate in substantive areas such as academic and cooperative education curricula and student counseling?

Designating MCHS a high school conforming to BOE mandates gave the school leverage in its negotiations (mainly tactical) with LaGuardia. But LaGuardia, MCHS staff understood, could not address all issues. In any case, MCHS staff perceived LaGuardia as more supportive and nurturing than the BOE. Could, the designers asked, "the power of the site"—the leverage coming from its community college campus location—offer independence from otherwise highly regulated school life? Would students, faculty, and staff seek and use this independence, or had they so internalized the norms of 110 Livingston Street—all knew BOE headquarters by its address—that MCHS would soon become little more than a small urban high school featuring selected, sympathetic staff?

Answers came quickly. Greater freedom for MCHS students resulted in more absences from the classroom, but not from the premises. The results included pranks, noise, and disruption. The influence of older students, designers assumed, might encourage their younger peers to internalize salutary collegiate norms. But the larger-than-anticipated age spread between LaGuardia and MCHS students—reflecting a national trend toward an older community college population—resulted in considerable resentment among LaGuardia students. Negative editorials in the LaGuardia student newspaper singled out the pranks and the noisy halls. Imposing tuition at LaGuardia further increased college student resentment since MCHS students who enrolled in college courses escaped the charge (Greenberg, 1982b).

Opening LaGuardia's extracurriculum to MCHS students helped to reduce the tension. Staff members suggested other palliatives: a larger Big Brother-Big Sister program; expanded high school–college peer counseling classes—empathetic LaGuardia students worked as counselors to help MCHS students identify problems and increase self-confidence—more MCHS student cooperative internships at LaGuardia, and vice versa; and a regular column about the high school in the LaGuardia student newspaper. The Office of College Security also helped by maintaining open lines of communication, participating in orientation and internship programs, hiring MCHS students for part-time and summer work, and offering a law course for high school credit (Denniston, Lumachi, & Rosenberg, 1984).

Tension diminished in subsequent years as MCHS 11th and 12th graders brokered between new arrivals and LaGuardia students. But reduced student freedom was the immediate tried, true, and more certain answer. "The second quarter program allowed time for many students to have independent study," noted one evaluation. "Students were unable to accept the self-discipline necessary for success and were uncomfortable with the 'free' time. This quarter the curriculum is much tighter. All concerned seemed happier" (Poteat, 1975b, p. 3). MCHS eventually reorganized its daily schedule to eliminate free time during the first six daily periods, thus increasing the structure of the student's day and reducing noise in the halls.

Pranks ceased to be a point of contention by the time Arthur Greenberg became principal in the school's third year (1976–77). The most vociferous LaGuardia student objectors had graduated or otherwise departed, and subsequent cohorts of LaGuardia students saw MCHS as one of the "givens" (Greenberg, 1993). But in the short run, community college student resentment hindered collaboration between LaGuardia and MCHS and raised questions about the unity of a late adolescent peer group. The issue reappeared at several replication sites a decade later, exacerbating community college *faculty* anxiety about the innovation.

Of greater long-term importance, the freer community college environment resulted in high absenteeism. The problem was anticipated. About 58% of the applicants to MCHS were absent more than two weeks of the previous school year. Only 23 of the 155 1973–74 enrollees were absent less than five days while in 9th grade. The median was 10 to 15 days, and 40% were absent more than 15 days (Fiorello H. LaGuardia Community College, c. 1975). But, observers argued, the freer LaGuardia environment for MCHS students exacerbated this proclivity. Attendance rates declined as the weather improved, and students singled out house meetings as expendable activities.

Lacking "an inner discipline" and, some added, peer counseling and support, students showed high rates of absenteeism and poorer performance in their college courses (Poteat, 1975b, pp. 8–9). Ironically, in a school in which older students were to be salutary influences for younger students, Poteat called a year-end meeting to find "ways to prevent the new 10th graders from being adversely affected by students who have not adjusted to Middle College" (Poteat to Middle College Advisory Committee, in re June 3, 1975 meeting, MCA, "First Year" file).

Absenteeism remained a conundrum, and staff disagreement on the appropriate mix of freedom and control kept the issue in the forefront. When the MCHS student newspaper asked, "What do you think can be done about cutting in Middle College?" answers included capping permissible cuts, building a gymnasium, and holding classes in major subjects in the morning. The newspaper's cover featured a "Middle College 1975" New Year's baby resolving, "I will not cut any more classes" (*Horizon*, 1975, p. 1). Faculty and staff were tempted to gravitate toward the structure their students experienced in prior schooling. By March 1975, evaluators noted improvement in classroom control, behavioral problems, and hall noise. "Some learning is taking place," the evaluators wrote. "In addition, the administration appears to be functioning more smoothly . . . [and] . . . there appears to be some tightening up in procedural matters" (Ruth G. Weintraub to Martin Moed, March 7, 1975, attached to Dan J. Ehrlich to Joel Millonzi and Ken Berger, March 7, 1975, MCA, "AED Reports" file). But MCHS was intended to foster independence and responsibility; too much structure would defeat the larger goals. At times, LaGuardia's norms counteracted "slippage" toward the traditional; at others, dealing with LaGuardia *forced* creativity.

Community expectations also pulled MCHS toward the traditional. Contemporary writing on alternative high schools emphasized "the consideration of a school's particular outcome goals rather than on the availability of standard achievement tests, self image scales, etc." (Center for New Schools, 1972, p. 341). But teachers were used to testing. In any case, unadulterated "progressive" educational philosophies and evaluations did not sit well in New York City public education, and MCHS could not neglect standardized testing. MCHS students, noted Poteat,

> will ultimately be compared with their counterparts in traditional school settings. . . . Since society at large still measures success by means of tests, whether standardized or local, it is important that Middle College students be exposed to these methods of measurement and have opportunities to develop test taking skills. (1975b, p. 4)

Two years later, external demands and internal ambiguities led Arthur Greenberg to conclude that MCHS had turned too far from the community college; freedom *from* had not led to freedom *to*, but instead to a regression toward the traditional.

Getting Through a Day

But this was hindsight. It took less than a month for MCHS and LaGuardia staff to grasp the consequences of working with a "high-risk" student population. Long-range planning for teachers was sacrificed to the need for daily support for most students. "Curriculum development for the 11th year, long range planning, staff governance, student–parent–teacher involvement, and articulation with the college proper," noted Peltz (1974), "must be provided for during time which is separate from the normal school day" (p. 5).

Demands on the seven full-time MCHS faculty members remained intense—each instructor taught 25 hours per week and supervised other activities needed to fill out a student's program. But MCHS students, staff concluded, required one-on-one instruction that the faculty could not provide. Nor did conditions improve; demands on administrators, many of whom also taught, mounted because of the need to work with multiple constituencies, and because MCHS, responsible for all BOE mandates, lacked the specialized staff that handled these tasks in larger schools. "More time was needed to explore the house concept," Peltz wrote. "Very little was learned about the community surrounding LaGuardia as a source for understanding Middle College students." Teachers, he added, "needed further training in group dynamics. Much more time should have been devoted to the teaching of reading skills in the content areas" (Poteat, 1975a, p. 7).

Morale remained high despite these problems. Perhaps a "Hawthorne effect"—positive outcomes resulting from participating in an experiment— saw the students and faculty through the first weeks. Observers praised faculty and staff as "capable, optimistic about the program, and dedicated to making it work" (Academy for Educational Development, 1974, p. 8). Students feared the loss of élan when Peltz left. "As of now the atmosphere between the students and teachers is fantastic," wrote the students of house 122. "We . . . are afraid that the new A.D. will disrupt the relationship" (Students of house #122 to the students of Middle College, October 11, 1974, MCA, "First Year" file). "[I]t is difficult to recall visiting an institution in which the morale was better," an observer reported that fall. "There seems to be an absence of backbiting and jockeying for position, which is par for the course at most institutions" (Ruth G. Weintraub to Martin Moed, December 13, 1974, MCA, "AED Report" file). "Teachers enjoy working with the students and the informal relaxed atmosphere of the program in general," added a later assessment. "The teachers are a bit more realistic about what can be accomplished in the program. The first year has been a learning experience for the teachers, too" (Weintraub to Moed, March 7, 1975, attached to Dan J. Ehrlich to Joel Millonzi and Ken Berger, March 7, 1975, MCA, "AED Reports" file).

When they could catch their breath—the school's 92.5% retention rate after the first year added to the pressure—faculty and staff members contemplated the significant gap between design ideals and school realities. Slowly, they began to address key, controllable issues. High on the list: growing isolation between LaGuardia and MCHS faculty and staff. Many at LaGuardia, Poteat noted, were unaware of MCHS. "Confidence builders" were the suggested solution, including joint staff meetings, informal activities, and curriculum development. Attending LaGuardia faculty meetings, she noted, "would not only prove beneficial to Middle College staff, it would enable the college to better understand the goals of the Middle College" (Poteat, 1975b, p. 7). MCHS faculty invited LaGuardia colleagues as guest speakers; the faculties later progressed to joint committees on cooperative education and on student interaction in the extracurriculum.

Some MCHS administrators cultivated informal relationships with their LaGuardia counterparts. But Poteat, considered a LaGuardia department chair in the proposal, remained at arm's length from other chairs. The Middle College Advisory Committee—composed mostly of LaGuardia administrators and a few teaching faculty—*was* a forum for interaction. But the school's designers intended this committee to include "educators with expertise in innovative program planning as well as parents and business and community leaders" (Poteat, 1975b, p. 6). The school's external relations remained underdeveloped for several years.

Curriculum and instruction, the house system, staff development, and funding topped the list of desired internal improvements. Perhaps nowhere was a regression to the traditional more apparent than in curriculum development. BOE approval to run MCHS as an alternative high school required modifying the envisioned interdisciplinary curriculum to meet city graduation requirements. A 1974 memo, calling for students to complete between 21-5/12 units and 24 units in three years, showed greater curricular structure than earlier proposals. Students would complete four units of English, two of math, 3-8/15 of social science and American history, three in a three-year sequence, 1/2 of health and safety education, 2-1/5 of science, 1-1/2 of art and music, and 3/5 of practical arts. Here, units were based on MCHS attendance for three 12-week quarters per year; students would spend the fourth quarter in activities related to the cooperative education curriculum (*New York State Requirements*, c. 1974). "Interdisciplinary instruction has not taken place as described in the plan," wrote Poteat (1975b) at the end of the first year. "The present group of 10th graders are taking traditional subjects developed around the theme, 'Who Am I'. However, no attempts have been made to tie subject areas together under this theme" (p. 2). During its early years, MCHS confined most interdisciplinary work to career education.

But this component was itself in trouble. Shenker and Lieberman sold the middle college concept to western Queens by noting LaGuardia's focus on cooperative education. The program proved difficult to implement since it required relationships with many employers and agencies in the community. Cooperative education was not part of the curriculum during the first year and the school did not hire a full-time work–study coordinator, called for in the plan (Poteat, 1975b).

LaGuardia and community leadership eventually helped MCHS to address this issue. The school first adopted some halfway measures: a staff member found part-time positions for 11th graders and tried to incorporate their work experiences into the academic curriculum. Guidance counselors offered workshops, organized field trips, and brought in guest speakers. During the first year, MCHS created a task force to seek ways of implementing career education, but a joint MCHS–LaGuardia faculty committee made little progress and Poteat later recommended hiring a curriculum developer. Full implementation awaited Arthur Greenberg's arrival two years later (Poteat, 1975a).

Poteat also noted difficulties with tutoring. The proposal included a tutoring program pairing LaGuardia and MCHS students. But inadequate academic skills and irregular appearances by LaGuardia student tutors hindered rapport with MCHS students. Poteat (1975b) recommended that selected current MCHS students serve as tutors when they reached 11th grade; they would be "ideal tutors for the younger students and for each other" (p. 7).

MCHS faced two pressing personnel issues: Staff was inadequate and untrained. The school had a guidance counselor, but did not have a psychologist, psychiatric social worker, or psychiatrist—all called for in the proposal. These absences placed additional burdens on the school's teacher-counselors, who were to teach five classes while handling "intensive remediation, interdisciplinary instruction and all areas of counseling" (Poteat, 1975a, pp. 4–5). The plan also envisioned teacher-counselor help in implementing cooperative education.

By the mid-1970s, the teacher-counselor notion had gained popularity among reformers of urban education (Doll, 1972). An alternative environment in which teachers did not have to act primarily as disciplinarians, some reformers suggested, would allow their growth into the role of counselors—or at least of "friends" to at-risk students. Reformers called for including counseling and clinical work as part of a teacher's regular load freeing time by delegating administrative, security, and bureaucratic functions to paraprofessionals (Wilson, 1971). Reallocating tasks would result in more attention to the academic and developmental needs of students and in greater personal and professional fulfillment for teachers.

The problems associated with this new role quickly became apparent. The teaching staff met the hiring criteria outlined in the plan and held New

York City teaching licenses. All but two held tenure, but no one had in-depth counseling credentials at the time of hiring. The truncated orientation period preceding the school's opening gave faculty members little guidance on how to shift from counseling, expected during the house period, to instruction, expected as soon as the next period (Academy for Educational Development, 1974). Overcommitted days precluded on-the-job role development, and understaffing meant faculty responsibility for "house, group counseling, serving as liaison with home, maintaining student records, academic counseling, remediation, teaching four classes in a major discipline and one elective course," and weekly staff meetings. At year end, observers continued to cite counseling—its indeterminate nature and the inadequate preparation of teacher-counselors—as a key problem.

Inadequate staff training meant problems for the house. The house concept never really took off. Lieberman (1991) bluntly noted, "It was butchered by faculty and principals" (n.p.). BOE unit allotments meant that houses included 20 to 25 students instead of the envisioned 15. Faculty discomfort with the teacher-counselor role contributed to dissatisfaction with the house period. Some houses were unstructured; others served only an administrative function. Later, the length of house periods was shortened (Academy for Educational Development, 1974).

Lieberman attempted to salvage the house at a December 1974 staff meeting. The house, Lieberman said, should encourage academic independence and self-reliance. Students, she added, should be encouraged to make decisions about their own studies and their careers, not about the school's educational policies. Students would learn consensus decision making by determining the activities of the house; these activities could include social service, artistic performances, and projects to improve student life at the high school. But group counseling sessions were substituted for the house period, which remained an unfulfilled component of the proposal for another decade.

Funding, the key hurdle faced by the designers, remained a problem. The issue was no longer the source, but the amount. MCHS faced a "Catch-22": "The Board of Education requires LaGuardia to accept students in the Middle College program who would not ordinarily go to LaGuardia," noted an evaluation, but "the Board of Higher Education funding level for remedial students is based on the needs of students who would go to LaGuardia" (Minutes of Staff Conference, December 2, 1974, MCA, "Miscellaneous, 1974–75" file).[2]

After the 1975–76 year, Carol Poteat accepted a promotion to the BOE's central office. The challenge of the new job attracted Poteat, noted most interviewees, not a push out of MCHS. So did the accompanying salary increase—an MCHS director was paid at the rate for an assistant principal in charge of a high school annex. Poteat argued her post was more analogous to the head of an independent alternative high school. But MCHS was not independent, and Poteat noted an additional "crucial and demanding" level of responsibility "as liaison between the Board of Education and the college. He/she must be aware of the procedures and policies of both institutions and be able to effectively draw upon the resources of both" (Poteat, 1975b, p. 5). The director maximized flexibility by working *with* the BOE while using the freedom offered by the community college location. Middle college replications often went through one or two principals selected by the traditional seniority system before identifying a leader who used the dual governance structure to advantage.

Shortly after the first school year ended, Poteat received a thank-you letter from the grateful parent of a top MCHS student. "I am writing to thank you for all the wonderful teachers of your staff, for help making me the proudest mother in the world," the parent wrote. The student was lucky, he told his mother, "to have teachers that really teach and care about their students." He understands his classwork and homework, unlike his last school, which he disliked." She continued: "I can feed him, clothe him, love him, take care of him when he is sick, but it takes great teachers to make a man out of him and one they will be proud of also." Poteat commented: "To borrow (and alter) a line from *Fiddler on the Roof*, 'after a long hard year it's nice to know'" (Poteat to "All Staff," June 24, 1975, MCA, "First Year" file).

MCHS could cite such successes. But could its staff do for a school what it did for this student? After two years of operation, the jury had yet to render a verdict.

THE GREENBERG YEARS: ACADEMIC REFORM

A friendly critic—Baird W. Whitlock, former president of Simon's Rock Early College—visited MCHS during the 1976–77 academic year (Whitlock, 1978). An enthusiastic disciple of *16-20*, Whitlock brought Simon's Rock from an associate's to a bachelor's degree-granting college during the mid-1970s. He followed the experiment at LaGuardia with great interest from afar, although expressing skepticism that below-average students, some with learning disabilities, could do college work.

Whitlock's ambivalence turned into "considerable shock" during his visit. The proposal, he asserted, was in no way realized. "What does exist," he wrote, "is a three-year high school on a community college campus" (Whitlock, 1978, p. 140). Insiders could predict his indictment: traditional—not interdisciplinary—courses, poor attendance resulting in failure of students to develop basic skills and vocational interests, and an indifferent community college faculty. Whitlock attributed these failures to BOE and teachers' union regulations accompanying the alternative high school designation. Time-consuming mandates, he claimed, precluded faculty collaboration required to implement a complex academic program. Whitlock noted improvement during the program's second year. More able students showed better academic results, some MCHS students registered in regular college courses, student pride increased, and communication between high school and community college faculty members improved. But, he contended, the mandate to operate as a high school—rather than as a grades 10–14 school—would always constrain MCHS.

Whitlock's experience at Simon's Rock colored his observations. He believed, for example, that a middle college required "better-than-average students" and that "student motivation is an internal quality, not a result of structure" (Whitlock, 1978, p. 141). But other observers also questioned the applicability of an innovation, designed for one type of student in one setting, to another type of student in a different setting. MCHS and LaGuardia staff agreed with many of Whitlock's specific criticisms, although they offered a more optimistic prognosis and did not see as a fundamental flaw the need to operate as a high school for at-risk students. Arthur R. Greenberg belonged in this category.

A Great Event

When he arrived as its third principal in Fall 1976, recounted Greenberg (1993), MCHS was a "high school that just happened to be on a college campus" (n.p.). Greenberg, previously an assistant director—the title given assistant principals at alternative high schools—at a school without walls in New York City, applied for the MCHS directorship after seeing a posted vacancy notice. Arriving just as the school, now with about 300 students in grades 10–12, was about to graduate its first class, Greenberg, like Whitlock, found few realized components. Conversely, he reported, much of what he might have expected was just not there. "Middle College had no sense of mission—the facilities of the community college were not utilized," Greenberg noted. "There was little collaboration between the faculty and the administration. There was a lot of wishful thinking and optimism, but no reality check." MCHS may have reached individual students, but successes resulted mainly from teacher dedication, not school structure.

A key problem, he noted, was the persistence of normative dissonance: LaGuardia personnel never learned the culture of a public school. MCHS, he observed, suffered from a lack of anticipation, not malevolence. MCHS staff, Greenberg echoed Whitlock, lacking the time to cultivate consistent interaction with the community college, moved inward and "did things that high schools were used to doing."

Some LaGuardia officials feared having a tiger by the tail, Greenberg added, but Shenker's support was consistent, although he was distant—Greenberg's term was "properly aloof." Greenberg met with Shenker once or twice a year, described school activities, and reported a satisfactory level of support from LaGuardia staff. Hearing that Greenberg was satisfied, Shenker ended the meetings, never offering direct feedback. Martin Moed, second in command at LaGuardia as the dean of faculty and dean of the college, was the key player, noted Greenberg. Moed was close to Shenker. "He was very supportive, with Joe's support," Greenberg recalled. Moed gave MCHS financial support, created an articulation agreement in cooperative education, and established a new liaison with the LaGuardia registrar's office.

Perhaps most important, Moed gave Greenberg entrée to LaGuardia's faculty and staff—especially the department chairs. Department chair meetings were a key arena for decision making at the college. But Poteat, who, Greenberg asserted, had a cool relationship with the LaGuardia chairs, rarely attended these meetings. Greenberg initially felt a lack of support, but soon became "one of the boys," noted Lieberman. He met with each chair individually; asked for input and ideas, especially about ways to collaborate; and always attended chair meetings. Greenberg worked, for example, to establish better relations with LaGuardia's science department, whose chair complained that MCHS students wrecked his labs and believed that MCHS was anarchic. Greenberg promised there would be no recurrence. Greenberg reported a conscious attempt to have things to offer to the college, especially in the general area of high school–college relations. "I tried to be a team player," he noted.

Greenberg took a few months to learn about his inheritance—the school's problems, the cast of characters, and the potential resources. Most students were "nice," but, as the MCHS department chairs sensed, persistent absence from school and class cutting reflected a lack of student commitment. Students, in turn, frequently denounced the absence of a student government, which, according to the proposal, was to have addressed discipline. The house, Greenberg added, did not work. But the situation was not hopeless; students could develop a stake in the school and experience academic success if given the proper types of support.

Two members of the staff, Tom Sena, a career education teacher, and Winston St. Hill, the assistant director, were Greenberg's rivals for the MCHS directorship. Greenberg had to win them over—a delicate task accomplished after several summertime "try to work with you guys" discussions. Greenberg came to rely heavily on both staff members; not only didn't they sabotage, he noted, they were "terrific."

With the help of sympathetic LaGuardia department chairs—some taught at MCHS—Greenberg identified community college faculty members who would work well with MCHS students. LaGuardia faculty members currently teaching at MCHS, he knew, lacked the thorough screening given MCHS faculty before hiring. Some LaGuardia faculty, Greenberg reported, used inappropriate pedagogy; student boredom and impatience resulted.

Greenberg completed this diagnosis during Fall 1976, but the "Great Event" began when Greenberg left the school in midyear for back surgery. "Flat on his back" for two months, mostly in recovery, Greenberg reflected on what he had seen during his brief tenure as MCHS principal. He called a staff meeting upon his return, five months into his incumbency, and soberly described the issues facing the school. "It's difficult to admit that things aren't right," he recalled saying, "but this is what I think you believe: the systems and curriculum are inappropriate, the college connection is not being made, there is no student investment in the school." "If this is real," Greenberg concluded, "then there's lots of work to do. Let's do it." You could hear a pin drop during the hour and a half presentation, he recounted. Applause followed a stunned silence. "I can't tell you how I needed to hear someone say this," remarked one staff member. The time on his back, Greenberg commented, was the "best thing that could happen" (1993, n.p.).

The Institute

The following summer (1977), Greenberg ran an institute to redesign MCHS. All institute committees included faculty members and students. The institute created a college-style registration process and a new record-keeping system. But most of all, it designed a new academic curriculum, featuring interdisciplinary courses.

Curricular Innovation. The Bongo Theater Travelling Herd led the list of innovations. Participation in this interdisciplinary program permitted its 90 or more students to earn credits in most curricular areas by writing and staging live and televised productions on social issues based on academic source material studied in depth early in the course. At-risk students, noted MCHS administrators, often were excluded from participating in extracurricular activities for academic or social reasons. But these activities could re-engage students academically, so it made sense to ensure their incorporation into the curriculum (Cullen, 1991). Bongo, under Cecilia Cullen,[3] Greenberg's successor, compiled and published *American Dreamland*, an oral history of Queens, and performed a play based on this history throughout the borough. The program cultivated extensive peer support and drew extensively on LaGuardia's resources, especially its theater.

MCHS gradually shifted to nonsequential coursework, when possible. The staff, for example, redesigned American Studies, a year-long course taught chronologically, into three thematic courses that students could take in any order: government and constitution, cultural pluralism, and American foreign policy. Options increased—students gained the ability to elect their subjects, especially to decide when to repeat failed courses—thus advancing the goal of student "ownership," while facilitating implementation of the cooperative education component (Lieberman, 1986, p. 111). By the late 1980s, MCHS eliminated nearly all sequential work, except for some mathematics courses.

Student Governance. The summer institute also addressed student participation in governance and discipline. Previous attempts to launch the Faculty–Student Governance Committee, called for in the proposal, had failed. Many MCHS students, Poteat concluded, had previous bad experiences with student organizations and governance, and did not know each other well enough at the outset to choose a trusted leader. Believing the MCHS academic program was more effective at developing leadership and governance skills, she remained content with occasional testing of the waters (Poteat, 1975b). An institute committee created a student-faculty disciplinary structure resembling LaGuardia's, featuring student-chaired boards to hear disciplinary cases and pass judgments. Under Cullen, student government became part of the curriculum for students wishing to earn social studies credits. Student representatives took turns as meeting chairs, served as a review board to adjudicate infractions such as absenteeism, and sent recommendations to the school administration. Students called before the board could bring a teacher-advocate to speak for them (*Middle College High School at LaGuardia Community College*, 1989). The summer institute also changed the MCHS admissions system to permit current students to screen applicants, further adding to their feelings of ownership.

The institute shortened house periods from 40 to 20 minutes—they would later be shortened again to 10 minutes—thus becoming more like traditional "official" or home room periods. This change, Greenberg believed, reduced teacher discomfort with the "teacher-counselor" role without losing face. Instead, MCHS increased reliance on a more traditional guidance program emphasizing one-on-one meetings between guidance counselors and students.

Relations with LaGuardia. Would greater internal cohesion come at the cost of external relations? LaGuardia faculty members were directly involved in only the cooperative education and counseling components of the institute. Greenberg used his growing network of informal contacts to regularize procedures for enrolling MCHS students in LaGuardia courses. Ending the right of 10th graders to enroll in college courses, he elaborated on prior reforms by restricting enrollments to graduating seniors, juniors and seniors with satisfactory academic records, students who satisfactorily completed the prerequisite sequence of courses—precalculus for students completing intermediate algebra, for example—and students with a specific skill or talent, such as typing, art, piano, and language (Denniston et al., 1984). Enrolled students earned high school *and* college credits.

Noting that few MCHS students took these courses, Greenberg emphasized high school credit bridge courses, taught "college style," often by LaGuardia faculty members who served as adjuncts. Examples included introductions to data processing, business administration, law, and library research, and typing, elementary Spanish, guitar, economics, and arts (Denniston et al., 1984, p. 9). Participating LaGuardia faculty members did not object to this extra teaching, which was covered by the MCHS budget. Lieberman secured a LaGuardia bylaw permitting teaching at MCHS to be counted as "community service" in evaluating LaGuardia faculty members for promotion, an incentive she considered necessary for their participation. In turn, Greenberg obtained adjunct appointments at LaGuardia for several MCHS faculty members. Two-way faculty traffic, he noted, improved knowledge of the curriculum of each school. Faculty members would become "cousins, not brothers and sisters," he added, and college faculty resentment would diminish as MCHS student enthusiasm produced improved conduct.

Cooperative Education. Implementing the cooperative education-internship program was the institute's most important contribution. Under Peltz and Poteat, said Greenberg, this component was mainly "a road paved with good intentions." But, with Greenberg's blessing, career education became "the central and integrative theme of a student's program at Middle College" (1993, n.p.). The curriculum, designed by Tom Sena, included three internship-related courses, three full- and part-time monitored internships accompanied by internship seminars, and a new internship supervisory structure.

A developmental, not a vocational, motif united these elements. Tenth-grade MCHS students enrolled in Sena's Personal and Career Development (PCD) sequence, a two-quarter interdisciplinary program that included anthropology, economics, geography, history, political science, psychology, and sociology (Middle College High School, c. 1977). Students took the first half of PCD upon entering the school and completed the sequence in a subsequent quarter, depending on the scheduling of their first internship, which, in turn, depended on the number of credits earned in 9th grade. Designed to move from the concrete to the abstract, PCD began with a unit on the self. Building on the "Who Am I?" theme pervading the MCHS curriculum, the unit taught students to identify their strengths and weaknesses. PCD moved to defining and analyzing primary—family and peer—relationships, and then on to secondary, more abstract, relationships, including the community, neighborhood, city, and work.

Conceived as a progressive "school and society" course emphasizing inquiry and investigation, PCD aimed *not* at acquisition of specific internship-related skills—although the final unit, which teachers *had* to complete, addressed these skills—but at acquisition of "observation techniques, collecting and using evidence to form and test hypotheses, using questions and seeking their answers, and analyzing and evaluating data" (Middle College High School, c. 1977, p. 3). Considered part of the social studies sequence, PCD emphasized identification and clarification of values, especially with respect to work, and development of positive interactions with members of primary and secondary groups. The pedagogy emphasized small-group discussions and cooperative learning, seen as reinforcing and recapitulating the program and course goals.

Eleventh-grade students took "Decision-Making," originally designed by the College Board, and considered by the school's planners as the best existing, readily adaptable course (Gelatt, 1973; Gelatt, Varenhorst, Carey, & Miller, 1973; Lieberman, 1995). Students used a "rational decision-making process" to "examine closely in light of their first internship experience, their personal strengths and weaknesses, aspirations and fears, and skills and potentials" (Lieberman, 1986, p. 11). The students then applied the results of this self-examination to choosing a second internship—a new area or further exploration of the area identified in the first internship—and to clarifying career goals. Sena's curricular design discouraged students from making career choices until at least completion of the decision-making course, which was intended to help suggest a career cluster.

The decision-making course also provided a forum for social critiques. A late 1980s class met during a LaGuardia student tuition hike protest. "The teacher," noted an observer, "used [the protest] as an example of an important life decision that college-bound students must make." The class "listed tuition and college expenses at public and private institutions in the area . . . [It] speculated about society's moral responsibility to provide for financial aid and whether this aid would be available to them when they started college." Sometimes the implicit tension between self-definition and social critique led to frustration, as when "the most disaffected students," grouped in a section of the decision-making course, attempted to reconcile the desirable and the possible in budgeting with the pay they received from hypothetical jobs (Gregory, Sweeney, & Strong, 1989, pp. 79, 80).

The unpaid, credit-bearing internships centered on three "career clusters"—human services, business technology, and liberal arts and sciences—drawing upon LaGuardia's curricular strengths and the city's economy. Students alternated academic work with these internships, which were not automatically assigned. Instructors in the PCD and decision-making classes assessed student readiness and willingness to participate in internships. The public and nonprofit sectors sponsored most 10th-grade internships. Internship selection, wrote Lieberman (1986), at the 10th-grade level was "relatively informal and intuitive, guided sensitively by the career education supervisor" (p. 11). Most students worked at full-time internships, but students needing remedial work in basic skills had part-time internships after daily classes at the school. MCHS teachers could work with remedial and regular students in small classes—15 and 27 student maximum, respectively, in the 1980s—with one-third of the MCHS student body in off-site internships, and other students enrolled in college classes at LaGuardia.

The goals of the internships mirrored the developmental stages identified for the three cooperative education courses. Sena viewed the 10th-grade internship as an introduction to work for students who had not yet held a job; Lieberman viewed it as an opportunity for self-assessment. Official documents listed the goals for the first internship as developing "work values, job satisfaction, and elementary coping skills."[4] The second internship stressed "the application of decision making skills at the worksite, particularly in relation to interpersonal relationships" (Lieberman, 1986, p. 11).

Concurrent weekly career education seminars reinforced these goals. Students discussed and evaluated their experiences in light of the concepts they learned in PCD and the decision-making course. A "coping skills" module stressed "developing appropriate inter-personal skills to handle on-the-job problems." The sequence on "identifying work values and their influence in career planning" used the internship as a "laboratory" to help students in "exploring and developing their work values and needs which are identified and discussed in the classroom" (Middle College High School, c. 1977, p. 1b:4).

Seminars and internships for 12th graders drew together "insights and skills into a design for the future." Students did not take another career education course between the second and third internships. Instead, they conferred with their career education supervisors, who by this time had worked with them for two years to design a "career action plan" that "almost always includes post-secondary education" (Lieberman, 1986, p. 11). Monitoring for all internships included on-site visits by the internship coordinator.

Twelfth graders could still explore other clusters or another field within a cluster. But Sena expected these students to reconcile the desirable with the possible. A student in the health service cluster, for example, might focus on a career in medicine. "The student," noted one description, "can now realistically assess his or her abilities and perhaps decide that within the field of medicine a paramedic or lab technician is a career that is most attainable" (Middle College High School, c. 1977, p. 1b:5).

MCHS administrators preferred progressive and developmental to careerist and vocational language. "Theoretically the internship provides a formative cognitive experience, which moves some students through the Piagetian stages and provides the experiential dimension to facilitate advanced thinking skills" (Lieberman, 1986, pp. 12–13). But centering a high school curriculum around cooperative or career education—terms often used interchangeably—raised questions about student tracking and occupational sorting. Did "realistic assessments" mean that MCHS might divert students with career interests in medicine from careers as physicians and nurses into jobs as paramedics or lab technicians? Most academic and vocational tracking in high school, critics noted, was downward, despite the rhetoric of raised aspirations (Armor, 1971; Cicourel & Kitsuse, 1963; Clark, 1960a; DeLany, 1991; Erickson, 1975; Rosenbaum, 1976; Schafer & Olexa, 1971; Turner, 1960).

Staff used two related "high-ground" arguments to justify student-centered career education. First, realistic assessments meant that students must know "where they are, where they are going, and how to get there." The high "at-risk" level of MCHS students meant that career education would "divert" few students from higher-level career tracks. Without MCHS, they argued, many students would end up unemployed or in unskilled positions.[5] About 75% of MCHS students, staff noted, averaged 25 hours as grocery baggers, fast-food servers, or baby sitters in addition to their academic work and internships; career education, staff added, served as a counterweight to the low expectations typical of at-risk students (Lieberman, 1986).

Second, the MCHS curriculum was designed to demonstrate to students that skills they needed to participate successfully in identified careers required college-level study. "Does the Middle College aim to encourage students to take mainly the vocational route?" asked a 1989 publication. The answer was an unequivocal "no." In fact, the publication continued, "one of the goals of the Middle College is to attract more students to higher education." "The career education program," the document concluded, "orients students to the world of work, and the academic courses help them to process their experiences and acquire job-seeking skills. If a student chooses not to go to college but to go to work after graduating, he or she will be better prepared to do so" (Callagy, 1989, p. 30). Pointing to PCD, MCHS staff could argue that extensive attention to the Maslow hierarchy and to value choice demonstrated a student-centered education that promoted aspirations. In any case, MCHS students reported learning more in PCD than in other courses and saw the internships as key curricular components (Middle College High School, c. 1977).

To unify the cooperative education curriculum, two staff members were designated "career education-internship teachers" who advised each student throughout the three-year sequence; supervised the internships, including on-site visits; and taught PCD, the decision-making course, and the career education seminar. Off-campus interaction allowed teachers "to relate to students on an affective rather than an academic/intellectual plane" (Gregory, Sweeney, & Strong, 1989, p. 86).

"The courses are a forum for questioning and discussion, complaints, reflection, and support from teachers and other students," noted an observer. "They teach practical skills. . . . Perhaps more important, the courses give students much-needed personal support." Students "came up with surprisingly good solutions," the observer continued, when "grappling with adult problems." "Their concrete plans and more clearly defined visions of the future" reflected their training in decision making and goal setting. Students completing the internship curriculum, the observer concluded, "appear to be accomplishing their objectives" (Gregory et al., 1989, pp. 86, 87).

Some students expressed dissatisfaction with their internship experiences. "They said they are not 'real jobs.'" Other students noted "conflicting personal or home problems [and] office politics or less-than-understanding bosses." These problems, said a teacher who viewed the school as a counterweight to dead-end careers, brought them to MCHS in the first place. "Here, at least," the teacher added, "they come. I know them very well. I've been with them for three years." This teacher and an observer "often shared a wink . . . when students feigned cantankerous responses to her. Some pretended to pack their books and leave, but stopped at the door and returned to their seats at her command."

Other students reported more positive outcomes: "I have always wanted to earn the trust and respect of others," said one student. "I *have* earned it by doing what is asked for in an internship even though we aren't paid for it." "I have a few goals for my future," the student added. "One is to go on to college and major in business. Hopefully, I would get accepted in Baruch College or Hunter College." "After I finish college," this student concluded, "I would look for a job in what I majored in. I want to have my own responsibilities" (Gregory et al., 1989, pp. 80–81).

Through cooperative education, MCHS strengthened its relationship with LaGuardia. Greenberg (1993), for example, persuaded the college to accept the 12th-grade internship as meeting a cooperative education requirement for LaGuardia students. By the 1980s, MCHS regularly selected 25 students for college-level internships, and LaGuardia provided high school-level internships for 60 students (Denniston et al., 1984). More than two decades later, MCHS retained the goals of Sena's curriculum, although a focus on academic achievement during the 1990s led MCHS to reduce the number of internships from three to two, and to reduce PCD to a one-quarter course. The decision-making course was devoted to college readiness: reading biographies prior to writing the college essay, identifying colleges, and beginning the application process (Middle College Charter High School, 1999; Middle College High School, 1999).

The New MCHS in Action

The MCHS that opened after the Summer 1977 institute, contended Greenberg, was a different school. The place "took off." Students liked the redesigned courses—the internship program was a "huge carrot"—and attended more regularly. Teachers taught what they wanted, and found greater response from their students. Grades improved; so did morale. Greenberg's (1982a, 1982b) evaluation of MCHS, offered at the end of his tenure, reflected the realization of key aspects of the original proposal. Academic "bridge" experiences, and access to LaGuardia's academic support services and physical plant, familiarized MCHS students with a college campus and exposed them to positive college student role models. The resulting opportunities for academic success and improved self-concept, Greenberg concluded, outweighed the risks: the distractions of a campus and excessive fraternization with—or lingering resentment expressed by—college students.

MCHS faculty members, noted Greenberg, benefitted from interacting with college faculty and from the more abundant resources of the college. Enrolling higher-ability MCHS students in college courses, he added, freed high school instructors to offer basic skills instruction to other students at more favorable student–faculty ratios. MCHS faculty, Greenberg added, might envy the lighter teaching load carried by community college faculty members. But, Greenberg noted, the academic benefits, increased recruitment derived from close articulation, and improved relationships with K–12 administrators, parents, and the community could outweigh attendant financial, space, and disciplinary problems.

Would other community colleges sponsor replications? Not for another five years, well after Greenberg left the school. A successful model was necessary, but so were the many reports criticizing American secondary schools, philanthropic interest, and the continuing need to convince skeptics that the middle college concept was applicable to *at-risk* youth. Other models of educating at-risk high school students appeared easier to implement. But Middle College High School at LaGuardia was noticed. School systems, suggested the Carnegie Council for Policy Studies in Higher Education (1980), could use the design "to create more challenging environments for high school juniors and seniors who are bored with their schools or on the verge of dropping out" (p. 186). Other favorable reports followed. The staff took special pride in the assessment of Gene I. Maeroff (1981), *New York Times* education correspondent: "a magnificent example of cooperation" (p. C4).

The school began to show results once the key components of the academic and cooperative education programs were in place. For 1978–79, the enrollment was 443 students—all identified as "pre-dropouts"—the attendance rate was 84.4% (citywide = 79%), the dropout rate was 14.5% (citywide = 46%), and the college enrollment rate of MCHS graduates was 85% (citywide = 87%, but note the much greater citywide dropout rate). About 43% of MCHS graduates continued at LaGuardia, 28% attended other CUNY branches, and 15% chose SUNY or independent colleges. The others entered the workforce or the military (Greenberg, 1982c).

Greenberg emphasized the academic and career components of the original proposal, but Lieberman's design also included a strong developmental component. During the next decade this component became the focus of efforts to strengthen the school.

"CECE'S" ERA: SCHOOL MEMBERSHIP
AND ACADEMIC ENGAGEMENT

Affective curricula permeate every level of Middle College's culture.
　　　　　—Center for Urban Ethnography (1990, p. 69)

Cecilia L. Cullen—another Board of Education appointee—succeeded Greenberg as MCHS director in October 1981. Although expected by many at LaGuardia to spend only a few years at MCHS, she continued to lead the school at its 25th anniversary in 1999–2000. During her tenure, the academic and cooperative education programs continued to evolve, but Cullen focused on promoting the affective development of MCHS students.

The smallness of MCHS, Cullen recounted, initially captured her. The large size of typical urban comprehensive high schools, prior experience told her, strongly contributed to increasing dropout rates. Influenced by the developmental emphasis in the proposal for the school, by 1980s trends in school organization—especially site-based decision making—and by research on retention of at-risk youth, Cullen promoted the growth of community. "Larger schools, increased staff specialization, and diversified staff," she wrote, "have contributed to student alienation" (Cullen, 1991, p. 19, citing Goodlad, 1983; Grant, 1985; Newmann, 1981; Powell, Farrar, & Cohen, 1985; Sizer, 1984).

The Affective Tilt

She adopted two constructs from the research of Gary Wehlage: "school membership" and "academic engagement," premised on the assumption that at-risk students needed to see their school as an extended family or organic community, with teacher-counselors performing quasi-parental functions (Cullen, 1991, pp. 16–17; Wehlage, 1983; Wehlage & Rutter, 1986; Wehlage, Rutter, Smith, Lesko, & Fernandez, 1989). School membership—the social bonding of students and the communication of concern—was necessary for, and came prior to, internalizing official goals. Cullen adds,

> When schools are successful in promoting school membership, then students feel that they belong, that teachers care about them and their peers accept them. For teenagers, this means that they feel as if they belong to a family; they quickly assign parental roles to their teachers and counselors. (1991, p. 31)

Academic engagement—the "psychological investment required to comprehend and master knowledge and skills taught in school" (Cullen, 1991, p. 17)—arose from school membership. "Students with high attachments to teachers and counselors have a personal stake in meeting the expectations of those adults." From this attachment, she concluded, "a commitment to stay in school and to reach the goals of a high school diploma develops." Rewards, not penalties, nurtured academic engagement (Cullen, 1991, p. 32).

The family metaphor took center stage at Cullen's MCHS. Upon her arrival, Shenker recalled, she asked to be called "Mrs. Cullen," but by the end of her first day, everyone referred to her as "Cece." She soon accepted and justified this informality. "To promote school membership," she wrote, "the Middle College creates a positive relationship between the adults and the adolescents." "Everyone is on a first name basis," she added. "By breaking down the conventional boundary of authority inherent in the title, Mr. or Mrs., the student receives a clear signal that the adult is open to a more familiar relationship" (Cullen, 1991, p. 33).

Cullen began the school's tilt toward the affective by revising and enhancing counseling services. In 1981, she noted, counselors still saw individual students from 8:00 A.M. to 10:00 P.M. Cullen added a third counselor and an assistant principal for guidance (the student–counselor ratio was 132:1 by the early 1990s), and allowed group counseling to grow until about one-third of the student body participated in daily group guidance sessions.[6]

A visit from representatives of Daytop Village, a Staten Island-based drug rehabilitation center emphasizing peer support, led to the hiring of an MCHS counselor from that program and to a shift to group guidance. Students in crisis, Cullen argued, needed peer groups that could develop honest self-assessments by balancing near-confrontational directness and support. "The goal of group guidance at Middle College," stated a late-1980s evaluation, "is to help students with the most serious problems to develop coping strategies that will enable them to adjust to difficult home situations and to avoid becoming so enmeshed in personal problems, that they cannot function either socially or academically" (Center for Urban Ethnography, 1990, p. 55).

Each guidance counselor met in daily class-like, peer-counseling sessions with three teacher-referred groups of ten to 14 troubled students. Some groups met around specific topics. "Spark" discussed drug abuse; "Alateen" dealt with alcohol-related issues, and "Cutters Anonymous" addressed absenteeism (Bangert-Drowns, 1984). Guidance counselors also met with parents in monthly support groups and participated in drug and suicide prevention activities at other schools. Group counseling, Cullen concluded, held greater sway than teachers, teacher-counselors, and one-on-one counseling. The practice became a signature at MCHS and at many replication sites by the early 1990s.

Cullen also reversed Greenberg's policies of attenuating the teacher-counselor role and the house. She divided MCHS into three "families," each of which, in turn, was divided into 12 houses, each with 15 students. The need for 36 house leaders meant that all faculty members, administrators, and counselors—that is, all adults at MCHS—had charge of a house for a three-year cycle. "[T]he faculty's expertise varies widely in this area," wrote Cullen, but she expected each house leader to become "the primary adult in the student's passage through high school." All house leaders helped to design curricula for the houses—eventually compiled into a guide—covering academic advisement, building student self-esteem, and nurturing student government. These curricula focused on "hot-button" issues, including "AIDS, sex, birth control, local government elections, the census, study tips, SAT preparation, and communication with parents" (Cullen, 1991, p. 45). Later, the houses moved toward team-teaching and faculty collaboration. Cullen, and eventually a faculty-dominated personnel committee, made ability to perform the teacher-counselor role, including academic and personal counseling, a key criterion for hiring new faculty members.

The house period remained a "degenerated"—Cullen's word—ten-minute "home room" until 1988, when she used the school's shift to 70-minute class periods to expand weekly house meetings to that length. The houses included students from 9th through 11th grades—MCHS began to admit 9th graders in that year. These changes permitted all students to attend two 70-minute classes four mornings per week and a double house period on the fifth morning—all before their internship. On the fifth day, students also would attend the 70-minute seminar that always accompanied the internships. Twelfth graders moved into Senior House, which emphasized college counseling.

When teacher-counselors and other house leaders asked for direction in using the expanded time allotment, Cullen reallocated half the weekly period to family meetings of house advisors. She assigned a guidance counselor to each family, who discussed issues raised by students and who provided support for student counseling—the counselors emphasized academic advisement during the program's first year. Cullen—noting that she was "intimately involved with my house"—concluded that teachers could become successful house leaders. But she also expressed restiveness with continued variation in teacher effectiveness in performing the role (Cullen, 1993; Haberman, 1994; Schreiber & Haberman, 1995).

One-on-one peer counseling also assumed a central role in the revamped guidance structure. Motivated, empathetic peers—some LaGuardia students enrolled in peer-counseling internships—were matched with MCHS students with similar problems. Guidance staff trained these mentor-peers to cultivate self-confidence in their charges (DeRosenroll, 1988; Hansen, 1992; Kuner, 1984; Varenhorst, 1984a, 1984b). Evaluations of MCHS did not measure the impact of the experience on the peer counselors, but analogous research on one-on-one academic tutoring often showed what some MCHS staff suspected happened to these peers—significant affective gains *for the tutors* (Benware & Deci, 1984; Fitz-Gibbon, 1992; Light & Glachan, 1985).

Favorable publicity from the tilt to the affective—seen as contributing to high graduation and college attendance rates—led the New York City High School Principals' Association to renew the charge that MCHS was "creaming" the western Queens student population (Denniston et al., 1984, p. 2). The Board of Education responded by mandating a random selection procedure aimed at all Queens high schools but intended to forestall creaming. The lottery, contrary to association expectations, *raised* the percentage of the MCHS entering class with reading scores more than two years below grade. Students admitted through the lottery also showed a higher persistence rate, although the school reported much better results with junior high school recruits—the preferred target group—than with high school dropouts admitted in midyear "as a cooperative response to the community" (Lieberman, 1986, p. 5). Cullen subsequently obtained lottery exemption by demonstrating that MCHS chose students from only the lowest ability levels.

MCHS did not cream—the association was wrong—but it did select. By the mid-1980s, the school received over 600 applications annually, a ratio of four at-risk students for every opening. From the outset, the school interviewed candidates for admission, an uncommon practice in New York City high schools. The interviews and the sense of being chosen, staff learned, increased "buy-in" by students with a history of failure (Cullen, 1991). The lottery exemption, combined with heightened student interest in the school, permitted MCHS to reject applicants who appeared incapable of thriving in the less-structured world of the community college.[7] When, a few years later, the BOE permitted involuntary transfer to alternative public high schools of students caught with guns, LaGuardia president Ray Bowen obtained an exception to this policy for MCHS.

By the late 1980s, Cullen—finding that the academic accomplishments of most students increased after participating in group counseling—had expanded the "power of the peer" theme from the realm of guidance to a motif that permeated the school (Cullen & Moed, 1988). Observers noted her attempts to infuse or structure the affective needs of students into new and existing academic courses—and even into the school's governance structure. Cullen used the 70-minute periods to encourage student–faculty interaction and to discourage lecturing, to push for interdisciplinary—often combined—classes and team-teaching, and to espouse pedagogies moving students from the personal or the particular to the universal, from the concrete to the abstract. "In a number of classes," wrote one observer, "teachers attempt to influence the students' value systems, particularly to get them to think in less violent terms, diffuse anger, and respond to incidents in their lives with some measure of thought." One teacher, the observer added, "calls this 'personalizing' and said that it is accepted as good teaching at the school, though it generally is not the subject of conversation among the faculty" (Gregory et al., 1989, p. 75).

Curricular Innovation (Again)

Collaborative learning, noted Cullen, was the academic component of a positive peer culture. Peer teaching, she added, attended to the affective and cognitive needs of students and broke down teacher isolation. Cullen moved toward an interdisciplinary curriculum featuring peer teaching.[8]

"The African-American Experience," a thematic, team-taught English course designed in 1986, built upon the school's by then well-established "Who Am I?" motif. The course, arising out of a student request for a club for African-American students, incorporated questions of identity into the academic curriculum. Between 1986 and 1990, topics included the transition from indentured servitude to slavery in colonial America, the literature of protest, Malcolm X, the nature of personal relationships among African-Americans, the Tawana Brawley case, and children's attitudes toward racial relations. The course, noted a 1990 evaluation, enabled students "to connect with its content on a personal level" and was "affectively attractive to students" (Center for Urban Ethnography, 1990, p. 56).

The social sciences offered other team-taught, interdisciplinary options. MCHS and LaGuardia teachers jointly adopted and team-taught a high school version of the American Social History project, originally designed for college use by CUNY's Center for the Advanced Study of Education. The course combined basic English skills and social studies content. Students who passed CUNY's freshman skills exam received high school and college credit for completing the course successfully.

"Motion" was introduced in 1989 as a team-taught, collaborative learning course that moved from completing physical tasks—students stood on a beam balanced on a fulcrum to learn weight and distance relationships, for example—to deriving abstract concepts. The course emphasized depth of conceptual understanding. It moved, noted an evaluation, "at a relatively slow pace that would allow students to really learn the important physical and mathematical concepts of motion." Learning by reward was the second goal; task completion counted more than testing in evaluating student performance. The motion course also stressed group-work, "thus investing in one another's accomplishments" (Center for Urban Ethnography, 1990, p. 57).

Affective goals included giving "students the opportunity to experiment with taking responsibility for their own learning . . . by both giving students choices in what, and how much they learned of a given unit, as well as a deliberate teacher interaction style of answering questions with questions to get students to 'do the work.'" Students chose a task from a list on a chalkboard and worked in groups of three or four to solve worksheet problems. Teachers, moving from group to group, helped with tasks or "debriefed" students, that is, determined whether students were on the way toward mastering the concepts underlying the task (Center for Urban Ethnography, 1990, pp. 57–58). A year later, MCHS, helped by LaGuardia faculty, expanded the course into "Exploring Motion," a one-trimester immersion course offering credit toward mathematics, physics, literature, and physical education.

A late 1980s evaluation commended the ability of MCHS teachers to "structure their course content and classroom interactions with students to engage their interest and learn the subject at the same time" (Center for Urban Ethnography, 1990, p. 59). But the report provided ample evidence of an affective tilt—it posited multiple levels of student support, moving from ensuring regular attendance to guidance as key to successful functioning as high school students, and then to instruction where teachers nurtured "affective as well as academic needs" (Center for Urban Ethnography, 1990, pp. 55, 57). Seniors praised their teachers for caring. "[T]hey care about you and help you in any way they can. They really want you to do well," noted one student. "I liked the way the teachers teach their students and the way they care for the students," added another. "The fact that the teachers are like your friends—you can really talk to them," said a third. About 36% of the 1988–89 entering cohort chose MCHS for its affective reputation; 34% cited academic reasons (Gregory et al., 1989, pp. 89–90).

Had MCHS sacrificed course content to secure positive affective outcomes? Some seniors concurred. "I think classes should be more challenging," responded one student. "The teachers are too easy and some are not even interesting," added another. "It hasn't prepared me for college," noted a third. "Nonthreatening" content delivery might mean no content delivery. The focus of "The African-American Experience" on "a relatively finite content," stated an evaluation, "served the affective purposes of the course well, because it enabled a serious analysis of the nature of racial discrimination without having to 'cover' a wide variety of historical facts." But the evaluator raised questions about academic achievement. "Students were asked to write paragraphs about indentured servitude they had found in library sources." The next day, "they were allowed to go to other rooms to write up their notes." Half the class found no information. One student "asked the teacher if they were 'in trouble,' who responded 'of course not' and gave them alternate assignments" (Center for Urban Ethnography, 1990, pp. 58–59).

An internal consensus—and recognition of external concern for school accountability—formed around the need to strengthen the curriculum. Cullen, citing a student who received many As but could not pass her exams, convinced MCHS faculty members to attend to the school's core disciplines. The price: a reduced career education component. Graduates would complete substantial work in English, global and American studies, economics, biological and physical sciences, foreign languages, mathematics, art, music, and physical education. The school still espoused and offered interdisciplinary work, but curriculum development also focused on promoting active learning within a subject.

A strengthened math curriculum became a centerpiece of change. MCHS adopted the Interactive Mathematics Program (IMP), a spiraling, inquiry-based, four-year mathematics sequence used by about 250 high schools in 21 states. IMP addressed National Council of Teachers of Mathematics standards in traditional high school math, and optional topics such as statistics, probability, curve fitting, and matrix algebra. Solving IMP's open-ended problems, advocates argued, deepened mathematical understanding by integrating the specific focus of a unit with mathematical knowledge acquired in prior units. IMP's interdisciplinary approach impressed MCHS faculty: The program facilitated active learning through interactive group problem solving—no 70-minute lectures and rote algorithms here. The faculty also praised IMP's emphasis on performance criteria, portfolios, writing assignments, and oral presentations, although students also took exams. Last, IMP permitted the pairing of MCHS and LaGuardia math teachers.

Compiling portfolios became a key assessment mechanism throughout MCHS. Students collected longer-term projects in each subject into portfolios and reflected on their academic growth as shown by the projects at special house meetings held during each cycle. MCHS also required students to create synthetic projects during the final course of every sequence. Students, for instance, wrote a critical analysis of a classic text for English, a personal statement for the college application in the decision-making course, and an investigative report for science. These end-of-sequence projects formed the basis of the "graduation collection"; students elected three projects for oral defense before a committee that included the advisor, another faculty member, and a peer or family member selected by the student. Evidencing a growing commitment to reflective practice—outside "experts" were out—faculty workshops later analyzed sample portfolios to suggest improvements in instructional strategies. "Critical friends reviews"—assessments conducted by representatives of peer schools—were also based on these portfolios.

Students with B averages and about half the credits needed to graduate were eligible—although not automatically entitled—to enroll in LaGuardia courses. They earned dual credit for completing regular courses with a C grade or better, and high school credit only for passing college-level remedial courses. The proportion of MCHS students opting for college courses remained between 5 and 10%—26 students in Fall 1998. Wobbly student performance led MCHS to institute a mentor program that assigned a teacher to consult with college faculty, attend classes, confer with students, and conduct weekly skills sessions (Ort, 1998).

Faculty Governance

MCHS had to effect many delicate balances—balancing a focus on cognitive and affective growth being central. Cullen, observing LaGuardia's governance, asked whether a strengthened role for MCHS faculty might result in continuous improvement in both domains. LaGuardia faculty, she noted, had considerable discretion in selecting department chairs—so much so that Shenker, usually seen as a strong supporter of faculty prerogatives, ran into trouble with the CUNY Faculty Senate when he overruled a department's choice in 1985 (Maeroff, 1985). Could not, she asked, MCHS teachers likewise select their own colleagues, thereby spreading out the workload while facilitating acculturation? Scrutinizing the informal governance structure of MCHS—an inheritance from Greenberg's tenure—Cullen decided that fostering shared governance and obtaining faculty "buy-in" were no small feats in a city marked by periodic confrontations between a hierarchic central administration and a militant faculty union. But, she hypothesized, interaction between high school and college faculty—through curriculum planning, teacher exchanges, and team-teaching—might help to overcome MCHS faculty reluctance to assume responsibility for personnel and governance.

In 1988, a year before the New York City school system under Chancellor Joseph Fernandez began to experiment with shared decision making, MCHS created teacher-chaired curriculum, climate, and personnel committees (Blase & Blase, 1996; Marczely, 1996). Faculty, paraprofessional, and secretarial participation was mandatory, but staff could choose their own assignments. Committee membership changed annually, and membership on the personnel committee depended on recruitment needs. Committees elected their own chairs annually; an assistant principal served as facilitator. Cullen, as principal, could make a final decision if a committee could not achieve consensus on a matter needing resolution. She also could veto a committee decision, although she did not exercise this right. Committees met for 90 minutes monthly during regular school hours; a shift to a four-day-per-week schedule permitted by team-teaching freed faculty members for committee participation. The committees dealt with "second-order changes"—some voluntary, some mandated—including defining short- and long-term institutional goals; shifting the school's daily, weekly, and annual calendars; reallocating space; establishing criteria for student assessment; and redefining staff roles.

Many changes occurred after a 1988 mandate to turn MCHS into a four-year school, a mandate prompted by reshuffling of grades in feeder junior high schools. This controversial move would have provoked more debate if implemented a decade earlier when some observers still questioned the admission of 10th graders. Ninth graders, often 15 and sometimes younger, critics noted, had even less in common with community college students; their presence might divert attention from and reduce resources available to older students. Cullen accepted the mandate, but continued to argue for a broad age grouping. "Middle College was designed," she wrote, "to test the hypothesis that 14 year olds have more in common with 19 year olds than with 12 year olds" (Cullen, 1991, p. 29).

Cullen attempted to turn problems associated with the mandate into opportunities. And the mandate did pose problems. Instructors, for example, found the new, team-taught, double-period humanities core (English and social studies) course, devised for incoming 9th graders, "exhausting and frustrating to teach." "They are not," noted an evaluation, "accustomed to the immaturity level of thirteen and fourteen year olds." "There was frequently a "highly charged" atmosphere in the classroom," the evaluation added, "which seemed to be required to keep the students involved for two 70-minute periods." The class needed both teachers, said the evaluation, for content and for class management (Center for Urban Ethnography, 1990, p. 58). The curriculum committee—responsible for approving new courses and textbooks—attempted to reduce frustration by mentoring staff to use team-teaching as a control *and* a support mechanism.

The curriculum committee later implemented major changes in student evaluation. Uneasy with reliance on standardized tests and teacher grades, and influenced by the total quality management movement, Cullen (1993) called for a shift to an outcomes-based student assessment, based on portfolios demonstrating mastery of specified competencies. MCHS staff used workshops to develop lists of desirable student competencies, skills, and outcomes and to compile an assessment manual. The committee incurred teacher resentment by assigning responsibility for devising outcome measures to individual teachers, without providing additional compensation. Cullen offered to intervene, but committee members decided to approach their colleagues again with more options and support, but without yielding on the mandatory nature of the assignment. Eventually, the committee compiled beginning, middle, and final instruments, including portfolios, to assess student outcomes and to provide for improvement.

The climate committee—responsible for school morale and student attendance—staged public events, displayed student work, and organized student–faculty activities. Cullen attributed a 10% increase in class attendance to committee creation of a reward system for students with perfect attendance and passing grades in all subjects (Center for Urban Ethnography, 1990). The committee later fell into disuse.

The personnel committee implemented much of Cullen's shared governance vision. It emulated college-level practices, first by conducting the initial screening for faculty positions—Cullen retained the right to make the final decision—and later by hiring on its own, using criteria defined through a collaborative process. The committee then contemplated an expanded role that included peer evaluation and mentorship (Grant & Murray, 1999). Contractual provisions posed obstacles, although the personnel committee negotiated a waiver of the teachers' union policy of transfer by seniority in 1990. Unsuccessful candidates who would have had the right to transfer to MCHS teaching positions under seniority rules were given enough time to transfer elsewhere (Cullen, 1991).

Committee member inhibitions posed a greater problem. "Don't put me in a position where I have to decide who to fire," said one committee member. "I don't want the responsibility of evaluating my peers." Teachers could not at first visualize playing formative, not summative, evaluative roles. Some tension dissipated when Cullen volunteered to undergo the first review; more was diffused as the assessments became integrated into the school's collaborative ethos.

Decisions, learned committee members and their colleagues, had far-reaching consequences. Adopting governance models more typical of college than of high school faculty, MCHS staff often questioned the relevance of general BOE edicts to the school's specific circumstances. "The teachers in the school have become more political animals," noted an evaluation. "Their success with the personnel issue demonstrated to them that as part of the staff of an alternative school it was their responsibility to their students to stand out on a limb and fight for alternative policies when appropriate" (Born, 1991, p. 62). Committees often proposed novel, beneficial solutions; collegial approaches and counseling, for example, reduced the misuse of school supplies by a staff member who had received many administrative warnings (Born, 1991). Committees also served as counterweights to classroom isolation and provided leadership opportunities to many colleagues.

Could shared governance become a permanent feature of the school? The personnel committee, Cullen believed, would play a key role by hiring colleagues who believed in changing current practice through collaboration, rather than by administrative fiat. Eventually, the staff agreed to include all key areas of governance via a school-based management committee that comprised the principal, an assistant principal (the slot rotated), a paraprofessional, two elected members of each of the three governance committees, the chapter chair of the United Federation of Teachers, and slots for students and parents. Student and parent participation in most governance activities was disappointing, although one evaluation noted that parents were vocal and influential *when* they attended meetings (Born, 1991). The personnel committee retained its key role in governance after MCHS became a charter school in 1999.

Changes occurred in fits and starts; not all innovations succeeded. But MCHS, a participant noted several years later, showed that a high school could provide a richer learning environment for students by creating a professionally supportive working environment for the staff. Real changes do not occur "in environments that infantilize teachers and push them into patterns of defensiveness and conservatism," or "when they are meant to serve only one segment of the school community." "When the group agrees on a policy, the observer concluded, "all things are imaginable, and most are possible" (Born, 1991, p. 64).

These changes in governance required senior administrators to redefine their roles; edicts just would not do. A principal, Cullen reflected, must be a professional developer who trusted her staff enough to turn over considerable authority. "It's ridiculous in a group of adults," she added, "to have one controller. All should know what I know to make decisions that affect the school." Collegial collaboration, she contended, would translate to teacher–student collaboration, if facilitated by the school's administration. The administration, she wrote, "needs to articulate the vision and be the consensus builder. You don't prescribe how." With site-based management, she added, "it's easy to be sidetracked. You have to be grounded in what's good educationally. . . . Have them work collaboratively with each other and then have then transfer that into working with students in the classroom" (Born, 1991, p. 58).

"At meetings," one assessment noted, "[Cullen] is most often the voice of mediation, facilitation and reiteration—asking 'What do you want? How do you want me to address this issue? Is this what I'm hearing you say?'" She "continually holds up the banner of consensus, redefining and reiterating the staff's decisions, problems and objections, making us all more aware of the power of our responsibility. It is truly a case not of we against them, but of us together" (Born, 1991, p. 58). Cullen attributed many of her beliefs about leadership, motivating people, brokering, and power to Joseph Shenker, whose leadership style was at odds with the top-down orientation of many other community college presidents.

"The school's success with at-risk youth depends, in large part," said a 1990 evaluation, "on the success of its support structure. . . . [A]t least some teachers . . . creatively structure both their course content and classroom interactions to engage students in ways that are sensitive to their needs and, at the same time, facilitate learning." As for outcomes, MCHS "students show higher in-school retention, credit accumulation rates, and attendance," when compared with a similar control group, but lower school-wide average monthly rates than other high schools in Queens, and average rates compared with other New York City alternative high schools. The evaluation found significant differences between MCHS and control group students in Regents Competency Test (RCT) pass rates—100% vs. 53% in the Reading RCT, despite similarities in Degree of Reading Power scores. About 86% of surveyed graduating seniors planned to attend college the next fall. Two-thirds of respondents, the evaluators added, "credited Middle College with influencing their plans by encouraging them to go to college, providing them with internship experiences, and helping them to be more hopeful and motivated about their future lives" (Center for Urban Ethnography, 1990, p. 69).

Skeptics might question whether the success of MCHS in the affective sphere depended on the design of the school or the dedication of the staff. "The extent to which student support services are dependent upon special individual qualities may be cause for future concern," wrote Arthur Greenberg in 1987. "Any support system which is constructed around the unique sense of obligation borne by key, and not easily replaced, personnel may be crippled by staff changes" (Greenberg, 1987, p. 167). A governance mechanism featuring a powerful oversight committee and a personnel committee charged with minimizing the problems attendant upon staff turnover allowed MCHS to hedge its bets.

CONCLUSION

By the early 1990s, MCHS employed between 25 and 30 teachers, including adjuncts from LaGuardia; the staff also included paraprofessionals, school aides, outreach program personnel, three assistant principals for guidance, organization, and supervision, and a principal. The staff's growth under Greenberg and Cullen enabled MCHS to realize key components of the original plan, including cooperative education and attention to affective development. MCHS enrolled five hundred 9th through 12th graders—more than half from low-income families often on public assistance—recruited from seven feeder schools in western Queens. Throughout Cullen's early tenure, the racial and ethnic composition of MCHS remained relatively constant. By 1996, the proportion of first- and second-generation Hispanic students increased to 47%—reflecting demographic changes in western Queens and expansion of the recruitment area to include the entire city (Center for Urban Ethnography, 1991; Ort, 1998). Whites made up another 28%; African-Americans, 18%, and Asians, 7%.

Nearly all students entering MCHS in 1988 wished to attend college—69% aspired to at least a bachelor's degree, although only 57% expected to attain this goal. About one-third of the entering students had repeated at least one grade; most entered with no high school credits. Half of the 1988 entrants heard about the school from a peer; MCHS had achieved credibility among its students. Just over a third cited the school's reputation for affective growth as its main attraction; another third cited the academic offerings. Few students, in contrast, cited the internships or the opportunity to take college classes. But this was not a surprising result since students came to appreciate these activities once on campus.

As predicted in 1973, MCHS students "saw contact with older students as an impetus to growth. They also liked the freedom, access to a wide range of facilities and resources, and the responsibility afforded by the college context." "College students," said one student, "help to motivate you to act more mature—I like mixing with college students." "It's more like a college than a high school," said another. "[It] makes me feel older." "I feel comfortable with having the freedom and responsibility that comes with being here," said a third. "It makes it better than a regular high school," noted a fourth. "You can use college facilities and have more options" (Gregory et al., 1989, p. 97).

MCHS had realized an updated version of the 1973 design, but what about the future ("Unique Community College Collaboration," 1993)? The school, staff understood, required continued semi-autonomy from the Board of Education. Even when MCHS and the BOE espoused the same principles—such as a commitment to site-based decision making—working definitions could differ. MCHS therefore took advantage of administrative benign neglect, established at the outset. Early opposition from the Queens school superintendent arose from her belief that it was unsafe to have 10th graders on a college campus where there were "untoward social influences." But by the time Greenberg arrived, her successor, who participated in the 1973 negotiations with Lieberman, saw MCHS as a safe haven. "He didn't know what was really happening," said Greenberg, "but was benignly supportive." When Greenberg invited him to visit, the response was: "You don't want me at your school. If there's a problem, call." Greenberg added: "He didn't intrude" (Greenberg, 1993, n.p.). The school's success, the distance from BOE headquarters and the indifference of some administrators, and the ability to select its students gave MCHS the needed independence.

The relationship with LaGuardia was less bureaucratic and problematic; informal relationships made the project work. When Shenker left LaGuardia to assume the presidency of the Bank Street College of Education in 1988, Ray Bowen, his successor, endorsed the high school. Bowen—present at the creation of MCHS—returned to LaGuardia after stewardship of Shelby State Community College in Memphis, Tennessee, where he nurtured a replication of the high school. Cullen and Lieberman, now LaGuardia liaison, interacted frequently, with Lieberman pushing for fuller realization of the original design. In contrast, Martin Moed's successor as dean of the college was not sympathetic to the high school. Moed, Cullen noted, always replied to her requests by saying, "Yes. How can we do it?" But when a LaGuardia faculty member, assigned by Moed to work on the MCHS career education program, left the school, the new dean denied Cullen's request for $3,000 to buy services and hire adjuncts. Cullen went over his head in this instance, but used the tactic sparingly.

What would happen to MCHS when successors could not count on Cullen's network of informal relationships? Consistent support from the LaGuardia administration meant financial assistance, equitable space allocation, and support for innovation. But the realities of academic collaboration—which Cullen considered the key strategy for regularizing close relationships—fell short of aspirations. The move of MCHS in the late 1980s to its own building added to the challenge.

Some MCHS faculty members hesitated when discussing academic relations with LaGuardia: "There are really very few organized means toward school–college articulation," asserted one staff member. "Some opportunities are offered for staff to work with college personnel, but they are voluntary and limited." "Part of the school's professional development program," this staff member added, "should be geared to general articulation with the college departments, admissions policies, freshman programs, etc." (Gregory et al., 1989, p. 96).

But MCHS and LaGuardia faculty members served as adjuncts at each other's schools, team-taught, and jointly devised curricula and prepared grant requests. Deploring curricular overlap, Cullen and Lieberman built bridges, first via articulation committees and by adapting the American Social History Project for high school use, and then by MCHS–LaGuardia team-taught bridge courses in English, math, and science. MCHS staff also worked with a LaGuardia faculty member to learn techniques for integrating basic skills into content courses. Collaboration, Cullen believed, best grew inductively in an atmosphere of opportunity, if both schools retained committed faculty members.

Overcoming ups and downs in key relationships, Cullen believed, also meant making MCHS *useful* to LaGuardia. Cullen, like Greenberg, contributed to the functioning of the community college. She, for example, established a campus day care center, participated in the search for Shenker's successor, and helped to create a campus center for business, career, and values, based on affective components of the MCHS cooperative education curriculum. LaGuardia faculty members cited specific contributions from MCHS faculty: "study skills, reading curriculum, how to deal with the transition to college, teaching methodology, affective aspects of education" (Gregory et al., 1989, p. 97). MCHS also helped LaGuardia externally: Being useful, Cullen knew, included promoting LaGuardia's reputation for innovation. In turn, that reputation helped ensure that no one would tamper with the high school.

The mere presence of a high school on a community college campus, MCHS staff concluded, did not guarantee a minimum level of collaboration. Two divisions of the same postsecondary institution might have shared a campus for years, but neither cooperation nor collaboration *automatically* followed. Two independent, hierarchic institutions were even less likely to collaborate; and, if forced to do so by the lure of external reward or threat of sanction, the resulting projects were unlikely to succeed.

Many LaGuardia staff probably did not feel threatened by MCHS since, unlike other two-year colleges, the college never had to establish its identity apart from a high school, and because MCHS had adopted some collegiate practices. But Cullen may have perceived correctly that success depended on the ability of each school to internalize a collaborative norm that permitted staff to negotiate from strength. Symmetric relationships permitted activities beyond the tactical "academic alliances" of the late 1980s (Gaudiani, 1990). But collaboration would not lead inevitably to integration; Cullen did not advocate the grades 11–14 scheme urged in *16-20*.

MCHS, Cullen believed, best lived at the border—far enough away from the college and the school system to avoid constant scrutiny, to ignore both, and to play them against each other, if necessary. Living at the border led both college and system authorities to assume that MCHS was under the other's supervision, thereby maximizing autonomy and permitting experimentation. Seeing MCHS as a "safety valve" also may help to explain BOE tolerance.

An opportunity to increase the school's autonomy appeared in 1998, when the New York State Legislature permitted the Regents to issue charters that freed converted public schools from many local and state regulations.[9] The Regents granted MCHS and neighboring International High School conversion charter school status the following summer; both applications listed LaGuardia as an institutional partner. Charter status enabled the LaGuardia partnership to include academic and support services such as payroll and purchasing (Middle College High School, 1999). A board of trustees would govern the school; the site-based management committee would continue to recommend academic, staffing, and business policies. Few policies would change immediately; the school would focus on a smooth transition from BOE supervision. The charter, granted in August 1999, thus ratified the direction of governance that had evolved over a quarter century.[10]

The school's success demonstrated, Lieberman, Shenker, and Cullen wished to assess its potential as a model for the reform of secondary education. Was success based on unique circumstances, or was replication possible? With Ford Foundation funding, they set out to learn the answer.

4

Replications

Middle College is a national treasure; it should be replicated nationwide.

—Ernest L. Boyer, President,
Carnegie Foundation for the Advancement of Teaching.

By the mid-1980s, the model provided by a stable, visible Middle College High School at LaGuardia was ripe for export. Foundation and government officials, such as Carnegie's Ernest Boyer, expressed interest in a high school for at-risk students that "worked" at a time when the nation's entire public education system appeared "at-risk." The movement went regional in 1985 when the New York State Legislature voted renewable grants to replicate the model elsewhere in New York City.

State funding prompted Janet Lieberman, still at LaGuardia, to set her sights on the national stage. In 1986 she received the first of several Ford Foundation grants that resulted in the opening of seven geographically dispersed replications. Five sites remained in operation a dozen years later, and about 20 additional sites opened during the 1980s and 1990s—including schools at two of the City Colleges of Chicago (Olive Harvey and Truman College) that opened (in 1985) before the Ford initiative.

Could other late-1980s reformers successfully open and run a school, modeled on conditions in New York City and on educational thought of the 1970s? The model, Lieberman and Cullen concluded, was replicable if a tenable host community college and the local school district adopted the entire package, thereby eliminating many ups and downs experienced by MCHS at LaGuardia. But some sites chose selectively from the rich menu offered by Lieberman and colleagues, and sites that adopted *in toto* still experienced implementation problems. Examining the state- and Ford-sponsored replications allows us to explore the relationship between "adopt" and "adapt," and how local educators navigated difficult political currents.

THE NEW YORK CITY SITES

MCHS did not close after five years, as Governor Malcolm Wilson had stipulated. Instead, in 1985 the New York State Legislature funded five replications in New York City. The legislature intended one school for each of the five boroughs, but when the horse trading ended, Queens got International High School (IHS), also located at LaGuardia, Brooklyn College Academy (BCA) opened at Brooklyn College, and the Bronx got two schools—Lincoln Academy of Science (LAS) at Hostos Community College in the South Bronx, and University Heights High School (UHHS) at Bronx Community College (BCC). The fifth school—to be supervised by the College of Education at City College in Manhattan—never opened despite a foundation start-up grant. Staten Island was excluded.

International High School

International High School, originally Middle College II, targeted recently arrived immigrants—perhaps 7,500 students in contiguous Queens school districts—whose limited English proficiency placed them at-risk of dropping out (Lieberman & Callagy, 1990; *Middle College II*, c. 1984). Janet Lieberman spearheaded the initiative for IHS, which proposed to accept graduates of local junior high schools, age 17 or older, with one to three years residence and a minimum 6th-grade education in their native country. The LaGuardia location, Lieberman noted, "encourages [older] students to enroll as they escape the embarrassment of being over-aged in a younger setting" (*Middle College II*, 1984, p. 12).

The school featured an assistant principal who reported to Cecilia Cullen, the nominal principal; 14 teachers—the student-faculty ratio was 20:1—and several professional staff members. The IHS faculty spoke 11 languages; most were at least bilingual and had cross-cultural experiences. Roughly equal numbers of Hispanic, Asian, and "other" students spoke 27 languages; the number of languages spoken increased substantially in the 1990s. Classes were taught in English, but students and teachers translated when necessary, and students could complete the foreign language requirement by taking a course offered in their native language. IHS students could enroll in MCHS and LaGuardia courses; they completed internships arranged by MCHS (*Middle College II*, 1984).

When IHS, like MCHS, was charged with "creaming," it restricted admission to referred 10th-grade students scoring below the 21st percentile on the English version of the Language Assessment Battery and residing in the United States for less than four years. IHS students reported relatively low economic status and parental education, although most families were intact. A 94.8% attendance rate (1986–87), a negligible dropout rate, and higher student aspirations and ability levels distinguished the school. To ensure a cordial reception from the LaGuardia community, Shenker and Lieberman enlisted several LaGuardia faculty members to teach IHS courses. The opening of IHS elicited resentment when some LaGuardia faculty were forced to move out of the main building. But Shenker allowed the school to use his office as a classroom for a year, and resentment dissipated when IHS and MCHS received dedicated space in 1988 (Bush, 1992; Lieberman, Nadelstern, & Berman, 1988; Tyler, Gruber, & McMullan, 1987).

Brooklyn College Academy

Opened hastily in 1985–86, Brooklyn College Academy faced start-up problems that also affected other replications: short lead time, low staff morale and high turnover, high student absenteeism—37.9 days per student average in Fall 1985—and college faculty and student resentment, especially over lost space. The school also suffered from a poorly selected student body; staff members accused the Board of Education of making BCA a "dumping ground" for students with disciplinary problems. The academy featured a more traditional curriculum than MCHS, although it also de-emphasized course sequencing. Brooklyn College instructors taught language, fine arts, and chemistry courses at first, since the BCA budget did not permit hires in these areas.

The rough first year prompted BOE and BCA officials to consult with Lieberman. In Fall 1986, the academy hired a new principal—previously an MCHS assistant principal—who set out to build morale among existing staff and to hire six additional faculty members. Admissions policies were modified to favor 14- and 15-year-old, over 17-year-old, freshman-year students. Staff phoned absent students and provided movies and a meal at a breakfast club. Average attendance increased in the school's second year (22.3 days absent), but BCA's 80.9% attendance rate (1986–87) was the lowest among the replications.

A link to the school of education at Brooklyn College provided BCA students with tutors and adjuncts, and offered faculty inservice workshops. BCA also moved to avoid large blocks of free time; the 35-minute periods used at the time by MCHS replaced the 80-minute periods that coordinated with the Brooklyn College academic day. Relations with the college improved; students participated in many college events; the BCA advisory committee took an active role in governance; and staff worked to integrate the academy into college facilities to ensure the school's survival if state funding ended.

Lincoln Academy of Science

Located at Hostos, a bilingual CUNY community college, Lincoln Academy of Science served a largely Hispanic constituency. Planning for the school languished during early 1986, but an interim president of Hostos, who took office in July 1986, appointed a liaison charged with opening the school by the middle of the 1986–87 academic year. The BOE chose a principal, who in turn chose the school's mostly inexperienced teachers and staff from a small candidate pool and within a short recruitment period. LAS moved into one floor of a main building at Hostos in February 1987 with 70 students, mostly from neighboring junior high schools. The school, confronted with ongoing space problems, projected gradual growth to 450 students.

Originally intended to take advantage of programs in allied health, business, and mathematics at Hostos, LAS changed its orientation to college preparation. Most students took seven or eight classes a day and could enroll in after-school internships—located at neighboring elementary schools or at Hostos—for high school credit. Confrontations with the college, the BOE, and CUNY's central administration, often precipitated by short lead times, continued into the school's second year. But the principal also reported improved student attendance, academic performance, and staff morale (Tyler et al., 1987).

University Heights High School

University Heights High School also opened in February 1987 with about 150 students. Bronx Community College and Hostos had agreed to target different student clienteles. But the ethnic breakdowns—60% Hispanic, 35% African-American at UHHS; 70% Hispanic, 29% African-American at LAS—were nearly identical for the first two years.

A longer lead time permitted better curricular and administrative planning and more careful recruitment. Applicants had to be at least 15 years old, read at a 6th-grade level or above, and appear, along with their parents, for an interview. Space was at a premium—some college staff blamed the space needs of UHHS for the cramped conditions on campus—so the school projected enrollment increases of 50 students per semester to a 450 cap. Gradual growth permitted the formation of new "family groups," essentially houses, instead of adding new students to existing groups, a potentially disruptive practice. BCC students objected to the high school, noting space and discipline concerns, but the dean of students at the community college reduced tensions by touring the relatively placid school with the objectors.

UHHS offered a three-tiered curriculum featuring traditional high school courses, computer literacy, and preparation for the Regents Competency Tests on Tier I; coursework, internships, volunteer service, and preparation for CUNY Freshman Skills Assessment (FSA) on Tier II, and high school and college coursework, passing the FSA, and career counseling and choice on Tier III (Tyler et al., 1987). But neither UHHS nor Brooklyn College Academy—the only replication located at a four-year college—offered cooperative education, despite Lieberman's insistence. Noting that the parent colleges did not feature cooperative education, as had LaGuardia, staff at these sites—along with Shenker—favored adapting programs offered by the hosts (Shenker, 1992).

The debate over cooperative education raised a key question: What was necessary for a replication to succeed; what was sufficient? Lieberman viewed the Brooklyn and Bronx initiatives as college campus-based alternative schools, whose philosophy and supervision came from the BOE. BCC's president, she noted, called UHHS a "tenant." Few BCA students, she added, took college classes, little faculty collaboration occurred, and physical integration was nonexistent. She termed the results of the consultation after the first year a "bailout."

But national attention to MCHS at LaGuardia as a solution to the contemporary educational "crisis" and its export to other CUNY divisions led other reformers to consider the model. Staff members at the Ford Foundation, long interested in reforming urban education, also noted the potential for replication.

THE FORD FOUNDATION AND THE REFORM
OF URBAN EDUCATION

How long a modern society and economy could expect to thrive, and how long a republic could flourish, with so large a part of the populace substantially undereducated—and, more than this, largely disaffected from the institutions and the process of education—is not clear.

—Ford Foundation (1984, p. 12)

A Lighthouse

Why did Ford Foundation staff sponsor a national replication? Since its founding (in 1949), Ford espoused several themes pertaining to the reform of American education: equality of opportunity, comprehensive—not piecemeal—reform, and the need to restore deteriorated high school–college relations. The egalitarian streak appeared in the Gaither Report, Ford's charter document. Equal educational opportunity, the report stated, "is not only a fundamental democratic principle; it is a prerequisite to the social mobility and fluidity which are basic to democracy," and to equal economic opportunity. But, "prejudice and discrimination abridge the educational opportunities of the members of our minority groups." And moreover, "the advantages of education are also walled off behind economic barriers, which are even more prevalent though perhaps less well publicized" (quoted in Ford Foundation, 1972, p. 7).

The Gaither Report emphasized the need for coordinated services to achieve equality of educational opportunity. But, the report added, attaining coordination and unity of purpose of local education was extremely difficult. "How to solve these problems in the interest of society as a whole, and how to do so without at the same time undermining freedom of education itself, constitutes a problem of a still higher order in the application of democratic principles" (quoted in Ford Foundation, 1972, p. 7). Ford subsequently designated education as one of five priority areas; comprehensive interventions remained a priority throughout four decades.

Ford's interest in improving high school–college relations—not necessarily targeted at disadvantaged students—began with creation of the Fund for the Advancement of Education (FAE), its prime vehicle for educational reform during the 1950s. Proposed by Robert M. Hutchins, who left the University of Chicago to become an associate director at Ford, FAE explored ways to shorten the time needed to complete high school and college, especially proposals to reduce "time-marking" during the high school senior year.

Grades 11–14, said FAE staff, should follow the example of the College of the University of Chicago by emphasizing liberal education. Through 10th grade, FAE staff continued, a student "is largely preoccupied with acquiring the minimum essential tools, skills, and information necessary to function in society, and after his second year in college he is increasingly required to major in one field." But, staff added, "between the 11th through 14th grades, his horizons are wide and exhilarating, for during this time he is encouraged to consider new and complex ideas and concepts." During these years, if ever, "he will acquire a taste—hopefully, a lifelong appetite—for broad liberal learning." Breaking a continuous learning process between two schools, FAE staff concluded, forced students to make up work they should have completed in high school or, conversely, required them to repeat work (Fund for the Advancement of Education, 1961, p. 87).

Between 1951 and 1954, FAE offered scholarships to bright students from weak high schools if they began college early (Ford Foundation,

1962; Fund for the Advancement of Education, 1953, 1957, 1961; Scott & Hill, 1954; Woodring, 1970). High school principals opposed the plan, fearing that colleges would cream their best students, their student government and social leaders, and—less frequently stated—their best athletes, along with accompanying average daily attendance (ADA) funds. FAE ignored this opposition, and *They Went to College Early* (1957), the fund's evaluation, reported mixed, although mainly positive, academic results. Early admissions freshman-year students did slightly less well than a control group of older students, but better than their freshmen classes as a whole. The experiment ended when no organization took over the scholarship program. During the 1950s, growing demand from able high school seniors deterred many colleges from recruiting sophomores and juniors, regardless of ability—and the baby boomers were close behind. Worse, from FAE's standpoint, few underclass students applied to colleges that would admit applicants early.

Advanced placement (AP)—recipient of most of the $4.9 million that FAE committed to improving school–college relations—was more successful. College-level AP courses were taught in the high schools, not in colleges, by high school teachers; therefore they received a friendlier reception from secondary school staff. The College Entrance Examination Board assumed responsibility for AP in 1955 when FAE funding ended, and the program spread to over 800 colleges by the end of the decade (Fund for the Advancement of Education, 1961). AP received another boost when the North Central Association approved advanced college standing for college-level work completed in high school. Advanced Placement developed rapidly in areas under NCA's jurisdiction, although less rapidly than in the east (Geiger, 1970). One FAE consultant praised AP for improving articulation, not for shortening the time to complete the baccalaureate (Woodring, 1970).

On the equity front, Ford "philanthropoids" focused on southern school desegregation during the 1950s, but a decade later the foundation shifted its attention to urban educational systems with growing numbers of minority students. Improving these systems, Ford staff concluded, required "bringing together a sufficient number of the new practices to create a *critical mass*—a chain reaction of change that would overcome the inertia of school systems and produce significantly different educational institutions." Piecemeal approaches such as "implementing only team teaching without a new curriculum, or installing a new curriculum without flexibility in scheduling," staff added, "would not make the significant impact needed to reverse the decline in the quality of American education" (Ford Foundation, 1972, p. 9, emphasis in original).

Great Cities–Gray Areas (GCGA) promoted "compensatory education" programs for potential dropouts in urban school systems that addressed cognitive and affective development. The Comprehensive School Improvement Program (CSIP) sponsored "lighthouse" projects—innovations that might ignite educational change elsewhere. The program took an anti-lockstep approach: "Curriculum in all content areas should be built on a continuum from the beginning to the completion of formal education, rather than be frozen by grade levels or age of pupil" (Ford Foundation, 1972, p. 9).

CSIP also emphasized strengthened school–college relationships, especially in teacher education. The program sought to introduce and integrate innovative curricular and instructional practices, including team-teaching, using nonprofessional personnel, flexible scheduling, variable size pupil groups for instruction and new space arrangements, and using educational television, programmed instruction, language laboratories, and educational data processing. The program also built on prior Ford initiatives, including advanced placement and early admissions, nongraded school programs, and school–college partnerships for curriculum improvement and teacher preparation (Ford Foundation, 1972).

Could "lighthouse" sites inspire the diffusion of innovation throughout a school district? Districts, evaluators found, might adopt specific ideas, but reject comprehensive change undertaken in an innovative spirit. Instead, an "umbra phenomenon" prevented "those close to the 'lighthouse' from being clearly guided by it." Innovative programs, wrote CSIP evaluators, often threatened employees in the larger systems who were reluctant "to admit that others within the system are innovating successfully when they are not," and who resented the recognition accorded recipients of foundation grants. Reformers, meanwhile, "often adopt 'superior' attitudes . . . are possessive about their projects, and for reasons not entirely under their control . . . tend to alienate colleagues in the parent system." Distant districts, in contrast, were more likely to adopt CSIP innovations. Distance, the evaluators found, provided legitimacy and proof of viability, reduced the threat level, and raised the possibility of external funding. A network of innovative subsystems, the evaluators concluded, might stimulate educational change—an insight not lost upon reformers, including Ford project officers, during the 1980s (Ford Foundation, 1972, p. 31).

The comprehensive approaches to school reform demonstrated in GCGA and CSIP activities found their way into Title III of the Elementary and Secondary Education Act (1965). But could Ford staff successfully mesh the key themes defining their work in educational reform? Could a comprehensive package of high school–college activities promote equal educational opportunity? In 1978, the foundation awarded grants to six cities to help urban colleges and universities serve central-city populations.

In 1983 Ford turned to community colleges—"the crucial point of access for millions of students wishing to pursue higher education," including 90% of all postsecondary Chicano students in California—as academic hubs that might best implement integrative activities. Reversing the atrophied liberal arts transfer function, Ford staff concluded, might be the centerpiece of its community college work. Emphasizing terminal vocational programs at the expense of promoting transfer, staff believed, had discouraged urban, minority students from attempting liberal arts baccalaureate programs that increased chances for upward mobility. Conversely, improving the academic quality and quantity of community college liberal arts offerings, staff speculated, would entice minority students to move through the higher education "pipeline" and help to ensure their successful transfer into four-year colleges. At the state level, appropriations formulas might emphasize academic over nondegree programs (Ford Foundation, 1983).

Ford launched its Urban Community College Transfer Opportunity Program (UCCTOP) in 1983. First, 24 urban public community colleges received small grants to identify potential transfer candidates while still in high school, improve counseling and academic advising, redesign liberal education to improve preparation for transfer, and negotiate articulation agreements with four-year colleges. Ford then substantially increased funding designated for five model programs, including "Exploring Transfer," a program initiated by Lieberman and Coltun Johnson, a Vassar College dean, that introduced students at public community colleges to selective, independent four-year colleges (Lieberman & Hungar, 1998; Roundtree, 1995).

The foundation's "pipeline" metaphor emphasized the need for structural change. Ford officers not only looked from two-year to four-year colleges, but also looked to secondary schools and earlier. "The dwindling of minorities in the middle and upper reaches of America's educational pipeline," a report stated, "is calamitous" (Ford Foundation, 1984, p. 12). A 1987 task force, charged with suggesting methods of expanding minority student access to liberal arts colleges, emphasized the needs of the secondary schools—not the recruitment needs of colleges (Task Force on School Cultivation, 1987).

By the late 1980s, Ford and other foundations saw the community college as a key path to the baccalaureate, especially for minority students. Lieberman's interest in replicating MCHS at LaGuardia showed potential for increasing the flow through the "pipeline." Ford staff could focus on improving precollegiate education and urban life while deflecting criticism that it gave low priority to reforming colleges and universities (Shapiro, 1987).

Ford staff took special interest in an initiative that featured comprehensive structural and curricular strategies for educating and raising the aspirations of minority and working-class students. Did the success of

MCHS at LaGuardia arise from idiosyncratic, nonreplicable factors? Could often isolated and sometimes hostile community college and K–12 bureaucracies successfully negotiate complex agreements? Would the schools include "key" components, including interdisciplinary coursework, cooperative education, and affective support? Adapting models was risky, staff concluded, but history suggested that change in urban education required comprehensive reform and that collaboration on the transition between high school and college must focus on at-risk students. The potential benefits outweighed the risks, concluded the staff; anyway, foundations should sponsor risky experiments with potentially high payoffs.

Implementing the Model

The success of a replication depended on how well community college and school district staff implemented the model; successful implementation, in turn, depended on resolving several key issues.

Planning and Leadership. MCHS at LaGuardia opened after two years of planning. Replications had less time to plan since their opening typically followed close upon financial authorization. Among the first replications, Shelby State Community College in Memphis, Tennessee, showed the longest lead time—about six months. MCHS at Los Angeles Southwest College, in contrast, had less than two months and had a firm budget only well after its opening. Hasty planning and opening also resulted in inadequate space and in less-desirable, off-site, or ancillary locations.

Choosing the first principal by conventional criteria, including seniority, adversely affected several sites. The principal, and often faculty hired by that leader, might be out of synch with the nontraditional mission and character of the school. The schools at Contra Costa College and Los Angeles Southwest had immediate leadership changes; Contra Costa needed three principals to find someone who worked successfully with the school district and community college staffs. Replications required an experienced "reformer-from-within," not a well-intentioned outsider or a traditionalist insider.

Resistance. Resistance from community college faculty and students emerged just after the replications at Shelby State and El Centro College in Dallas opened, and a bit later elsewhere. College faculty members, especially if not involved in planning, objected to the presence of students who were up to ten years younger than many community college students. These students, objectors added, were difficult to teach and had little chance of admission to the community college. Observers noted frequent mismatches between at-risk students and two-year college faculty who taught high school or "watered down" postsecondary-level courses requiring innovative, time-consuming methods (Palmer, 1994). Some fears were proven false; college instructors often could not distinguish between high school and college students unless told in advance. But short lead times did result in inappropriate student selection at several sites, and 16-year-olds often did act like 16-year-olds.

To some extent, such resistance reflected a fear that diminished quality anywhere affected an entire institution (Clark, 1980). This fear was not confined to faculty members at two-year colleges. At four-year colleges, faculty often were accused of resisting campus-based, short-cycle programs and off-campus extension centers. But here, status issues were also involved: How did faculty and staff at high schools located at community colleges with up to several generations of history deal with colleagues who knew of—or perhaps even fought—the battles involved in achieving independence from a high school and a K–12 district? Most principals worked hard to overcome community college faculty resistance.

Resistance from community college students often accompanied faculty resistance. Several schools, including MCHS at LaGuardia, had to overcome initial negative publicity in the college newspaper. One principal, for example, used her friendship with the newspaper's faculty advisor to obtain more friendly coverage. But student transience meant, as LaGuardia's Joseph Shenker predicted, that new generations would find the high school part of the "givens."

Administrative Relations. Even in the absence of overt resistance, administrative relations with host colleges required constant attention. A school needed active participation by at least some community college faculty and staff. Strong relations between the principal, the community college president, and senior administrators at both schools were important at the outset when even well-connected principals who understood the culture of a community college faced resistance from other constituencies. At some sites, community college administrators consulted school staff before making decisions affecting the replication; at other sites, "surprises" reflected the absence of ongoing administrative relationships.

At LaGuardia's MCHS, the principal's status as a community college department chair took on increased importance. Would the same pattern hold at the replications? Meetings of department chairs, noted one principal, allowed her to discuss germane issues *and* to contribute to the community college, by advising on student recruitment and on teaching a developmental population. But another principal, working with a top-down community college administration, said that department chairs rarely met, so her title meant little. The informal conduit provided by the community college liaison, the LaGuardia experience suggested, complemented formal department chair status. Liaisons, for example, could help principals obtain favorable accommodations by explaining college governance practices.

Adopt or Adapt? Should local faculty and staff adopt the entire package, thereby downplaying idiosyncrasy, or were the components separable and the concept adaptable to local conditions? Could schools, for example, follow the example of the New York replications by omitting key elements, such as cooperative education, if the host community colleges did not feature this program? Could replications successfully admit 9th graders, a practice opposed by Lieberman but adopted by MCHS at LaGuardia? What was necessary and sufficient in the design to attain at-risk student success and eventual college attendance? And in any case, did replications gravitate toward or away from the model over time? Answering these questions might help address a more basic issue: Could a consortium establish accreditation standards, and perhaps criteria by which to judge other reforms? Or would standardization contradict key tenets of nontraditional education for at-risk students (Gamson, 1989)?

The Lighthouse Effect. Would a lighthouse have ships to guide, that is, promote "systemic" change in a school district, or would it promote "threatening" reforms? Would success increase the district-wide influence of less-conventional faculty and staff, or result in their "exile" to a marginal corner? Would others dismiss the accomplishments of a replication by noting that living in two worlds gave these schools *de facto* independence? Indeed, would districts allow these replications to exploit the relative freedom of the community college? Or would paralysis result from subservience to two masters with different agendas? Last, was one replication per school district enough to stimulate change?

Lieberman and her colleagues, Ford funding in hand, selected sites likely to support a successful replication, offered these sites the benefits of their experience, watched for the lighthouse effect, and reflected on the results.

SELECTING THE INNER CIRCLE

[Students] want to be heard about what they feel is important in their education. Courses should be changed so they are relevant to them . . . . It's also important that they learn

what college is all about. Other places should benefit from
our experience over ten years. We've been through it, so we
have the best understanding there is about it.
                          —A guidance counselor at MCHS at LaGuardia
                                         (Klohmann, 1987, p. 63)

    Soon after Ford authorized the first replication grant in 1986, Lieber-
man and Cullen convened a conference—attended by over 80 administrators and faculty members representing more than 30 high school–college
pairs, including 18 UCCTOP colleges—to determine interest in a replication. MCHS at LaGuardia received many follow-up visits, and 12 pairs—
several including UCCTOP colleges—applied for support that included
start-up funds for pairs willing to make firm commitments, and consulta-
tions for potential administrators and teachers.
    Applications went through Lieberman and Cullen and her staff at
LaGuardia's MCHS. Lieberman thereby "accredited" replication sites and
could withdraw that status if circumstances warranted. With initial funding
for six replications, Lieberman wished to identify sites demonstrating sufficient commitment and financial resources. Site visitors and the screening
committee might evaluate commitment by judging the enthusiasm of the
community college president and the school district superintendent. They
also might consider the target student population; the proposed faculty and
administration; space; commitment from outside agencies; funding arrangements and state approval; prior collaborative track record and other
pending proposals for school–college integration; governance provisions;
the proposed curriculum, including "cooperative education or other motivational programs"; meeting high school graduation requirements; and the
coherence of components (Lieberman, 1987a; *Rating Sheet*, 1988). Frequent changes in the list of anointed sites reveals the difficulties experienced by many applicants in meeting these criteria.
    Lieberman and her colleagues visited all community colleges eventu-
ally chosen for replication and at least eight sites not chosen. The first
evaluation meeting, held in January 1987, provided technical assistance
for a September 1987 opening of three schools—Miami–Dade Community
College, Shelby State Community College, and Illinois Central College,
Peoria (Leonard Britton and Robert H. McCabe to Lieberman, December
11, 1986, MCA, "Evaluator Meeting, 1987" file). Shuffling among the
chosen began almost immediately. Lieberman replaced Miami–Dade,
which failed to meet the conditions of the grant, with Union County Community College, Cranford, New Jersey, which received "extensive support
and technical assistance" (*Summary of 1987 Evaluations*, 1988).

Subsequent approaches from Dallas, San Diego, and Los Angeles—school districts with sizeable minority populations—prompted Lieberman to request a grant to assist three more sites. Ford agreed to provide additional funding in October 1987. The jury was still out, Ford staff noted, on how many school–college pairs ultimately would express interest and whether the school was replicable. But attendance at the conference and the number of first-round applications convinced Ford staff that many enthusiastic school districts considered this a realistic model for at-risk students, although some sites might not adopt all key features. Staff noted two other strengths: energizing officials and staff at potential sites and involving local donors in the enterprise (*Recommendation for Grant/FAP Action—Supplement 86-585*, 1987).

The evaluators tentatively identified a second trio for opening in September 1988—Cuyahoga Community College, Cleveland, Ohio; J. Sargeant Reynolds Community College, Richmond, Virginia; and San Diego Community College. The evaluators later rejected further assistance for Cuyahoga, which, the selectors concluded, showed minimal evidence of progress and an inadequate design. This decision subsequently was reversed, although later events bore out Lieberman's reservations.

Reynolds encountered secondary school resistance (students would remain enrolled in their current high schools), proposed an unacceptably small student body (weighted toward over-age students), and provided weak criteria for faculty selection ("those who have demonstrated a *willingness* to *volunteer* time in working with high risk students"). The school, the evaluators added, would become a punitive solution for dropouts (Ford Foundation Project, 1988, p. 4). Noting substantial progress since the initial contact, the evaluation committee accepted the application of San Diego Community College, despite a request from its new president to defer the school's opening. Neither site ever opened.

The evaluators eventually accepted bids from Dallas and Los Angeles, the two other districts that triggered the supplemental grant. Dallas opened its El Centro College replication in Fall 1988; Los Angeles had to work through some thorny local politics and win a statewide competition, sponsored by the community college chancellor, before confirming a September 1989 opening at Los Angeles Southwest College (LASC). Contra Costa College (CCC), Richmond, California, also received assistance after winning a second slot in the same competition.

Lieberman encouraged three other sites to devise detailed plans. The application from Cincinnati Technical College featured a year-long cooperative education component (proposed because of a lack of space and deemed potentially problematic) as part of a career education program (deemed generally acceptable). The evaluators also included South Mountain Community College, Phoenix, Arizona, on the list of accepted sites. Again, neither college opened a replication.

The school proposed by the Detroit public schools—a rare instance where the school system, not the college, took the initiative—would have allowed Lieberman to examine a collaboration between a four-year institution—Wayne State University—and a high school. But evaluators remained concerned about support from "unstable" leadership at the university, and in 1988 Wayne County Community College replaced Wayne State in the partnership. A year later, a presidential change at the community college led to the withdrawal of the proposal (Lieberman, 1990).

The funded colleges—which included several UCCTOP grantees— were located in large and medium-sized cities with high concentrations of minority students. Trainers, mostly faculty and staff from MCHS at LaGuardia, worked in teams to model collaboration and to reassure new faculty and staff. "The spirit will be cooperative," wrote Lieberman, "a sharing of knowledge and curriculum, and collegial, an opportunity to learn from each other." On-site training that supplemented pilgrimages to LaGuardia enabled trainers to avoid the distractions of New York City and to demonstrate that "learning takes place in a social context and that learning communities exist in groups" (*Summer Training*, 1987, p. 2).

When the dust settled, replications had opened at Shelby State Community College, Illinois Central College, Los Angeles Southwest College, Contra Costa College, El Centro College, Cuyahoga Community College, and Union County Community College (Battersbee & Warren, 1991; Lieberman, 1992). MCHS at LaGuardia, with more than a decade of operations, offered technical advice, encouragement, savvy personnel—and a design. Lieberman, Cullen, and colleagues moved from gatekeepers to advisors; a middle college consortium eventually assumed the latter role.

FIVE SUCCESSES

Shelby State Community College, Memphis, Tennessee

Ray Bowen's experience as LaGuardia's associate dean of faculty (1971–1975) made Shelby State Community College (SSCC, opened in 1972) a prime candidate for a replication during his presidency (Anderson, 2001; Rhoads & Valadez, 1996). Bowen, a biologist and an African-American, assumed the SSCC presidency at a time (1982) when observers agreed that the college was in poor shape. Most students needed remediation; the average ACT score for incoming students was 11.4 (nearby four-year Memphis State reported 20.5). Many SSCC students (average age = 27) were therefore enrolled in developmental programs; the attrition rate was nearly 75% (Ray, 1987). Remediation was unavoidable; the state mandated these studies for all eligible students, and Tennessee's community colleges were Open Admissions institutions. But the need to remediate, observers noted, created a morale and image problem among SSCC faculty members, and contributed to declining enrollment on the midtown campus. Ironically, this decline made space available for a Middle College High School that might create more image problems. Drawing on insights from his LaGuardia years, Bowen attempted to convince a 70% White community college faculty to accept a high school populated with predominantly African-American students.

SSCC had no history of high school collaboration. But strong personal chemistry and an upcoming increase in the requirements for admission to colleges governed by the Tennessee State Board of Regents prompted Bowen and Willie Herenton, superintendent of the Memphis city schools, to consider collaborations to "mitigate the dropout rate and any potential adverse racial impact resulting from those 1989 requirements." Herenton's district was the 12th largest in the United States with 107,000 students and a 78% African-American student population (*Middle College High School*, 1987).

Bowen invited Herenton, later the mayor of Memphis, to the 1986 LaGuardia conference. They returned enthusiastic. A replication, both believed, could lead to greater changes in Memphis; three years later, for example, Herenton proposed a self-governing, inner-city district, free from most requirements. The new school and the community college would have congruent missions: "The MCHS program will also be consistent with the SSCC mission," noted the school's mission statement. "At Shelby State, a great deal of emphasis is placed on innovative approaches to developmental education appropriate for the large numbers of underprepared students" (*Mission*, 1987, p. 4).

Bowen's relationship to LaGuardia led Lieberman to make SSCC a first-round choice. Planning was already well underway, and Herenton had helped Bowen establish key relationships with members of the Memphis Board of Education (MBE) and the Tennessee Regents, who would approve the proposal (Bowen to Lieberman, August 28, 1986, MCA "Evaluators Meeting—1987" file, and Thomas J. Garland to Bowen, December 22, 1986, MCA, "Shelby State Community College" file). The First Tennessee Bank then donated $50,000 to underwrite staff salaries during the six months prior to the school's opening; the bank also provided officers to teach economics and related courses. Local financial assistance—not available at all sites—permitted LaGuardia staff to offer on-site technical training to seven teachers and three staff.

Joyce Colbert Mitchell became the school's first principal. A Memphis native, Mitchell was a teacher and counselor in the Memphis schools before her appointment as the system's bilingual supervisor. These positions, she said, prepared her for the MCHS principalship; so did her *lack* of experience as an assistant principal, since she came to the job with fewer preconceived notions (Mitchell, 1993). SSCC faculty members who participated in her recruitment supported Mitchell when resistance emerged from their colleagues. Her durability—Mitchell was still principal 12 years later—stood in contrast to the pattern of short-tenure founding principals typical of other replications.

Shelby State's enrollment decline and good rapport between Mitchell and SSCC's liaison, the dean of institutional advancement, helped the high school secure desirable space on SSCC's 22-acre midtown campus. Interpreting middle college to mean "in the middle of a college," Bowen asked the liaison to integrate the high school's 12 classrooms and 11 offices among the nine buildings. Math and science classes would be in the "M" building, English and art classes and the principal's offices in "E," social science and French in "F," gym in "D," and the cafeteria in "C." A 60% enrollment increase at SSCC later raised fears of battles over space; Mitchell responded by placing more students in college classes. The resulting increase in SSCC's enrollment-driven funding helped to offset some resentment expressed by SSCC faculty.

Early assessments ratified Lieberman's decision to include SSCC. "Shelby is a wonderful campus and the staff is very competent and eager," wrote a LaGuardia consultant. "If it is possible to replicate Middle College it can be done at Shelby State." Mitchell chose a strong staff, subject to a 50–50 racial composition provision in the school district's desegregation plan. She eased the staff, the consultant noted, "into the environment, the expected student body, their guidance roles and the newness of the Middle College concept." "Their qualities of eagerness, strong academic backgrounds and interests in a variety of disciplines," the consultant concluded, "is important to the success of M.C. They are a very open group of people" (Terry Born to Lieberman, July 28, 1987, MCA "Shelby C.C.—April 4–5" file). Mitchell's ability to work with the SSCC faculty, the consultant optimistically added, produced cooperation: "She has gone out of her way to calm the [faculty] by acquainting them with her staff, their intentions and showing them what an asset Middle College will be on campus." SSCC faculty members, especially department heads, met frequently with their high school colleagues; joint visits to LaGuardia helped, but some members of the SSCC faculty remained unenthusiastic.

MCHS at Shelby State Community College opened in August 1987 with a hundred 10th graders ("Middle College Hoping," 1987). But support and planning, Mitchell noted, did not eliminate all significant problems. The time, effort, and energy required to address MCHS faculty recruitment and development, resolve financial concerns, improve student selection mechanisms, and reduce SSCC faculty resistance, she said, came at the cost of creativity. "You become a plant supervisor during the day, curriculum innovator at night," Mitchell commented. These problems were resolved, she added, at the cost of three personally and professionally draining years.

Long lead time did not, in Mitchell's view, produce an ideal faculty. Some ideas of MCHS teachers, concurred the LaGuardia consultant, "were too narrow in scope and showed teachers to be very tied to traditional, small scale projects." "More extensive work in faculty recruitment and readiness" led her list of second thoughts. "A middle college will only be as successful as its faculty," she said. "If the kids like you, they'll do anything for you. If not, life will be miserable." When asked, "What might have been done differently?" she responded, "There are only a handful of really gifted, non-traditional teachers, so I'd look for flexibility" (Mitchell, 1993, n.p.).

New teachers, she added, must know what they're getting into. "Teachers should buy into the concept at the outset; that's easier than changing on the job." Recruitment interviews should include tough questions: "What about grading? What if a student throws an "F" paper back at you? What about maximizing student involvement?" The ideal MCHS teacher, Mitchell concluded, had from two to ten years' experience—novices had too much to learn; seniors might have other obligations or suffer from burnout. Negativism was infectious, she counseled new recruits. "Don't listen to older teachers uncritically."

But, Mitchell added, the teachers were not entirely at fault. The rigid rules imposed by the Memphis Board of Education did not help. Like Cullen, Mitchell asked the school's faculty council to participate in hiring decisions—the only faculty members at a replication to assume the task at the time. The time spent listening to faculty problems paid off, this request suggests, even at the cost of innovation.

Financial uncertainties—and salary cuts—continually threatened the high school's existence. Multifarious planning activities, evaluators concluded, enabled school and staff to weather the school's first crisis in early 1988, when the MBE almost eliminated the school. Long-term survival, Bowen concluded, depended on its ability to supplement average daily attendance monies with funds from other sources. Soon after opening, MCHS applied for state funds earmarked for innovative programming for at-risk students.[1]

Fiscal conditions only worsened. MCHS weathered a second crisis in 1990 (Waters, 1990a), but in July 1993, the Memphis board abolished the high school, planning to reabsorb its students into other schools. Students, parents, and community members protested this unanticipated move, and 280 students sat in at MBE offices. Mitchell appeared on television, locking the school's doors. But telling Mayor Herenton, "I have to do what I have to do," Mitchell led the behind-the-scenes resistance to the school's closing, declining an offer to move to another school. The school survived the threat.

Admissions criteria resembled the requirements used by MCHS at LaGuardia, and changed little over the years: one or more grade retention, absenteeism in excess of district norms, "home problems," over-age for grade placement, academic potential, and a counselor or an agency referral. Enrollment was voluntary: "No one is making you go to MCHS," students were told. Students completed an application, provided a transcript or report card, secured a recommendation from their home school or from another person, and showed evidence of parental support, based on knowledge of MCHS. The school might be a surrogate home, Mitchell noted, but parents still had a key role to play for students in crisis. Mitchell outlined the school's expectations, including a parent contract, at an interview prior to admission. But she recognized that unconventional work schedules and teacher unwillingness to call home or to meet parents after hours often hindered parental participation, despite good intentions.

There was a difference, Mitchell added, between high-risk and at-risk; admitting too many students with severe problems would hurt MCHS and its relations with SSCC. Students therefore required careful screening for the ability to adjust to a college environment. But other high schools, fearing creaming and competition, were reluctant to refer students. Some students appeared only after the 20th day of the academic year, when school enrollments were tallied for funding purposes. Nor did MCHS receive adequate support from feeder middle schools. Mitchell relied more on counselors, whom she knew from her prior work, than on principals. But her contacts did not always produce results. "A counselor," she said, "may not let you see certain students." Middle schools gave no help during the second round of student recruitment; many counselors, aware of the school's financial problems, made no referrals. The smaller second-year entering class included many high school repeaters recruited from summer schools. That meant less ADA money and more disciplinary problems.

Inappropriate students, noted Mitchell, heightened SSCC student and faculty resistance—her most time-consuming, persistent problem. SSCC enrolled many students with bachelor's degrees who returned for vocational work in the health professions. These older students (average age = 28) displayed impatience with the less mature MCHS students. Experience at LaGuardia, Bowen claimed, helped him to anticipate and address student resistance. Staff repeatedly explained the mission of the school, adding that its students came from their neighborhoods and perhaps included siblings of friends or relatives. SSCC student resistance decreased with each graduation, but other sites with similar age gaps reported as much initial resistance as interaction.

Mitchell was less prepared for faculty resistance. "You can wait out student resistance," she noted, "but not faculty objections." Mitchell tried to communicate with faculty during the planning period. "There was a lot of curriculum collaboration," prior to the school's opening, she said, "but faculty talked shop, not 'discipline.'" SSCC faculty members complained they did not know about the enterprise. Some faculty members, Mitchell said, ignoring the word "prevention" in "dropout prevention program," conjured fears of delinquents and thieves on the SSCC campus. Faculty criticism was public, persistent, and strident: "The timing couldn't be worse," a faculty member said in 1987. "At a time when we're having image problems, when we're perceived in the community as an extended high school, they're actually turning the campus over to high school students" (Ray, 1987, p. 62).

Disciplinary incidents quickly escalated, and Mitchell responded with time-consuming investigations of each complaint. But she believed the inquiries would never suffice. Some objections, she noted, were disingenuous; charges that SSCC faculty were not informed about the program, for example, even if true, did not explain continued resistance. As for "image," SSCC already had an at-risk population; its developmental programs enrolled students from similar backgrounds. Race, Mitchell suggested, might have affected the attitudes of some SSCC faculty. "There was great joy, dancing in the hallways," when budget cuts threatened the school in 1990, an SSCC professor told a reporter. "These kids go down the halls making noise, kicking holes in the wall, making faces in the windows, they're very disruptive" (Waters, 1990b, pp. B1–2).

Cultural similarities and curricular continuities, Lieberman believed, would help a replication to thrive on a community college campus. But most SSCC faculty resistance, Mitchell believed, arose out of differing norms. An emphasis on process at community colleges, for example, implied participation on many committees; a result-oriented high school culture involved shorter, less frequent meetings. MCHS teachers, she added, instead of exposing disagreements, established channels of communication. Some SSCC faculty, in contrast, invoked their "academic freedom" to criticize, citing a "duty" to "right the wrong." Their actions, Mitchell charged, came close to sabotage. Conversely, SSCC faculty members would not fight each other on this issue. "The vocal minority spoke," Mitchell noted. "The majority, including my friends, remained silent." Most SSCC faculty members, Mitchell added, saw her as an intelligent principal, trying to do her best. "But it's just those kids" (1993, n.p.).

Some faculty members saw the light. One ill-disposed professor, Lieberman noted, visited MCHS at LaGuardia. After two days, she returned with a camera to photograph the building and the classrooms, explaining that the pictures would show that "if all this can be done in such a dirty place, think what we might do in a clean one!" (Lieberman, 1992, p. 86). Later, the SSCC faculty senate leader shifted from opposition to advocacy when he enrolled his own child in MCHS.

Securing some converts and putting out fires, Mitchell concluded, would not resolve the normative conflict. The long-run answer, she believed, involved learning to live in two cultures and addressing the needs of both schools. The high school, Mitchell suggested, could advise the college on increasing enrollments. Mitchell's science teachers helped by developing an innovative precollegiate curriculum. Shelby State came to appreciate the expertise residing at the high school, Mitchell noted. Bowen's support, revenues from enrolling MCHS students in SSCC courses, and favorable publicity also helped. Last, the perceived success of MCHS added to its legitimacy.

"We're all educators," Mitchell concluded. "It's difficult to hear educators talk disparagingly about underachieving students." New principals, she added, should recognize that community college faculty members want a say over new programs; they should anticipate resistance. But Mitchell could do only so much. Within five years, she moved from "doing somersaults" to acknowledging continued faculty resistance as part of SSCC. A television documentary, filmed several years later, she noted, found opposition from the same faculty members.

Predictably, MCHS at Shelby State did not immediately implement all components of the design. The school, for example, early on hired a career education coordinator, but the program was not launched until a year after the school opened. The First Tennessee Bank facilitated an internship program, sending students to 40 sites. The bank itself received many interns and eventually hired some MCHS graduates. "Quality Principles," a campus-based course emphasizing work skills, complemented the four-day-per-week (20–25-hour) internships. House took even longer to implement; it began in the third year as a weekly counseling and cultural program.

MCHS at Shelby State began its college course component by enrolling its students in music and art classes. This strategy minimized competition between resistant SSCC students and MCHS enrollees, while allowing MCHS students to study subjects the high school otherwise could not offer. SSCC faculty resistance dictated a "permission of the instructor" registration policy. MCHS students received dual credit for college courses, although the school had to raise private funds to pay SSCC course registration fees. By 1992, MCHS generated significant revenue for SSCC by enrolling about 20% of its students in college courses; several courses were designed exclusively for MCHS students.

Status as an SSCC department chair and membership on the dean's council gave Mitchell a broader picture of the college, and an opportunity to address student and faculty resistance. Mitchell viewed participation in college activities as a necessary price to pay for living in two cultures, and for gaining input into decisions that affected the high school, such as redesigning rooms and facilities. Mitchell, like Cullen, gained leverage by harmonizing the MCHS daily calendar with SSCC's. The change eased room and facilities scheduling and facilitated MCHS student enrollment in college courses. The move also improved communication and collaboration—previously, MCHS faculty and administrators were available only after many SSCC counterparts had left for the day.

Ray Bowen envisioned citywide and regional roles for SSCC in Ford replication activities. He began by inviting Memphis public school curriculum developers to frequent meetings with MCHS and SSCC faculty members to discuss the transition from high school to college. In 1988, SSCC proposed a citywide partnership with the 23 Memphis high schools to develop and export MCHS curricular, academic support, and career exploration models (Proposal for Innovative Partnership Activities, attached to Bowen to A. Bernstein, October 13, 1988, MCA, "Shelby State Community College" file). The next year, SSCC hosted a workshop to convince officials at Tennessee's nine other community colleges and at colleges in neighboring states to open similar schools; a 1990 Tennessee House resolution directed state education officials to determine whether other districts could adopt the model (Reel, 1990). But Bowen's 1989 move to LaGuardia's presidency left SSCC in the hands of an acting president during the 1990 budget crisis, and a president who suffered a no-confidence vote from his faculty in 1994, soon after the third closure threat. During these crises, strong community support made up for weak presidential backing.

A Memphis judge, Mitchell noted, called MCHS the only decent alternative to the streets. The school, she agreed, was a response to "crazy urban life," and an alternative to building jails. Save some children, Mitchell said, and they would influence peers or at least members of their extended families. Asserting that faculty and staff needed a sense of mission to get through a day, she succinctly stated the mission of MCHS at Shelby State: All children had the right to the best possible education.

Illinois Central College, Peoria, Illinois

The Academy at Illinois Central College (ICC, founded in 1967) opened in Fall 1987, in Peoria, a company town where farm equipment maker Caterpillar experienced considerable downsizing. Officials attempted to maintain public school funding by reducing the district's high school dropout rate. In 1986, ICC, with no history of K–12 collaboration, began a soft-money tutoring program, serving 1,200 high school students during its first eight months. Concluding that many students needed full-time help, Karl Taylor, tutoring program director and chair of ICC's basic education department, decided to open an alternative high school for dropouts at ICC.

The ICC governing board approved Taylor's plan in late 1986, and a full-time acting principal was hired the following Spring. The academy opened in September 1987, with two administrators, and six part-time teachers—mostly from outside the school's service area. Its 72 students were 90% White and 60% poor. Ninety percent came from single-parent homes, and 75% had substance abuse problems. Apprised of the middle college model, Taylor applied for replication status. Lieberman approved, and the school began to implement the model in 1988.

Academy students 17 or older could complete a GED program and receive a diploma from the Peoria Board of Education. Younger students (ages 14–16) studied at the academy from three to 12 months, and then returned to a feeder high school located in the area served by ICC. By 1993, the academy had served students from 23 rural and urban school districts. Located in ICC's liberal arts division, the academy had full access to the facilities of the community college; it scheduled classes to minimize disruption to ICC.

The part-time status of the faculty—a condition mandated by the level of state aid—inhibited innovation and delayed key curricular components. During its first year, the academy offered no foreign language instruction or interdisciplinary courses, and only a rudimentary internship program. The school used traditional content courses until staff members developed courses in art, creative writing, current issues, mass media, social problems, and sociology. ICC's location away from the city center dictated a campus-based internship strategy, implemented in 1989, including positions in child care, clerical work, and horticulture, and at the audio-visual department, bookstore, and library.

Jimmie Moore, the school's principal, relied on Taylor and ICC instructors at the academy to reduce initial community college faculty resistance. He also scheduled lunches among ICC faculty, himself, and academy students. The small dedicated space—four classrooms at the outset—forced the academy to adopt a selective admissions policy that capped enrollment at 125 students. Small size, minimal space demands, and willingness to use ICC facilities during college slack time facilitated the academy's acceptance.

The academy hired its own faculty, but relative independence from the Peoria School District came at the cost of inadequate funding—the school indefinitely relied on overworked part-time faculty. All faculty taught five daily classes and led a home room, but had no preparation periods. Questions about viability diminished when the academy began to report its own ADA, instead of going through the feeder schools. The ongoing tutoring program created dropout prevention strategies for potentially at-risk students and built relationships with feeders.

The academy grew to include most components typical of a replication, including dual enrollment, house, and group counseling. It reported a 91% pass rate for diploma courses and an 89% pass rate for vocational courses (*Evaluation Report*, 1992). A community college initiative, the academy became a model for other replications, such as Flint, that were not confined to serving urban populations from a single school district.

Los Angeles Southwest College, Los Angeles, California

The 1987–88 budget submitted by the California governor to the state legislature included $65,000 in planning funds for two middle colleges; the 1988–89 budget contained $150,000 for their first year of operation. Future budgets included funding for subsequent years, but the schools were expected to become self-supporting on ADA funds after the fourth year of operation, when they reached the full complement of grade levels. State education officials wished to designate sponsoring community colleges in the northern and southern halves of the state. In mid-1988, these officials, after consulting with Lieberman, designated Los Angeles Southwest College the winner in the southern region.

The Los Angeles site took three years to open, and another two years to implement all components. In Fall 1986, Belmont High School, a year-round public high school in the Los Angeles Unified School District (LAUSD) with a predominantly low-income and minority student body and a 60% attrition rate, leased classroom and office space at Los Angeles City College (LACC) to relieve overcrowding. Through the efforts of Toni Forsyth, an assistant professor of English and director of the Transfer Opportunity Program (a UCCTOP program) at LACC, the Belmont principal, the LACC president, and key staff members discussed a dual enrollment and credit program permitting 11th- and 12th-grade Belmont students to register in regular sections of LACC vocational and skills courses. Most students in this "2 + 2" program were not "at-risk"— 2.5 G.P.A. and proficient English skills—but Forsyth looked to recruiting an "at-risk" subgroup ("Belmont High Comes Back," 1986; Forsyth to Lieberman, October 22, 1986, MCA, "Evaluators meeting, January 15, 1988" file; *Survey of Desired College Courses*, 1987; *Survey Questions*, 1987).

The collaboration did not evolve, as hoped, into a replication, but Forsyth, who attended the LaGuardia conference, continued her campaign by arranging trips to LaGuardia for Los Angeles Community College District (LACCD) staff. A year later, the LACCD chancellor freed Forsyth to work on the project from district offices. She identified a possible site at Los Angeles Southwest College, on West Imperial Highway, next to the Watts district. Opened in 1967 as a response to the Watts riots, LASC was perhaps the least successful of the district's nine community colleges. Enrollments declined 64% in the five years after Proposition 13 dried up funds for completing the campus; many students bypassed LASC for more attractive programs at other two-year colleges.

The turnaround began with Thomas G. Lakin's appointment as acting president in March 1986. Lakin, formerly vice president at Los Angeles Trade–Technical College, introduced hi-tech and transfer programs that produced a 60% enrollment gain in 19 months (Williams, 1987). He also established a partnership with Southgate, another overcrowded local high school, that brought 200 students to LASC for mentoring; a few students enrolled in college courses. This experience, and his attendance at the 1986 conference, nurtured Lakin's enthusiasm for a replication.

In 1987, Lieberman offered to help plan a replication with Forsyth and her colleagues (Lieberman to Forsyth, January 20, 1987, MCA, "Los Angeles City College" file). Evaluators "decided that there was great need, as well as great leadership present in Los Angeles," but expressed reservations about the impending departure of a supportive LACCD chancellor, the commitment to cooperative education, and the designation of separate space for the school in free-standing "bungalows" (*Ford Foundation Project*, 1988, p. 4). In Summer 1988, eight potential staff members received faculty training and technical assistance at LaGuardia, and Lieberman subsequently accepted a strengthened final proposal.

LASC officials envisioned a September 1988 opening, but several problems led to a year's delay. First, state start-up funding became available only in June 1989. Second, the proposal stalled during a Spring 1989 LAUSD teachers strike. Third, a LAUSD board member called for locating the school in east Los Angeles, a predominantly Hispanic area, and refused to vote to fund two replications in the city, even if the state agreed to additional start-up funds. The gambit was lost when administrators at the targeted community college declined to participate (Battersbee, 1993).

Fourth, LAUSD officials requested assurance that the project would not divert funds from existing interventions. An analyst, requested by Lakin to explain the budget assumptions, privately criticized LAUSD. "Their attitude seems to be, 'If it doesn't cost us much money, we will do it, but it's not a big priority; there is no urgency,'" he wrote. "Whereas the attitude . . . ought to be, 'This program will really work for our kids; let's see how we can make it happen'" (Joseph C. Malloy to Lieberman, May 21, 1989, MCA, "Contra Costa" file). Publicly, the analyst argued for including ADA income generated by MCHS students as nondiverted funds, since probably the students otherwise would have dropped out of high school. A sustainable budget emerged when it was recalculated using these assumptions, and LAUSD approved a final proposal in June 1989 ("Middle College High Schools Established").

With state planning grant funds released, observers assumed that Natalie Battersbee would become the founding principal. Battersbee had taught and administered in LAUSD for a quarter century and was then principal of Jane Addams High School, a LAUSD continuation school for at-risk youth. She and her assembled shadow staff took the technical training at LaGuardia. But LAUSD appointed another principal, and Battersbee's colleagues withdrew their applications to work at the school. The appointed principal had less than three months to hire and train three faculty members and a counselor, recruit students, develop the curriculum, and address space and external constituency issues. The short lead time also meant borrowing books, materials, and equipment.

Student recruitment consisted of hasty meetings among school staff, feeder school counselors and administrators, and potential students and their parents. The school recruited 75 10th graders; Middle College High School at LASC, like most replications, admitted one grade at a time. Selection criteria included academic ability, attendance and discipline problems, and a counselor's recommendation. But inadequate screening meant that to avoid becoming a "dumping ground," MCHS sent some problem students back to their feeders, including special education students and nonreaders.

Haste and inexperience resulted in a difficult first year. A standard curriculum awaited the new students. By November, disciplinary problems resulted in deteriorating relations with LASC, and LAUSD officials appointed Battersbee to the principalship, beginning with the spring semester. She, like Joyce Mitchell, immediately encountered college faculty and staff resistance. Staff at the 25-year old college, she argued, viewed new entities as objects of suspicion, especially as California's financial crisis intensified in the early 1990s. All that went wrong at LASC, Battersbee claimed, was blamed on the high school—the new, disturbing element on campus.

A space shortage at LASC did force the high school into portable "bungalows" at one end of campus. Transfer of the Southgate program to another college in 1990—available space, concluded LASC officials, permitted only one partnership—freed up bungalows more proximate to the main building. But discovery that LASC was located on the Englewood fault meant demolishing part of the college's only permanent building; college units then objected to allocating the new bungalow space to MCHS. Lakin met even stiffer resistance when contemplating space in the main building for high school activities. MCHS students eventually gained access to the community college gym, cafeteria, and science and computer labs, but tight space capped the school's enrollment at 260–300 students.

MCHS teamed with some LASC faculty to replace the inherited curriculum with interdisciplinary courses. "People of the World" included social studies, history, art, and science components. High school and college teachers jointly offered the CUNY "American Social History" curriculum, disseminated via foundation grants to replication sites; "Psychology of Racism" was also well received. The high school maintained good relations with the LASC math and science departments. Students who enrolled in college math and science courses, for example, had access to a special high school laboratory component taught by MCHS faculty. These warmer faculty relations did not compensate for distant administrative relations that emerged when Lakin—considered an "outstanding man" by Battersbee—left LASC. The interim president confined herself to verbal encouragement. Her successor saw MCHS as an asset, but financial and political problems within LASC limited her support.

LASC faculty and staff, Battersbee (1992) noted, did not know what to expect. "Sacramento," it appeared, "put up some grant funds, and told us what they wanted." By 1992, enrollment increases had allowed the staff to grow to 11 teachers, Battersbee, an office manager, and a half-time clerical staff member supported by LASC. But the early 1990s recession then produced sharp, statewide cutbacks in education budgets; annual evaluations by the LACCD chancellor's office made the school's future financing appear even more tenuous. In 1992, MCHS teachers took a 12% pay cut; Battersbee's was 17%. The teachers remained committed to MCHS, noted Battersbee, although they were asked to do more on less pay.

Disciplinary problems and vandalism occurred less frequently under Battersbee, who promised more appropriate student recruitment. "If they see themselves as special education students," she noted, "they won't succeed on the college campus." The admissions process took on the aura of selectivity adopted elsewhere in the middle college movement. Battersbee and her staff told counselors about the school and specified the kind of student they wanted. The admissions process included learning about the school, self-evaluation, and an interview conducted by Battersbee, who evaluated candidates by "fit" or viability.

Implementing the key components took several years. MCHS did not offer internships during the first year, but students subsequently took an internship each afternoon for one semester. Internships, Battersbee insisted, helped students understand the value of their education. A student who dropped mathematics, she recalled, asked for reinstatement when he realized he could not complete the layout specifications for his graphic arts and printing internship. The internship, she concluded, allowed the student to learn this lesson for himself.

Battersbee also implemented a credit-bearing "family" (house) component; topics included: Middle College High School and the college system, choices and challenges, earth rent, community service, self-esteem, conflict resolution, and values clarification. "All teachers understand," she noted, "that they also have a counselor role to fulfill." But she did most individual counseling at first—there was no group counseling—freeing her time by having a classroom teacher double as the assistant principal (Lieberman, 1992, p. 43). Only eight students enrolled in LASC classes during the first semester; but by the end of the 1990–91 academic year all 215 10th and 11th graders took at least one college class and half of the 11th graders enrolled in at least three (Battersbee & Warren, 1991). The shift made economic sense, but resulted in a high failure rate and in behavior problems ("LASW," handwritten note in MCA, "L.A. Southwest" file).

Inadequate funding, equipment, and staff, said Battersbee (1992), resulted in high student–faculty ratios, a lack of textbooks, slow implementation, unimaginative programming, and an inability to work on long-range policy. More money, she believed, could counteract damage brought about by urban poverty to 17-year-olds from a community with a 20% unemployment rate and a 48% high school graduation rate (Lise S. Spielman to Charlotte Arrick, undated, c. Spring 1992, MCA, "L.A. Southwest" file). Schools, Battersbee argued, must help students plan a life—not let life happen. Programs on female sexuality, for example, could help young women view themselves as intelligent, productive, and success-oriented, not as boys' playthings. A school, she added, also must become part of the community. When the school closed during the 1992 Los Angeles riots, Battersbee recalled, students demanded its reopening, feeling safer there than at home or on the street. The school taught students to abhor violence and to apply positive problem-solving techniques to save disintegrating communities. A service program, for example, enabled students to help needy community members (Phelps, 1992–1993).

At Middle College High School at Los Angeles Southwest College, staff overwork helped to overcome severe financial pressures. Given time, the school produced some outstanding students, from Battersbee's point of view. LASC then took some needed bows, and MCHS gained some internal legitimacy.

Contra Costa College, Richmond, California

At least seven community colleges expressed interest in sponsoring the northern California replication, including Contra Costa College, located on the East Bay north of Berkeley (Silverman, 1992; Silverman & Carlton, 1993). The area serviced by the Richmond Unified School District (RUSD), which overlapped the main recruitment area for CCC, had an 85% minority population, a relatively high unemployment rate (7.6% vs. 4.7% for Contra Costa County and 5.8% for California), a relatively low family-income level (35% of the residents of Richmond and San Pablo lived below the poverty line), and a low level of adult educational attainment (40% lacked a high school diploma).

RUSD—the state's 16th largest school district in 1988—served about 28,500 students; 25% were welfare recipients, and almost two-thirds came from minority groups. The district had five high schools and a continuation school, but critics noted little innovation. The late 1980s superintendency of Walter Marx was marked by new programs, but change came at a price. Weak financial management—"the money will come if you have a good program"—placed RUSD in bankruptcy soon after the replication at CCC opened.

Coincident with the state competition, Marx and the RUSD board solicited staff suggestions for reducing the district's dropout and suspension rates (Educational Research Department, 1986). Santiago Wood, the district's new director of government relations and development and former president of Vista Community College in Berkeley, expressed interest in the middle college concept, and obtained strong commitments for drafting a proposal from Candy Rose, president of the community college; Marx; the Richmond mayor; and the local Urban League chapter (Wood to Connie Anderson, July 19, 1988, MCA, "Contra Costa College" file; Rose to Anderson, September 23, 1988, Marks to Anderson, September 22, 1988, and Richard L. Griffen to Anderson, September 23, 1988, MCA, "Richmond Middle College" file).

CCC (founded in 1949) was the least prestigious of the district's three community colleges; its demographic base resembled Richmond's, and upwardly mobile students often bypassed CCC. RUSD and CCC had created an articulation council to sponsor projects for at-risk district youth, including concurrent enrollment programs, joint facilities use, and a year 13–14 program for RUSD special education students. The proposal to Lieberman and the state envisioned a 100-student class, including 40 students who would have to repeat 9th grade if they remained at their former school; the other 60 students would be 10th and 11th graders from the six high schools in RUSD (*Survey Questions*, 1988b).

Competing proposals emanated from community colleges located in more urban areas, but Lieberman was impressed by the vigor of RUSD's proposal, by the delegation that visited LaGuardia, and by the availability of public transportation to the 87-acre campus. Many RUSD students already changed buses at the CCC bus stop on their way to and from school. Police monitoring minimized disciplinary problems at the transfer point, and both RUSD and CCC supported the arrangement.

Lieberman approved the disbursement of Ford replication funds for the CCC–RUSD proposal in October 1988. But her questions about administrative space allocations, the place of the principal in CCC's governance structure, and the grade-heterogeneous admissions policy led to changes from off-campus to on-campus administrative offices and classrooms, from representation of the MCHS principal on the CCC academic senate to inclusion among department chairs, and from a student body composed of 9th-grade repeaters and 10th and 11th graders to "potential dropouts who would be entering the ninth grade" (*Survey Questions*, 1988b, n.p.; see also Lieberman to Cullen, September 30, 1988, MCA, "Contra Costa" file; "Middle College High School, Contra Costa College," 1988; Santiago Wood to MCHS Planning Group, October 12, 1988, and Wood to Laurel Barton and Joe Malloy, October 25, 1988, MCA, "Richmond Middle College" file).

CCC received the northern California designation—and an accompanying $65,000 planning grant—in November 1988, but implementation languished for much of 1988–89. A skeptical CCC faculty took two months to approve the proposal; formal approval of the CCC–RUSD agreement came even later. RUSD passed over an assistant superintendent who was involved in the planning and was listed as the project director in the proposal, to appoint a principal unfamiliar with the design (Candy Rose to Lieberman, February 15, 1989, MCA, "Contra Costa College" file). Staff hiring and student recruitment remained uncompleted by the end of Spring. The CCC liaison—a proactive position at LaGuardia and other replications—did not facilitate the project. Rose, said some informants, appointed this liaison because he had no other responsibilities; with good reason, they added.

Lack of headway and understanding got the school off to a bad start. Only 45 of 65 admitted students appeared at the school's September 1989 opening. Enrollment increased to 64 by the end of the school year, but not in time to forestall the layoff of the school's mathematics teacher and the resignation of the principal.

Myra Silverman, the replacement principal, had moved from New York to California in 1964. A quarter century of teaching and administrative experience in RUSD included service as a middle school principal, as a high school dean with responsibility for discipline, and in alternative education programming, including planning for Middle College High School at Contra Costa. The previous principal, she noted, knew neither RUSD nor CCC; she "couldn't get a staple, and didn't know ogres from the good guys." RUSD turned to her, Silverman speculated, to rectify the mistake of opening a school with a new staff amidst an established college. Unlike LaGuardia, she noted, CCC had a 40-year head start. Turning to seasoned staff permitted the school to capitalize on informal ties and friendships with colleagues at RUSD.

Silverman immediately addressed two problems present at most sites: hasty, unselective student recruitment and strained relations with CCC faculty. The first students did not meet the admissions criteria—many, said Silverman, were literally dragged off the street (*Proposal Narrative*, 1989). The resulting academic failures and disciplinary problems occupied staff and faculty time, and fostered a testy relationship with CCC. A lack of space, the need to reduce disciplinary problems, and Silverman's emphasis on "community" led her to reduce the target class size from 75 to 60 students, and the overall student body from 300 to 200. Silverman used her contacts among RUSD's guidance counselors and faculty to deepen the candidate pool, thereby crafting a class reflecting the district's ethnic composition, without resorting to quotas. Diversity, she believed, would minimize ethnic divisions—frequent interaction would lead students to treat classmates as individuals. Silverman reported only one conflict with ethnic overtones during her tenure.

Silverman strongly supported a 9th-grade entry year for the school, although she accepted a few sophomore and junior transfers in spite of Janet Lieberman's continued insistence that MCHS students not be "tainted" by attendance at another high school. The district, she noted, moved its 8th graders directly into high schools—a big leap, for which students needed a support. Quality, selection, and student buy-in, she insisted, would decline if students began in 10th grade. Silverman and her faculty colleagues would sacrifice salutary interactions with CCC students to work with malleable younger students who still felt they could do anything. By age 15 or 16, Silverman and her colleagues believed, student expectations might be irreparably diminished. MCHS faculty and staff capitalized on student enthusiasm by introducing an MCHS/CCC team-taught "you're in the army now" orientation class that discussed grade point averages and college entrance requirements, encouraged enrollment in CCC classes, and developed social skills. By 1993, Silverman expressed satisfaction with recruitment, a necessary, but not sufficient, step toward improving relations with community college faculty.

Tradition, said high school staff, caused much CCC faculty resentment. Faculty members would have found MCHS easier to accept, they argued, if MCHS predated their hiring. But most members of a very senior CCC faculty were not pleased with the school's arrival. Start-up problems, especially the principalship turnover and the ineffectual liaison, raised eyebrows. Suspicion of administration sleight-of-hand arose from placing weak students in college classes without orientation or notice. Incidents of poor class control by an MCHS teacher, and publication of a negative story in the college newspaper, added fuel to the fire. RUSD's bankruptcy—MCHS and other special programs were threatened with closure until state legislators obtained a bailout loan—added fiscal issues to faculty concerns. Already fighting the perception that CCC had become a "majority-minority school" with the attendant problems, some faculty feared the high school would undermine a push for improved community relations.

Building faculty confidence, Silverman understood, meant addressing symbol and substance. The newspaper's faculty advisor, Silverman's former student, helped to assign "constructive" reporters to cover the school. "Teacher-by-teacher" efforts by Silverman and Rose resulted in enlisting three faculty members who reserved some CCC course sections for MCHS students, conducting a belated faculty orientation, leading a tour for faculty members living outside RUSD to show Richmond's diversity, and holding regular gripe sessions. But fear of disruption dissipated slowly, and not without regression. In Fall 1993, an alternative school moved next to CCC without notifying Rose or Silverman. The ensuing disciplinary problems included physical attacks on MCHS students. Silverman, an RUSD employee, could not object to the school's presence, but an unconstrained Rose insisted on its immediate removal.

Community college faculty concerns shifted to the performance of MCHS students—mainly juniors and seniors—in college classes. Permission to enroll depended on student readiness and on the class itself—the academic expectations and meeting prerequisites. Many MCHS students, believed school administrators, were equal in ability to CCC students. To give high school students time to prove themselves, most college instructors were not told they had MCHS students until mid-semester. This policy was borne out when experimental use of separate grade sheets showed similar attendance and grading patterns for the two groups. Gradually, some CCC instructors asked for earlier identification of MCHS students to provide supplementary support. Recalcitrant CCC faculty, concluded MCHS administrators, had selective and faulty memories—objectors with vivid accounts of problematic MCHS students did not remember CCC dropouts.

School staff echoed Lieberman's list of academic benefits of college coursework: establishing relationships with college peers, identifying role models, and working to a higher standard. Silverman also noted financial benefits: RUSD gave MCHS the same allocation as other schools; reducing the size of a high school class therefore required significant student enrollments in college classes. "We could not run MCHS without kids in college classes," argued Silverman. A "win–win" situation resulted: MCHS students, for example, maintained the enrollments of the CCC physical education department; in turn, MCHS did not have to hire a physical education faculty member.

MCHS administrators, in turn, identified ways MCHS might benefit CCC—from providing lab assistants to demonstrating improved pedagogy. These moves reduced faculty negativity; a few years later, Silverman called herself "proud and amazed at the positive attitude of the faculty." "Faculty members don't feel defensive, or threatened by having high school students," she added. Silverman attributed lingering hesitations to the "inevitability" that, everywhere, some faculty just don't like students.

Developing the curriculum also helped to connect high school and college faculty. The curriculum at first followed RUSD college preparatory guidelines; sacrificed was staff development and curricular innovation. But change began soon after Silverman arrived: The MCHS science and math departments designed "Scath"; an MCHS faculty member taught a CCC course in natural science—jointly designed by the MCHS and CCC science departments—as an adjunct. "College support," designed for students in CCC courses, and the mandatory college skills class, facilitated the transition to college studies.

The internship was a persistent curricular thorn. Unlike MCHS at LaGuardia, staff noted, the structure and ethos of RUSD and CCC did not support cooperative education; the high school opened without this component. Silverman addressed the omission during the first year. Initial 9th-grader placements did not work well; post hoc assessments noted student immaturity and a discrepancy between aspirations and workforce "realities." MCHS staff henceforth kept 9th graders on campus and gave them a "realistic" view of the world of work. The revised program would begin in 10th grade with community-oriented internships in CCC offices or at local schools. Juniors would complete semester- or year-long, once-a-week internships at local businesses. Seniors would work full-time for a semester, although this schedule required students to catch up on missed academic work and teachers to collapse a year's work into a semester. Silverman, reluctant to assign all students to Chevron—the largest local corporation—made other contacts through the Richmond Chamber of Commerce.

The age disparity between MCHS and CCC helps to explain the resolution of governance and space allocation issues. CCC's governance structure did not easily provide for MCHS representation. Rose, a believer in shared governance, thought the MCHS principal belonged on the faculty senate. A less certain CCC faculty made the principal an observer, but the asymmetry of this arrangement quickly became clear. MCHS faculty could attend senate meetings as observers—few issues came to a vote—but scheduling problems hindered recruitment of a representative. Silverman attended smaller meetings at CCC that addressed instructional and administrative issues. MCHS faculty also could attend as "department heads," although departments contained only one or two colleagues. Faculty attendance, Silverman noted, helped to reduce the "outsider" perception. It also permitted MCHS instructors to observe the many roles played by college faculty, and the value colleges placed on faculty participation in governance.

Accommodating to a much older community college led to difficulties in resolving space needs. The school's administrative offices were to be located off campus. But by the end of the third academic year, Silverman negotiated an on-campus allocation of two classrooms, some administrative space, a library, several computers, and an office suite, including a room used for faculty meetings and for tutoring students. MCHS shared other classrooms with CCC; classes even met in the administration building and the faculty office building.

MCHS faculty disagreed on the desirability of dedicated space—some argued for an identifiable location; others believed that integration provided MCHS students with visible role models: successful students who looked like themselves—perhaps their relatives—and who came from the same community. But integration meant that MCHS departments had no place to call their own; holding social events required public relations work with people in the surrounding rooms. All discussion of space issues began with the question, "How will this affect the college?" MCHS tried to be as unobtrusive as possible: The school rejected a desired modification to its class schedule, for example, because of possible hall noise during class changes. The space problem was somewhat alleviated when CCC enrollments declined as student fees increased after the early 1990s recession.

Replications cannot begin completely de novo, argued an MCHS staff conscious of the substantial age differences between the high school and both CCC and RUSD. The brand-new school—trying to work within two established structures—reduced the bull-in-a-china-shop syndrome by recruiting a well-connected principal from the school district. Time helped to overcome institutional age disparities, but bare-bones budgets at CCC argued for immediate, demonstrable successes—a strategy precluding excessive risk taking and innovation.

But most problems were behind-the-scenes, and the age disparity also could work to the advantage of MCHS. RUSD routinely promoted large numbers of at-risk students from 8th to 9th grade, who then dropped out for lack of credits. The application process showed students they were "chosen" for this special school through an affirmative, selective process. Exposure to a 40-year-old community college, with a developed campus and population of older, successful, but otherwise similar students, would help to nurture a belief in the attainability of academic success and college enrollment.

But "chosen" students also could depart. MCHS demonstrated success after its first four years. Enrollments increased by 45% to 139 students by 1992–93, and the school had the luxury of a waiting list, despite a 28:1 student–teacher ratio. MCHS was selective, noted Silverman, but not all students developed resilience—the maturity necessary for success—or gained independence from time-consuming family responsibilities (California Community Colleges, 1993).

At MCHS at Contra Costa College, hasty implementation and shaky finances added to the weight of history. Myra Silverman brought stability, know-how, and connections to the school; she also bought time for the school to find a niche on a campus largely set in its ways.

El Centro College, Dallas, Texas

The initiative for a replication in Dallas came from the top. At the behest of R. Jan LeCroy, chancellor of the Dallas County Community College District (DCCCD), representatives of DCCCD and of the Dallas Independent School District (DISD) attended the replication conference at LaGuardia. LeCroy expressed interest in opening schools at each of the seven units in DCCCD (Lieberman to Bernstein, May 4, 1987, FFA, Grant file 86–587). A return visit to LaGuardia by a Dallas contingent in March 1987 included the president of El Centro College (ECC, opened in 1966), located in downtown Dallas, who volunteered to open the first, and only, replication. "A flagship [ECC was the district's first community college]," he said, "should have a flagship" (Curtis, 1993, n.p.; see also Ackerman, 1994; Gibbons, 1975; Rippey, 1987).

LeCroy's timing was fortuitous; growing numbers of 9th-grade dropouts prompted DISD to look for a retention program (LeCroy, 1984). A joint planning team requested technical assistance and faculty training from Lieberman in October 1987, adding that the community college, its district, the Texas Education Agency (K–12), and the Texas Higher Education Coordinating Board tentatively approved the school.

Lieberman accepted the Dallas application despite reservations about leadership in the school and the community college districts. Key officials departed during the planning year; their successors would have to assent to the replication. But by bringing Dallas officials to LaGuardia, the planning team leader gained the leverage needed for final approval. "We returned to Dallas and said to DISD they had to let us know something about their plans immediately," he wrote, "and lo and behold, I have now been meeting with them on an almost daily basis" (McCrary to Lieberman, April 22, 1988, MCA, "Dallas County Community College District" file).

DISD approved a school that would admit 80 to 100 9th graders, and grow by one class and 100 students per year to 400 students by 1991–92 (*Middle College Proposal*, 1988). The planning committee decided to begin with 9th grade, despite Lieberman's reservations, and to accept potential dropouts, not dropouts—a condition set by Lieberman. The decisions, speculated Christine Curtis, first principal of MCHS, may have related to a substantial 9th-grade dropout rate (Curtis, 1993; Rosa Johnson to Lieberman, August 19, 1988, and Lieberman to Johnson, September 15, 1988, MCA, "Dallas County Community College District" file). MCHS at ECC opened in September 1988 in the 7,000-student community college. First-year enrollments peaked at 94 9th graders shortly after opening and dropped to 77 by midyear (Cullen to Rosenberg and Lieberman, February 17, 1989, MCA, "Dallas County Community College" file). Enrollments reached 143 students in 1991–92, but limited space and budget cutbacks forced a cap of 125 in 1992—about one-third the size of most replications.

The two schools shared space in a nine-story, two-block-long former department store—location and adaptability of space led other colleges to recycle abandoned department stores at about the same time—featuring "the slowest elevators in the world." The high school initially was assigned four offices and four classrooms. The planning committee agreed to use the school district's expendable materials and supplies, and the community college's equipment. But sharing some facilities took time to arrange. MCHS students were prohibited from using the ECC computer lab unless a high school faculty member was present; awkward incidents eventually embarrassed ECC staff into reversing the policy. The gym was shared, and MCHS students had access only to intramural athletic programs. The library was also shared. But MCHS, needing more dedicated space, installed a false wall to divide the library. The high school remained in the department store building until 1994. A move across the street in that year into its own, larger space permitted enrollment expansion to 250 students.

Students had to meet at least one at-risk criterion to gain admission: absenteeism, multiple course failures, failing a standardized exam, being a year behind in school, pregnancy, emotional or social problems associated with the student's family, minor scrapes with the law, being a runaway, low self-esteem, or alienation from home or school. But all admitted students had to score in the 41st percentile or better on the DISD placement test. Word of mouth led to enrollment of many Hispanic students—the school was 45% Hispanic and 35% African-American in 1990–91—since the school was located in a predominantly Hispanic neighborhood. Within a few years, MCHS teachers and students interviewed applicants—as the planning team envisioned—looking for maturity, interest in college attendance, and "fit."

A staff of seven included a guidance counselor, a vocational education teacher, four classroom teachers, and Curtis. Born and raised in Houston, Curtis taught and administered in Texas and California schools before becoming a principal at an alternative high school in California. She applied for the MCHS position shortly after her return to Texas. DISD assigned faculty members to the school—a practice, complained Curtis, that led to appointment (and departure) of some incompatible teachers. The faculty grew to 12 teachers in 1990–91, but declined to ten during a later budget crunch. Capping enrollment reduced the effect of staff cuts, and in 1992, the district permitted teacher selection from a supplied list of candidates. Curtis, a disciple of Cullen's views on shared governance, asked staff members to interview potential colleagues. The result, Curtis (1993) noted, was "the best team I've had." Staff turnover continued, but now Curtis lost faculty to ECC.

"Top-down" decision making at the community college meant that ECC staff did not learn about Middle College High School in advance. A stunned community college faculty echoed the complaints made at other sites: "Control the kids," and "I didn't want to teach in a high school." Even some key ECC administrative staff knew about the school only through negative grapevine comments about its students. Minimal staff collaboration—ECC's liaison to MCHS changed shortly after the school's opening because of a lack of communication—and a reluctance among ECC faculty to teach MCHS students reflected this resentment; the high school's traditional curriculum featured no team-teaching.

The turnaround in faculty attitudes, as elsewhere, was slow. Curtis gained friends when some MCHS faculty moved to ECC. Tuition revenue from MCHS students also helped; so did the strong performance of MCHS students in ECC classes. As at Contra Costa, community college faculty did not know at first which students came from the high school; the good grades earned by MCHS students were often "eye openers." Curtis depended on the consistent support of a president, who remained at ECC throughout the development of MCHS, to overcome instability generated by a rapid turnover in vice presidents.

To coordinate yearly schedules and to maximize student interaction, the high school year mirrored ECC's two 16-week semesters—two weeks shorter than at other Dallas high schools—divided into two eight-week sessions. Students in their freshman, sophomore, and junior years took three classes and house for three sessions and an internship during the fourth session. Space for MCHS was available only between 12:00, when ECC's morning classes ended, and 5:00, when its night classes began. The packed afternoon teaching schedule offered few chances for student–faculty interaction during instructional hours. Tutoring, student–faculty conferences, and internships occurred in the morning. Incoming students were warned about the school's fast daily schedule, but some students could not pace themselves through eight-week sessions with no "down time."

Scheduling classes according to the ECC semester did not exempt MCHS from a required 60 clock hours per course per session. The resulting 90-minute daily class periods necessitated uncoordinated high school and college daily schedules. ECC students objected to the noise made by high school students during MCHS class changes. ECC students—whose average age was 27—also resented the propensity of MCHS students to push all the buttons in the building's ever-lethargic elevators.

MCHS seniors were slated to take three semester-long ECC courses each semester, thereby completing 18 college credits (McCrary to Lieberman, April 22, 1988, copy attached to Lieberman to Bernstein, April 27, 1988, FFA, Grant file 86–587). DISD paid tuition to DCCCD for their instruction. Seniors also took house, which, for lack of space, consisted of daily, half-hour, school-wide meetings. Four students attained senior status in 1990–91, took their courses at ECC, and earned their college credits. MCHS celebrated with an earlier-than-expected first graduation ceremony. But, beginning in 1992, MCHS students who wanted college credit had to take an entrance examination along with all other community college applicants. Only 17 seniors in the first tested cohort passed; MCHS had to instruct the other ten. MCHS students also took some courses at ECC, including gym and art, for elective high school credits. Internships focused on governmental and educational agencies. MCHS "adopted" an elementary and a middle school so that students might explore careers in education. Curtis (1993) told office managers what they were getting, and that MCHS "will kill 'em" if they were bad.

The smallest replication in a movement priding itself on smallness, MCHS at ECC used its size to advantage, through the daily all-inclusive house, a 17:1 student–faculty ratio, and its dedicated space. "Students at MCHS are special; the place is never dull, and it's especially rewarding at graduation time," said Curtis. "They see themselves as a family. They're cohesive and look out for each other, the teachers, and me" (1993, n.p.).

TWO FAILURES

Cuyahoga Community College, Cleveland, Ohio

The Cleveland school district was ambivalent about opening a replication from the outset; Lieberman conferred, withdrew, and reinstated recognition within two years. The district's funding permitted hiring only a principal, a guidance counselor, and three teachers. Worse, the funds did not go to Cuyahoga Community College or to the high school, but to the Jane Addams Business Careers Center, across the street from the college's metropolitan campus. Once a week, students began their day with a house meeting at the community college, a group guidance curriculum developed by the Cleveland schools. But the district required students to take electives, gym, and lunch at Addams each morning before moving to Cuyahoga for the rest of the day. Space was at a premium at the community college, so the district was under less pressure to relinquish its claim to part—eventually all—of the student's day.

Students expressed enthusiasm for the new school, but community college faculty voiced objection. The poor screening procedures used to admit the first students did not help, nor did the resignation of the first principal after six months. The second principal, although unfamiliar with the concept when appointed, was a quick learner and became a strong supporter. She reduced community college faculty concerns during the second year through diplomacy and improved admissions procedures. A 1991 report noted an average grade point average one full letter higher than a Cleveland public school control group; a higher attendance rate (91 vs. 58%), and a 53% lower suspension rate. The number of students in peer counseling increased during the second year; suspensions and fights decreased as a percentage of the student body (Lieberman, 1992; *Notes on Visitors*, 1989; *Survey Questions*, 1988a).

The Cleveland school district considered its MCHS a *program* offered by Jane Addams, not a separate school, thus violating a basic tenet of the middle college movement. The issue was rendered moot when the district closed MCHS at Cuyahoga Community College shortly after it graduated its first class in 1993—it had survived an earlier budget cutback—saying it was not needed.

The New Jersey Initiative

A State-Sponsored Consortium. Opening four replications in New York City in the mid-1980s signaled a jump from a singular reform to an innovation with district-wide potential. The interest of New Jersey government officials might have led to a "systemic" advance: a school at each of the state's 19 community (or county) colleges.

Contiguity to New York City may explain the interest of New Jersey authorities. As a CUNY vice chancellor in the late 1960s, Theodore Hollander, New Jersey's chancellor of higher education, was instrumental in designing Open Admissions. As a New York State Education Department official in the mid-1970s, he helped to obtain the needed approvals for MCHS at LaGuardia. Officials in New Jersey's Office of Teacher Education and Pre-collegiate Programs, located in Hollander's department, offered to coordinate a consortium of colleges to replicate the school (Leonard T. Kreisman to Lieberman, December 11, 1986, MCA, "New Jersey Department of Higher Education" file). New Jersey already awarded challenge grants—often used by states to effect district-level change—to several community colleges to work with high schools to help at-risk students. State officials encouraged these colleges to use the funds to create replications. By late 1986, several community colleges expressed interest, and Lieberman helped state, community college, and school district officials plan a consortium that pooled technical resources for training (Martin S. Friedman to Lieberman, January 14, 1987, MCA, "New Jersey Department of Higher Education" file).

The concept of a state-sponsored consortium disintegrated by 1988. Glassboro State (now Rowan College), a four-year college, almost immediately withdrew its application. Brookdale Community College, in Lincroft, used its grant to recruit general-track high school students to technical careers, using the resources of its advanced technology center (Lee Blaustein to Lieberman, October 5, 1987, MCA, "New Jersey Department of Higher Education" file). Lieberman rejected the application of Essex County Community College in Newark, because of inadequate funds for planning, vague space provisions, and a lack of cooperation and leadership (*Ford Foundation Project*, 1988; Lieberman, 1987b; Lieberman to John Dugan, April 28, 1987, Alice Dickens to Lieberman, May 7, 1987, and Lieberman to Dickens, May 13, 1987, MCA, "New Jersey Department of Higher Education" file; *Survey*, 1988).

Atlantic Community College. Atlantic Community College (ACC), in Mays Landing, wished to use its state grant to replicate the LaGuardia model at newly opened Atlantic County Alternative High School, although the school was not located on the ACC campus (Thomas V. Chelius to Lieberman, November 12, 1986, MCA, "New Jersey Department of Higher Education" file). It proposed to recruit "disaffected and disruptive" students, who would attend for two to four marking periods before returning to a home high school; it would not award its own diplomas. The curriculum featured few innovations; instead, "any course a student could take in the home high school, he/she can take at Atlantic County Alternative High School." The school did not provide for house, although it claimed to offer daily counseling activities. ACC would find campus jobs for students in lieu of cooperative education. The school would accommodate grades 9–12, but officials did not propose to admit one grade at a time (Lieberman to Friedman, January 20, 1987, MCA, "New Jersey Department of Higher Education" file). Restrictions in the state challenge grant, ACC officials claimed, hindered full implementation. But Lieberman rejected the application, seeing little evidence that the school district and ACC would collaborate seriously to remedy shortcomings once weaned from the grant.

Union County College. Union County College (UCC), with campuses in Cranford, Elizabeth, and Scotch Plains, was the only New Jersey college to open a replication. UCC (founded in 1982) resulted from a merger between Union College, an independent two-year college, and Union County Technical Institute (founded in 1960). UCC had a predominantly white student body (12% African-American; 5% Hispanic in 1983); 42% of the undergraduates were age 25 or older (State of New Jersey, 1984). Union County Middle College (UCMC) proposed to build on the existing internships in UCC's health and technology programs.

Student demographics raised issues of congruity between UCC and UCMC. UCMC proposed to "bus in" 80 African-American, central-city, 9th-grade students to a predominantly White suburban campus (Lieberman, 1990). The racial disparity between students compounded concerns about including relatively immature 9th graders; confrontations were predictable. A site visit prior to UCMC's opening resulted in a qualified endorsement from the evaluator (Stoel, 1987). The commitment of UCC officials raised few questions. These officials, noting projections of an enrollment downturn, began several programs for their urban constituency, including a learning center in downtown Plainfield. Community college funding was in place; UCC dedicated most of the state's $1.16 million three-year challenge grant to the project.

But long-term funding depended on passing a controversial school budget. "I'm not sure where that stands," wrote the evaluator, "given the super-conservative mindset of the power brokers in Plainfield." Overcoming that hurdle did not ensure success. "Even though Union has tons of money, they can't literally buy the program and kids away from Plainfield. There will have to be some cooperation to make the program work over the long run." The budget controversy, turnover in the Plainfield schools, and the school board's reluctance to appoint a principal with UCMC's opening only months away were bad signs. "Because Plainfield is in such flux," concluded the evaluator, "it is difficult to estimate how much support can possibly be forthcoming from the city and school system" (Stoel, 1987, p. 2).

Lieberman included UCMC among the replications, but key problems remained, including unclear admissions criteria, an unimaginative curriculum, a weak high school staff, and nonintegration of students, teachers, and staff into the life of the community college (Burt Rosenberg to Lieberman, December 15, 1987, MCA, "Ford Evaluators' Meeting—October 21, 1988" file; Lieberman to Hollander, February 5, 1988, MCA, "New Jersey Department of Higher Education" file). "After repeated attempts to reshape the school according to the Middle College plan," recounted Lieberman (1990), "we withdrew the affiliation" (p. 2). Union County Middle College soon closed.

In New Jersey, state agency funding and technical support did not substantially promote community college–school district collaboration. The absence of strong commitments from local officials is a key finding for those who consider actions by state governments at the heart of "systemic reform" (Cohen, 1995).

CONCLUSION

In 2000, about 30 replications, including five Ford-sponsored sites, were open; others were in development (Lawton, 1996). Some community college or school districts, such as the Seattle Community College District, did not submit applications to the Ford competition; others were colleges Lieberman initially avoided; still others, such as Mott Community College, Flint, Michigan, had rural *and* urban recruitment areas. Several explicitly vocational variants also emerged. Washtenaw Technical Middle College (WTMC, opened in 1997), in Ypsilanti, Michigan, and Tech Prep Middle College (TPMC), in Houston, Texas, were vocational schools for at-risk students that partnered with the *occupational* departments and divisions of the host community colleges. WTMC, on the campus of Washtenaw Community College, combined work-based learning with applied science and mathematics courses (Vandenberg, 1996). Occupational programs at community colleges often were charged with offering terminal education to students instead of promoting transfer to four-year colleges. TPMC, a grades 9–14 school, offered a curriculum leading to an Associate in Applied Science degree with advanced technology skills and to transfer to a four-year college (Pianelli, 1995).

Some nonstarters were community colleges with reputations for innovation. Others may have felt pressure from state officials or from a need to appease foundation officials who might later support their initiatives. In any case, a rejection from Lieberman or a failure to open might well have hindered a future venture—the "we tried that" syndrome.

Rather than catalogue the necessary and sufficient conditions for a successful replication, let's return to basics. Burton Clark's *The Open-Door College* (1960b) noted the difficulties of locating a new school among an array of existing educational institutions. San Jose Community College, the site of Clark's research, had to find a niche in an area that included a state college just three miles away and a technical high school with strong local union support. Many two-year colleges still had not secured their own academic niches a decade or two after opening. Urban community colleges— often with low prestige—might face declining enrollments and budgets, and deteriorating, inadequate plants. Caught in a contentious debate over mission—academic, vocational, and/or developmental—and accused of being "second best" whatever they decided, many community college staff members were touchy about secondary education, especially for at-risk students.

The need to fit into the cultures of school districts and community colleges with long histories and identified constituencies accounted for some problems. MCHS at LaGuardia had two historical advantages. First, LaGuardia—opened shortly before the high school—had no prior association with secondary education. Second, equity topped the reform agenda when the school recruited its faculty and staff. Most replications were less fortunate. Contra Costa College had a 40-year head start over its high school, and many Contra Costa faculty and staff saw the school's emergence from secondary education as a triumph. All replications opened after major changes to the definition of "reform."

Opening a site required intense school–college collaboration over curriculum, finances, and space—few replications received prime space; some locations diminished the school's effectiveness. Schools had some advantages when the initiative came from the community college. But somewhere between acceptance of the design and full operation, the college passed the torch to the school district. The district typically awaited multiple approvals and budgetary commitments before authorizing staff and student recruitment and curricular planning. To open the school, districts often relied on the "normal" processes targeted for reform; appointing a first "conventional" principal was often a harbinger. Greater continuity between design and implementation might have reduced the learning curve for several school districts and community colleges; new players would not have had to acquire the vision and learn the necessary operational steps.

Once opened, a school's long-term survival and success depended on the ability of the principal, upon whom the burden largely fell, to work daily within two cultures. Adjustment to the community college was the greater priority at the outset. Coming from public school systems, principals had to learn about, and be open to, opportunities offered by community colleges for flexibility, for anonymity—at least when not under college scrutiny because of student behavior—and for collaboration.

Most principals did not anticipate the often vehement resistance from community college faculty members and students. Hasty implementation meant taking shortcuts, including failing to inform concerned constituencies. This failure often exacerbated pre-existing tensions within the community colleges. Faculty members who already saw their presidents as authoritarian—unions were strong at many community colleges—who labored under heavy workloads or inadequate physical conditions, or who knew of the college's struggle to gain independence from a school district and a *parent high school*, might not appreciate a belated announcement that a high school for at-risk students had opened on their campus. A tight budget, low or declining academic "prestige," a deteriorating plant, or a changed racial mix in the student body—all might occasion vented frustrations.

Some student resistance originated in the substantial age gap between community college and high school students. The growing adult segment in the community college mix, combined with scheduling problems, hindered salutary student interactions. But the flaw was not fatal: The serious environment resulting from the presence of older students helped to overcome the tendency of 16-year-olds to act like 16-year-olds. Improved selection policies produced students able to take advantage of the independence and resources offered by the community colleges. Reciprocal internship programs also promoted interaction. And, once a replication grew to full size, age heterogeneity *within* its population may have achieved some of what was intended from community college–high school student interaction.

A talented, patient principal could eliminate community college resistance, or at least reduce it to a predictable, reluctantly accepted part of the routine. Host colleges were not monoliths; vocal opposition might interfere with—but would not necessarily prohibit—collaboration with others. Living under the same roof meant accommodation. Most principals worked to make their schools valued sources of students and faculty, and of ideas about teaching developmental populations. A community college, they reasoned, might remain aloof, even hostile, but eventually would point to the school as its contribution to the reform of public education.

Later threats often came from the school district. A third-year crisis, Lieberman concluded, was a near-inevitable part of the growth process. The concept, she said, was accepted on paper. But no one perceived the challenge a replication posed to the autonomy of a school district; it was not just another alternative secondary school. Countering school district resistance, argued Cecilia Cullen and Myra Silverman, required a principal who knew both worlds, could blunt confrontations, had reliable friends, and could establish working relationships—a "reformer from within." Most schools with such principals gained stability by their fifth year, sometimes at the price of some components. But the schools also could become places of internal exile, rather than forces for district reform. Learning how to instigate change instead of becoming marginalized became part of the lore principals taught to new members of the Middle College High School Consortium (Evans, 1995).

What kept the principals going, despite a lack of funding, time, and support? Many came from religious families and studied at denominational colleges; all had a sense of mission. Their schools, principals attested, influenced the students who saw the process through. The physical appearance of some students, noted Natalie Battersbee, greatly changed between enrollment and graduation; she noted softened facial expressions, changed body language, and greater self-confidence. "They stand taller," she said, "look you in the eyes, and speak in a different tone of voice." Battersbee gave out metamorphosis awards to drastic changers at Middle College High School at Los Angeles Southwest College. When these students visited the school after graduation, she added, "you feel blessed you've had input into their lives." A tough student, she recounted, later apologized to a coach for an outburst, then went to his old middle school, where he tutored the students and even helped them cross the street to avoid the gangs. "Once you open a student's mind and develop what's already there," said Battersbee, "you don't have to do anything else" (1993, n.p.).

The Sum of the Parts

*The life history of most demonstration programs seems to be
self-limiting. They generally tend to be small scale and short
lived, with professionals learning that results are not cumulative but rather seem to be disjunctive. There is a high turnover of personnel so that the consequences of a particular
demonstration face gradual extinction. The most critical argument is that after a decision to spread the demonstration
project throughout the system, it faces death by diffuse and
partial incorporation. In addition, there is an absence of
training to insure the implementation of new procedures,
nor are there effective devices of inspection and audit. In the
end, a considerable degree of frustration develops as old
practices and procedures are given new names.*
                                        —Morris Janowitz (1969, p. 20)

*Middle College establishes a new role for the community col-
lege, one as the principal reformer for secondary education.
All in all, it has taken twenty years, but the expansion rate
is increasing and the initiative in New York City will un-
doubtedly increase the impact in the immediate future.*
                                        —Janet Lieberman (1992, p. 21)

During the 20th century, Americans came to view the comprehensive high
school as the most efficient way to educate a rapidly growing number of
adolescents. By standards of efficiency, these high schools were successful;
in 1995, 87.1% of all 25- to 34-year-olds graduated from high school or
earned a GED. But many educators turned their attention to the dropouts.
Continued lower graduation rates among members of minority groups—
the wide gap for Hispanic students appeared particularly intractable—led
observers to ask whether alternative settings might better address the needs
of students most at-risk of dropping out (U. S. Department of Education,
1998).

For a quarter century, the middle college movement offered a different model for secondary education. This chapter discusses the accomplishments and possibilities of the genre, centering on four themes: evidence of "success," especially at MCHS at LaGuardia; adapting educational practices to the needs of at-risk students; gaining institutional autonomy; and shortening the time to a college degree.

DID IT WORK?
TALES OF THE (DATA)TAPE

Evaluations of Middle College High School at LaGuardia began the day it opened. Formative evaluations enabled the principals, Lieberman, and Shenker to track the school's early development. But beginning in the early 1980s, the evaluations also responded to external criticisms, including the charge of "creaming" (Denniston et al., 1984; Greenberg, 1982b). Some studies compared graduates of the school with graduates of the city's other alternative high schools, and of the academic high schools of Queens. Attendance rates for MCHS, for example, exceeded the rates for the other alternative high schools each year between 1979–80 and 1988–89, and equaled or exceeded citywide attendance rates for all but two years between 1978–79 and 1988–89. Between 1982–83 and 1988–89, the dropout rates for the other alternative high schools exceeded the MCHS rate every year; the dropout rates for all New York City high schools exceeded the MCHS rate in all but three years (Cullen, 1991).

Most academic comparisons favored MCHS. MCHS students exceeded the June 1986 citywide and alternative high school Regents Competency Test (RCT) scores in reading (68.2, 60.9, and 63.0, respectively), but fell behind these scores in June 1987 (50.0, 58.6, and 69.1). In math, MCHS scores lagged the citywide scores in both years, exceeded alternative high school scores in 1986, but came up short in 1987 (June 1986: 53.1, 53.8, and 42.4; June 1987: 48.2, 54.8, and 49.1). But the combined January–June 1988 RCT scores favored MCHS students over citywide test-takers in both areas: 83.5% to 78.3% in reading; 61.5% to 53.3% in math (*Middle College High School at LaGuardia Community College*, 1989, Appendix D, Tables 1 and 2). School comparisons did not control for demographic factors, including gender and race, although student demographics at alternative high schools approximated the composition of the MCHS student body. Few other high schools for at-risk students, evaluators added, compared favorably with citywide averages, which included many students not at-risk.[1]

Second-generation controlled studies aimed at greater precision. About 83% of MCHS students who were "candidates for graduation" received their diplomas (Clark, n.d., p. 2). Dropout rates for students entering high school in 1985 favored MCHS students over a randomly selected group of 1985 nonattending applicants to MCHS—16.84% to 29.63%. The post-secondary attendance rate for 1988 MCHS graduates was 76.7%, a slightly lower rate than reported for late 1970s graduates. The 1993 and 1997 rates were 81.0 and 73.0%, respectively. Most college enrollees attended a unit of CUNY, although not necessarily LaGuardia (Middle College High School, c. 1998; *Middle College High School at LaGuardia Community College*, 1989).

A survey of 137 (of 657) graduates (1977–1984, 21% response rate) found that 78% of the respondents continued to postsecondary education; 57% of the college attendees reported earning at least a year of college credit. But only 2% of the graduates of the first four classes obtained a bachelor's degree within four years of graduation (Cullen, 1991). About 69% of the respondents held full-time jobs; about half of this group reported skilled employment.

Telephone interviews of 176 of 801 graduates (1977–1986, 22% response rate) found that 78% of the interviewees had enrolled in a postsecondary program; 25% had obtained a certificate, license, or degree; and another 30% were still enrolled in their program (Clark, n.d.; Cullen, 1991).[2] About 60% of the interviewees were employed full-time; 30% of employed graduates held business, financial, or retail positions; 20% worked in clerical or secretarial posts; 14% did blue-collar work; and 11% were full-time students (Clark, n.d.).

Taken together, the data suggested, the modal MCHS respondent-graduate engaged in part-time, college-level studies and earned a credential normally awarded by a two-year college and leading directly to skilled or semiskilled employment. Not surprisingly, 21% of graduates listed "internships–career" as the school's most positive influence on their work lives. The other 79% listed affective factors: "personal growth"—22%; "nurturing faculty"—21%; "self-esteem"—18%; and "achievement motivation"—18% (n = 131) (Clark, n.d., p. 37). Observers continued to debate the "vocational" orientation of MCHS, but graduates attributed their job readiness largely to their affective growth.

MCHS students gave uniformly high marks to their high school experience—93% "strongly liked" or "liked" the faculty; 91 and 88%, respectively, placed "college atmosphere" and "small class size" in those two categories (Clark, n.d., p. 39). These findings confirmed studies of affective growth that cited "the power of the peer," school "smallness," and adult attention as key to developing the resiliency needed for transforming at-risk students and for their success in postsecondary institutions (Gregory, 1995; Horn & Chen, 1998).

Graduates finding fault cited the academic program. That program, wrote one evaluator, "may be its weakest area" (Clark, n.d., p. 40). During the 1990s, Cullen strengthened the academics by adopting new curricula in the social sciences and in mathematics, and, in turn, reducing the duration of internships. To institutionalize the academic gains, the Middle College High School Consortium—founded in 1992 by the principals of ten schools—implemented a "Critical Friends Review" program that invited consortium principals and faculty members to assess the strengths and weaknesses of each other's schools.

ADEPT ADAPTATION?

MCHS at LaGuardia, measured against New York City's comprehensive high schools, showed decided advantages in educating at-risk youth. But one aspect of the underlying rationale gave educators pause. At a time when many observers praised innovations targeted at at-risk students or called for site-specific and site-generated plans, consortium principals continued to argue for adapting key components designed for average or above-average students (Powell, 1997; Semel & Sadovnik, 1999). Worse, critics added, not all these components gained general acceptance at the types of schools for which they were intended.

Proposals to shorten the time to the baccalaureate and to reorganize American education into a 6-4-4 model, for example, had few takers. Beginning MCHS at LaGuardia at the 10th-grade level deviated from most earlier proposals; Baird Whitlock, for one, continued to argue that 10th graders were too young to succeed in this environment. Opening MCHS at LaGuardia and all replications as high schools with strong ties to community colleges resolved the issue, although critics charged that recurrent community college student resistance was a response to high school student immaturity. Lieberman continued to criticize the inclusion of 9th graders, a measure usually adopted for jurisdictional or financial reasons. But, she added, even the earliest drafts of the original plan included 10th graders—a key year for determining the educational fate of at-risk students. And if a school that grouped at-risk students aged 16–20 could inspire younger students to persist, community colleges with many adult students provided even more concrete models for younger students to emulate.

Limiting the size of a grade to 100–150 students reflected the values of smallness and "community" promoted by educators at Vassar and

Barnard, colleges that Lieberman attended. Smallness, advocates believed, facilitated student socialization and counterbalanced the impersonal multiversity, repeatedly identified as a root cause of late-1960s campus disturbances. By the late 1960s, even public colleges that accommodated baby-boomers by permitting lecture halls to overflow, sought ways to promote community through curricular reform and through a strengthened extra-curriculum (Grant & Riesman, 1978; Levine, 1980; Tussman, 1969). Observing student demonstrators at Hunter College demand more attention—part of the late 1960s student movement for greater control of their education—reinforced Lieberman's conviction that at-risk students learned best in a *gemeinschaft*—a small, supportive community.

Smallness facilitated belief in a family metaphor—students at many sites used these metaphors to express the need to look after each other—that facilitated peer counseling and permitted interdisciplinary classes to explore issues in depth. This belief had backing from research: A study of 1992 high school graduates at moderate to high risk of dropping out, for instance, showed that peer engagement—along with parental encouragement—influenced the probability of postsecondary enrollment (Horn & Chen, 1998).

Smallness reduced the direct threat to a school district, while posing an increased ideological threat. Comprehensive urban high schools, consortium principals suggested, were not the best way to educate at-risk youth. Indeed, some observers added, these schools, lacking many key features essential for educating this constituency, might be fatally flawed (Angus & Mirel, 1999; Herbst, 1996). These arguments gained listeners; by the mid-1990s, New York City featured over 100 small alternative high schools (Sizer, 1996).

Lieberman based the house concept on New York's Dalton School. But many observers, then and later, considered the Dalton model too demanding for untrained teachers. Without a change in preservice teacher education, critics argued, teachers would remain wary; even with such a change, teachers might be overwhelmed. Redefining the teaching role à la Dalton also raised questions about affinities—this enhanced role for high school teachers might appear foreign to community college personnel. Arthur Greenberg, arguing that the experience of most MCHS teachers bore out these concerns, nurtured other forms of counseling during his tenure as principal. But a less ambitious adaptation of the model persisted; MCHS teachers often used a "case worker" metaphor to characterize their practice of referring students to specialized support services as needed (Janowitz, 1969).

Consortium principals borrowed other practices associated with postsecondary or elite secondary education. Most sites, for example, required candidates to submit an application and a transcript, and asked students and their parents to be interviewed. The principals ostensibly required these steps to obtain needed information and to ensure that students and parents understood the plan. But the replications had already obtained the requested information from guidance counselors; the principals, like many college administrators, saw a formal admissions process as an initiation rite that helped to convince students they were part of a select group. In turn, everything at the schools, beginning with the decision to come, was voluntary. Volition, Lieberman argued, facilitated attendance and academic success. "No one has to go to MCHS," became part of the recruitment vocabulary.

Three principles guided the blend of unorthodox adaptations and indigenous innovations: committed sponsors, a comprehensive design, and devising strategies to perpetuate the school (Wechsler, 1989).

Commitment

Strong commitments of postsecondary partners increased chances for success. Most initiatives, beginning with LaGuardia's, came from host community colleges under no obligation to venture into an administratively and educationally thorny area. School districts, in contrast, rarely took the lead. Success required a personal commitment from the president of the community college, and, when applicable, the head of the community college district. "[T]he increasing numbers of at-risk students will greatly exceed the capacity of the 1300 community college campuses," wrote Cullen. "The community colleges that are most successful at providing a place on campus for high risk students are those with a clear mission and a strong leader" (Cullen, 1991, p. 129).

A committed president could not delegate responsibility too far down the hierarchy; a successful school had a strong community college liaison—someone who had the president's ear and who therefore had the authority to run interference with constituencies at the host institution. The president and liaison also had to understand the constraints on the school principal. As Greenberg—recall his characterization by Lieberman as "one of the boys"—noted, strong professional and personal relationships between key actors worked to advantage; an adept liaison could nurture their growth.

The community college usually took the initiative, but primary responsibility soon shifted to the principal, who typically dealt with lukewarm school district commitments and with changes from stronger to weaker— perhaps less committed—presidents at some host colleges. Many schools experienced at least one major crisis—usually over funding—three to five years after opening. The schools were more likely to win these battles when the principal, backed by community college leaders, effectively marshaled independent bases of community support. Noting the success of their schools in working with at-risk youth, the principals publicized popular features; in some schools, for example, cooperative education helped garner support from local business and labor communities. Community backing helped to save the replications in Los Angeles and Memphis, although it fell short in Cleveland.

Comprehensive Design

Strong leadership facilitated implementation of a comprehensive design that addressed the affective, cognitive, occupational, and social needs of at-risk students. Implementation required sustained interaction between MCHS staff and community college counterparts, including academic administrators—especially the president, the academic dean, and the dean of cooperative education—faculty members who often taught interdisciplinary teams or who borrowed new pedagogical techniques when teaching alone, and staff responsible for support facilities, including the library, gymnasium, cafeteria, and computer lab.

Time to Mature

An ambitious innovation, backed by the requisite commitments, still needed time to grow. At LaGuardia, some design changes came at the outset, such as conforming to a grades 10–12 model and supervision by the school district instead of the community college. Others, such as reliance on group guidance and peer counseling, came later. Lieberman used her planning time to anticipate some consequences of these changes, but neither MCHS at LaGuardia nor most replications accomplished all key tasks between authorization and opening. Principals and faculty often invented on the run. Greenberg's summer institute designed the unrealized components, including cooperative education, three years after MCHS opened. The essentials in place, MCHS staff and faculty could turn, not always *seriatim*, to strengthening weaker facets. After revising the curriculum in 1977 to feature interdisciplinary courses, MCHS at LaGuardia revamped the counseling system, improved space and support services, strengthened student and faculty governance, and revised academic and cooperative education components.

The replications also needed time to mature. The design, as presented to Ford grant applicants in the late 1980s, presented the results of 15 years of experiment and elaboration. But most principals recapitulated the experience of MCHS at LaGuardia, depicting their first years as moving from crisis to crisis, implementing the essentials, and defusing (if not ending) resistance. But they also delineated longer-term steps taken to address unrealized elements, cement their relations with the community college, and arrive at a *modus vivendi* with the school district. Community college support gave these schools time to weather the initial crises and to implement the comprehensive plan.

At replications meeting these conditions—committed leadership, comprehensive design, and time for implementation—the evidence of success was sufficient to relinquish an "experimental school" designation. By the late 1980s, educator interest threatened to disrupt the daily routine of MCHS at LaGuardia; the school had to restrict, and charge for, outsider visits.

But outsider interest did not automatically translate into replication, and not all potential sites could count on start-up funds. With a decade's hindsight, what can we say about the limits of the middle college movement and about the ease of exporting the design? Did successful replication require adopting the entire package? Were many urban community colleges realistic candidates to host replications? What about rural and suburban community colleges? Could the movement export or mainstream key homegrown or adapted components—innovative curricula, house, career education, and faculty governance mechanisms, for example? Last, were these schools lighthouses that influenced school districts?

Lieberman's experience with selecting Ford-sponsored replications suggested a smaller than desirable number of realistic urban community college sponsors. Frequent changes to the acceptance list reflected difficulties in understanding the concept, garnering needed support, and addressing academic, financial, political, scheduling, and space issues, even with funding for start-up costs and technical assistance. Eventually, though, urban replications outside the Ford program increased to include sites in Boston, Las Vegas, Seattle, and Portland, Oregon.

Extending the plan to other constituencies and types of colleges also proved difficult. The failure of replications to proceed past the design stage at urban four-year colleges, such as Wayne State University in Detroit and the City College of New York, virtually eliminated this group from consideration. The small satellite of Seattle's Middle College High School, located in a house on the University of Washington campus, was a rare exception. Some replications—such as Peoria, Illinois, and Flint, Michigan—served surrounding rural and urban constituencies. Others emphasized technical and occupational programs, such as Houston's Tech-Prep Middle College. But the number of "nontraditional" replications remained small; in 1997, urban community colleges serving urban students hosted most sites. "Since community colleges are located where the largest concentrations of high risk students exist, in large cities and in rural areas," Cullen (1991) wrote, "large numbers of students could be reached by having all community colleges start Middle Colleges" (pp. 128–129). But even with goodwill from all, experience showed, the number of sites will not soon realize this vision.

Did a complex design hinder the spread of the idea? Perhaps some were deterred, but the total package, believed most advocates, worked far better than the sum of the parts. During the late 1980s, Lieberman and her colleagues selected replications for Ford Foundation funding only if they proposed to adopt *all* major components of the design. Lieberman was wary of proposals alluding to a *program*, a categorization disqualifying the school from having a principal with discretion to implement the package. Such proposals often featured one or two favored components; picking and choosing, Lieberman noted, might lead to a failure to address key needs of at-risk youth. The Cleveland example, Lieberman argued, showed that replications with program status were doomed.

Was cooperative education—the most disputed component among movement advocates—essential for the success of a replication? "Career exploration is an integral part of education," stated the original proposal (*Middle College Proposal*, 1973, p. 3; see also *Middle College High School at LaGuardia Community College*, 1989). "Middle College has as its central focus," reiterated Arthur Greenberg (1982b), "the concept of career education" (p. 81). Educators who criticized traditional secondary education as "information-rich, experience poor," argued for including a cooperative education component (Cross, 1971). So did advocates of the "articulation hypothesis"—the belief that a failure to perceive linkage between education and employment led to student alienation and attrition. And so did observers who noted significant employment rates among high school students—often to the detriment of their academic studies.

Some non-Ford-sponsored sites rejected cooperative education. The strength of MCHS at LaGuardia, critics noted, was its congruence with the parent community college. Cooperative education attracted LaGuardia's clientele; LaGuardia staff believed it would do the same for its Middle College High School. It would have looked out of place, they added, *not* to have this component. Inclusion, argued critics, depended on the school's mission—what was necessary in a conservative section of Queens might not be necessary elsewhere. University Heights High School at Bronx Community College did not emphasize cooperative education; neither school nor college staff saw its absence as threatening success. Cooperative education took time to implement—three years at LaGuardia, two or three years at some Ford sites. Local staff who did not see the light, critics concluded, should not include it simply for the sake of the model.

Looking back on the movement a generation later, even Joseph Shenker (1992) reflected that cooperative education was the hallmark of LaGuardia, not necessarily of MCHS. But the number of nonbelievers diminished as internships, service learning, and cooperative education moved into more college and high school curricula. Opponents also had to address a key administrative issue: Cooperative education permitted reduced class sizes, since up to one-third of all students were out of school at any given time. Absent cooperative education, how would a school maintain small class sizes?

Staff at replications with cooperative education focused on a more specific question: Could at-risk students complete a time-intensive cooperative education component and a substantial number of college courses? Several replications opted for less-time-consuming curricula than Tom Sena's, and by 1989 several teachers and students at LaGuardia's MCHS advocated more college preparatory work by truncating cooperative education (Gregory et al., 1989). The reduced internship and PCD requirements, and the changes in the decision-making curriculum, came a few years later.

This debate occurred among staff who saw cooperative education as part of the general education of at-risk youth. But the moves in Houston and Ypsilanti to partner with community college occupational departments and divisions augured a shift in the debate. Preparing students for "real" jobs, these educators argued, made more sense than an orientation to the place of work in society. Instead of debating the inclusion of cooperative education, some educators may argue over the relative importance of education and training for at-risk populations.

Commitment to the package did not preclude export of individual components of the design, as adapted over a generation of work with at-risk high school students. Some exports were noncontroversial: Principals, for example, provided insights into developmental education that helped the parent community college and the school and community college districts. Other high schools were attracted to specific curricular components, including American Social History, Bongo, and PCD.

More important, if, as we contend below, community college mores and norms influenced the development of these high schools, there was also a "trickle up" effect. High school faculty and staff suggested that host community colleges re-examine some practices for relevance to their student clienteles. Community colleges prided themselves on a "student-centered" mission, but also had to respond to the content demands of four-year colleges to which their students transferred. When working with an at-risk population, cautioned consortium principals, one could assume neither that "traditional" practices were automatically applicable, nor that nontraditional education had to conform to these practices. At a time when some critics considered the nation at-risk, these principals suggested that a "reverse" flow of ideas might strengthen mainstream educational practice.

Middle colleges might influence the curriculum and the student development practices of community colleges, which in turn might influence the four-year colleges to which many students aspired to transfer.

The principals thus claimed to show how a small school could educate at-risk students often abandoned within large urban school districts. Claiming to nurture a replicable, although not a "systemic," reform—a lighthouse—consortium members enlightened each other and those community colleges and school districts willing to take a careful look. The consortium helped to socialize those coming late to the model, and to supervise the export of specific components, such as the American Social History Project curriculum.[3] Will the middle college movement "mainstream" key ideas, often considered questionable when first proposed? The remainder of this chapter offers some tentative speculations.

COLLABORATION, LEVERAGING, AND
NORMATIVE CONGRUENCE

Less Time, More Options, the report of the Carnegie Commission on Higher Education (1970a) urging greater school–college collaboration, came at the wrong time: The 1960s and 1980s witnessed more collaborative activities than the 1970s. During the early 1960s, the increasing proportion of the 18- to 24-year-old, baby-boomer cohort attending college, combined with *increases* in SAT scores, spurred some collaborations. The "new math" and the Physical Science Study Committee's reformed high school physics curriculum, for example, aimed to enrich the education of the most academically able students. The North Central Association increased congruence of accrediting procedures for high schools and colleges, encouraged college-style or AP courses and teaching methods, and permitted high schools to replace Carnegie unit requirements with flexible scheduling patterns (Geiger, 1970). The 1960s also witnessed collaborations between urban high schools and colleges, aimed at improving the education of a growing population of minority students. SEEK and College Discovery, two CUNY secondary school interventions aimed at increasing minority enrollments, began in the early years of Albert Bowker's tenure as chancellor.

But the "New Depression in Higher Education" of the early 1970s—budgetary cutbacks, first in the growth rate, then in absolute terms—reduced the resources available to some institutions and led to a turning inward (Cheit, 1971). Cuts in research funding increased the dependence of some colleges on tuition to make up the financial shortfall. And all colleges faced a declining birth rate that augured reduced numbers of students aged 18–24. Tuition-driven colleges stressed enrollment maintenance, not credit for prior work or accelerating students to their degrees.

By the mid-1980s, improved economic conditions and a sense of urgency about the academic preparation of students for college and the workplace prompted renewed collaboration between schools and colleges (Daly, 1985; Gross, 1988; Shapiro, 1986; Sirotnik & Goodlad, 1988). Cost savings and curricular changes that accommodated student consumerism, practicality, and vocationalism allowed many institutions to stabilize enrollments and look outward. Philanthropic foundations, including the Ford Foundation, encouraged collaboration to remedy declining postsecondary enrollment rates for minority students. Citywide coalitions attempted to create student "pipelines" to the baccalaureate by combining school–college collaborations with programs to facilitate transfer between two- and four-year colleges. By the late 1990s, Gear-Up, a federal "pipeline" program, incorporated lessons learned from the experiences of these coalitions.

Collaboration was also, in part, a response to external attacks on public secondary and higher education, especially to charges of disciplinary isolation and an emphasis on research over teaching. Reducing the normative distance between school and college might increase teacher professionalism, seen by some as a way to stem perceived declines in the academic performance of high school students. Last, some college faculty members favored improving secondary school education by collaborating on the remedial instruction of admitted students. By the early 1990s, several associations published directories to track the rapid growth of school–college collaborations (Wilbur, 1990).

But could schools and colleges sustain these collaborative activities? And could their efforts substantially reduce high school dropout rates and improve college access? Skeptics said no to both questions. Collaboration took time, and high school and college faculty members faced increased demands on their time—the reported work week for the average college faculty member increased by at least eight hours between the 1970s and the 1980s (Allen, 1994). Short-run needs, including the growth of a contingent workforce on the postsecondary level, would, critics believed, preempt the long-range academic planning required for sustained collaboration (Clift, Veal, Holland, Johnson, & McCarthy, 1995).

Many collaborations targeted average to above-average students and focused on strengthening high school curricula, especially improving relations between high school and college teachers in the same field. Smoothing the transition of students from high school to college was a secondary goal; time-shortened diplomas or degrees had a lower priority, and even fewer projects adopted a holistic approach to the needs of at-risk students who were considered unlikely to attend the college partner (Yount & Magrun, 1989). Urban school districts, needing to show immediate, dramatic results, often gave low priority to collaborations that might marginally increase the chances of college admission for an at-risk 9th grader. In Rochester, New York, attempts at collaboration between groups that competed in other arenas succeeded only when the goals were limited and agreed upon (Overacker, 1994).

Some researchers speculated that the personalities of the collaborators—not the specifics of their prescriptions—spurred successful ventures, thereby making their programs difficult to replicate (Heathers, 1967). The real goal of collaboration, others suggested, was not to implement—some said impose—an existing model, much less to attain systemic reform; successful collaboration required site-specific "action research" to design and implement an innovation.

Yet others questioned the institutional payoff: Collaboration, some researchers insisted, affected mainly the participants, not the sponsoring institutions (Clift et al., 1995). Long-term effects were difficult to assess since lessons learned diffused as participants moved into leadership positions elsewhere. Administrators at LaGuardia and its Middle College High School, for example, eventually staffed IHS, other New York City replications, and sites further afield, such as Memphis. But in an age of "accountability," administrators pressed to show immediate results might withdraw resources from projects that might some day demonstrate replicability, long-term success, or even systemic effects, but that promised fewer short-term gains.

Some scholars offered a more fundamental critique—the norms underlying K–12 education and higher education were unbridgeable. Writing when LaGuardia staff members were designing the school, Martin Haberman, a professor of education, offered no less than 23 reasons why schools of education could not successfully educate elementary and secondary school teachers. The underlying dimensions reduced to normative and structural incompatibility, perhaps even conflict: differing reward systems, conflicting personalities, integrative vs. disciplinary—or, alternatively, concrete vs. abstract—intellectual outlooks, the inapplicability of professional knowledge in comprehensive settings, the inability of college faculty members to relate theory to practice, and the inability of research to improve the organization of schools. And if teacher education, a supposedly strong, well-developed link, was problematic, what about cooperation between K–12 educators and other, less experienced (and perhaps less interested) college professors and staff? The work of four-year liberal arts college faculty, critics noted, emphasized research and participation in disciplinary associations, taking them further apart from their high school colleagues (Haberman, 1971).

Assuming normative and structural dichotomies did not prove their existence, nor does the experience of the 1980s justify condemnation with broad brush strokes. But Lieberman seconded some of Haberman's assertions. She questioned, for example, whether a four-year college could successfully sustain a replication, noting the failure of the school of education at City College. The reason, Lieberman argued, stemmed from CCNY faculty adherence to a laboratory school model of secondary education that prepared students for the parent college, often in a traditional mode that belied the "lab school" characterization. A replication, she added, required sustained innovation to educate an at-risk student body. As for other collegiate divisions and departments, administrative decentralization often inhibited collaboration among internal units, much less with external units charged with precollegiate education. The normative distance between high schools and four-year colleges, with the latter's stronger focus on the academic disciplines, Lieberman concluded, reduced chances for successful replication.

Lieberman and her colleagues therefore focused on partnerships between *community colleges* and high schools, two institutions with many similarities. Both were teaching institutions—most community college faculty members taught a great deal and enjoyed that work, and many community colleges barely tolerated research—that had comparable course loads and preparations. By the late 1980s, a large proportion of students entered postsecondary education through community colleges. Community colleges accommodated vocational and minority students, promoted community service, and showed curricular overlap with high schools (J. C. Palmer, personal communication, 1997). Critics questioned the growing emphasis on developmental education, but Lieberman believed this focus would increase the probability of successful replication.

No doubt, community colleges gradually had grown apart from high schools, although the separation was less than the distance between high schools and four-year colleges and universities (Pedersen, 1993). Community college staff members emphasized the serious, yet supportive, atmosphere of their colleges, and the attention they devoted to their mature, mostly appreciative students. Public high schools remained compulsory and accommodated college preparatory and terminal students. Community college faculty taught more hours than colleagues on four-year college campuses, where there are expectations for publishing and service. But they taught less than high school teachers.

"While both the Middle College and LaGuardia staffs have worked well together over the years," Arthur Greenberg wrote in 1991, "significant cultural differences between the institutions still are evident, although most of the time these differences do not appear to get in the way" (p. 46). Maintaining a spirit of cooperation, Greenberg stated, called for sensitive handling of contractual divergences, separate pay scales, and differing calendars. "In the cases of many other concurrent enrollment programs," he added, "the actual physical distances between school and college campuses and faculties help to de-emphasize these contrasts. In the Middle College model, we see almost daily reminders" (p. 46).

Lieberman and her colleagues did not see this asymmetry as undesirable; instead, LaGuardia and other urban community colleges could act as salutary counterweights to anti-academic peer pressure exerted on high school students, to administrative burdens shouldered by high school staff, and to curricular prescriptions placed on high school faculty.

But not everyone saw the light; resistant community college faculty and students saw replications as problems, not opportunities—or as opportunities to point out other problems. Strong community college presidents, for example, often made for tense faculty–administration relationships, especially on unionized campuses. Consortium principals might find themselves caught in battles not of their making, say, if a community college president approved a replication without adequate faculty and student consultation. Other resisters objected to diverting resources to even small "ancillary" projects—replications typically opened with about 100 students on campuses with enrollments in the thousands—when the recession of the early 1990s led to serious aid cutbacks to community colleges.

Time—especially the gap between the founding dates of the two partners—exacerbated normative differences. MCHS at LaGuardia had espoused as a virtue the short time span between institutional birth dates: "The relative newness and innovative openness of LaGuardia Community College," stated an early document, "make it an ideal setting for the Middle College program" (*Agenda: Middle College Advisory Committee,* 1973, p. 4). This setting included a zealous LaGuardia faculty and staff; malleable, although limited, space; and socioeconomically similar student cohorts. But most replications were founded between 15 and 50 years after the host. Middle College at Cuyahoga Community College, noted some observers, closed for lack of support from a college partner settled in its ways and from a Cleveland School Board that refused to free the school from the oversight of an older, traditional high school. But Contra Costa College also antedated World War II. Three years, three principals, and several financial crises later, it emerged as a relatively stable unit. Myra

Silverman at Contra Costa, with decades of work in the school district, successfully overcame the image of community college intruder—but at a cost of considerable time and effort.

One did not need to know the founding date of the host community college to object to the presence of younger at-risk students, apparently lower academic standards, and intensified competition for space and other resources. Many two-year colleges went their own ways years earlier; perhaps fear of reunification helped to explain some objections. Then again, so might race and ethnicity, or inadequate prior faculty and student consultation. But the age difference between the community college and the replication led some students and faculty members to view the school as a bull-in-the-china-shop.

Successful replications required adept personnel, beginning with the principal, who was responsible for gaining community college and school district support. MCHS principals, Cullen argued, must be savvy K–12ers—ultimate authority, after all, still resided in the school district—who knew how and when to leverage the environment to maximize autonomy (Cullen, 1993). As they gained experience and learned from each other, consortium principals devised several complementary strategies for navigating (increasingly predictable) storms.

First, they avoided being caught in cross-fires. Principals could do little about tense faculty–administration relations within a community college, but they could ally with supportive community college faculty and staff to demonstrate the school's virtues to those who criticized the innovation as imposed from above. Consortium principals also offered insights on educating at-risk students, a growing proportion of the community college population. They also noted the financial advantages of enrolling high school students in community college courses.

Second, the principals played off the school district and the community college administration, thereby reducing dependence on either. Few principals feared community college domination—the traditional fear of secondary school staff in collaborative relationships. Community college indifference or resistance was a more serious concern. The school district posed the real threat, noted the principals, since a successful replication was a not-so-implicit criticism of the comprehensive urban high school. By claiming that the school needed waivers to coexist with the community college, consortium principals justified requests to a school board for exemptions from inappropriate rules.

Balancing dual jurisdictions, Arthur Greenberg noted, required deftness, but the reward was flexibility. Rather than negotiate, MCHS at LaGuardia staff cited the demands of another bureaucracy for taking a desired action, or occasionally ignored all supervisory bureaucracies. When

New York's Board of Education nixed an innovation, Cullen (1993) noted, she implemented it anyway two years later, unbeknown to the BOE or to CUNY.

Subjecting a middle college to only one jurisdiction—inevitably the school district—consortium principals agreed, diminished leverage (and often resources) and made collapse or absorption more likely. Colleges within colleges, a popular early 1970s reform aimed largely at middle-class students, often tried to attain autonomy by replicating all academic, social, and vocational services to students on their own. But the implicit threat they posed to parent colleges, frequently combined with ineffective service delivery, often led to their demise, especially as student consumerism replaced a politicized culture. Innovative or "alternative" secondary-level schools within comprehensive high schools enrolling substantial numbers of at-risk students faced similar drawbacks.

Falling between the interstices of high school bureaucracy and college administration was not envisioned in 1973; Lieberman objected to funding arrangements subjecting the school to two jurisdictions. But consortium principals turned this supposed liability into a benefit, concluding that more institutional autonomy produced more effective school administration. And, as Shenker noted, dual supervision typified most replications, so successfully navigating between two (or more) worlds became part of the prescription for replicability. Consortium principals taught the associated lore to new principals and faculty members at the launching of each replication.

Third, playing off jurisdictions complemented, but did not replace, collaboration. After the intense collaboration typical of the design and early implementation phases, and presumably after by then having reduced or neutralized community college faculty resistance, consortium principals focused on internal improvements, while the community colleges moved on to other issues. Successful replications routinized collaborations between faculty members in the same or related subjects and between a strong principal and a committed community college liaison.

The principal's participation in community college governance—the faculty senate, department chair meetings, or the president's cabinet, for example—also helped to ensure continued collaboration, since these bodies made decisions affecting the high school. But collaboration took time that might have been used for personnel development, instructional improvement, or direct service to needy students. Carol Poteat's absence from department chair meetings and Arthur Greenberg's initial distance from LaGuardia's authorities may have resulted from decisions about optimal time allocation. Collaborative efforts between institutions might be limited by differing goals and histories; principals who focused on internal improvements did not face these obstacles.

This insight led to the fourth strategy: besides avoiding irrelevant battles, playing off bureaucracies, and routinizing collaboration, consortium principals promoted the absorption of higher education norms by school faculty, staff, and students. The freedom associated with collegiate life, the principals believed, might extricate at-risk students from mean streets and orient them toward postsecondary education. "The status associated with the college campus, as well as the superior work facilities for teachers," wrote Cullen, "supports a culture where teachers act more like professors than union workers in a factory" (Cullen, 1993, p. 127). Professional norms made the teacher's complex roles more palatable, promoted faculty involvement in the school's governance and culture, and exerted a salutary effect on the entire school.

Many community college faculty and staff, noted Cullen, took their relative freedom for granted, expressing a desire for the even greater freedom accorded to four-year college faculty with lighter teaching loads and an even greater say in governance. But, from the viewpoint of faculty and staff at more-regulated secondary schools, internalizing the professional norms of the community college offered the prospect of institutional autonomy. Teachers, as well as students, are less tightly controlled as the educational level increases, said a teacher at LaGuardia's Middle College High School in 1986. "At [MCHS] they treat teachers better—a little better. There is a laissez faire situation at the college level for students, so the high school teachers are treated better here because they are on a college campus" (Klohmann, 1987, p. 83).

Absorbing the norms of higher education, Cullen added, enhanced the effectiveness of other strategies used by the principals. Normative congruence supplied leverage on the local K–12 educational system, while strengthening the positions of MCHS principals within the community college governance structure. The greater mutual respect presumably arising from near-equality might also facilitate interaction and collaboration.

Take, for example, the comments of an MCHS teacher and two LaGuardia instructors, made prior to Cullen's late 1980s faculty empowerment campaign. First, the high school teacher:

> The college instructors are more independent as professionals. They have fewer restrictions in their work. They also have smaller class loads and free periods in which they can work with individual students. They have fewer courses to teach, so they can meet with students on an individual basis. They have office hours to do that.

Then, a LaGuardia instructor:

> I don't want to teach in the high school because I don't like high schools. I hated my own. [High school teachers] have a much harder job. When I

worked on the Committee for Common Concerns I found out I could learn an awful lot from them. But they have to play a charade—make lesson plans! That's an indignity.

And another LaGuardia instructor:

> The structure of the two systems is very different. At the college level there is less red tape, less control, a lot more freedom. The schedule and the work load are very different and the administration is also different. The college faculty have many more advantages than the high school faculty. . . . I could never have survived if I were teaching in the high schools. Working in that kind of bureaucracy would not have been possible for me. (Klohmann, 1987, pp. 85–86)

Whether or not perceptions of disparity accurately reflected the respective working conditions at the two schools, they could inhibit collaboration by the instructors expressing them. Successful long-term voluntary collaborations, Cullen understood, required greater symmetry between the working conditions at, and the norms of, the two schools, building on the strong agreement already existing between LaGuardia and MCHS faculty on institutional and personal goals (Klohmann, 1987). The shift toward normative congruence explains a mid-1980s remark by Joseph Shenker. "The connection with LaGuardia is important but not essential," he said. "It's the atmosphere at Middle College that makes the difference" (Camper, 1986, p. A-34).

Successful use of these strategies also explains why MCHS at LaGuardia survived when other collaborations failed. Dependence on charismatic leaders placed other innovations at risk if charisma papered over significant normative incompatibilities (Grant & Riesman, 1978; Levine, 1980; Orlans, 1990). In fact, MCHS depended less on charisma than on routinized creativity as high school and community college values grew congruent. Relationships in newer or weaker settings, in contrast, remained asymmetric, if benign. Community college resistance diminished as the high school grew to resemble the college. But this reduction often came at a price—a perceived threat to the policies and practices of other urban high schools and of the sponsoring school districts that threatened the school with closure.

To reiterate, LaGuardia contributed *time* for these strategies to work, an element often lacking at failed innovations. Principals did not have to implement everything at once; Lieberman, Shenker, and Moed ensured the school second, third, and subsequent years. Replications, often hastily opened, also needed more than a year's time to prove themselves: The lessons learned from MCHS at LaGuardia only partially offset the greater distances between replications and their much older partner community colleges. Many, but not all, replications received this support.

Discussing an innovative college that took ten years to develop, Grant & Riesman (1978) wrote: "Not a long time as historians would measure it, but much longer than most contemporary American educational innovators are willing to wait." Americans, they added, "expect to have committee meetings this month and a revolution next semester. . . . Most significant innovations in American education have not been successfully developed and institutionalized in less than a decade" (p. 171). Consortium principals could not have agreed more.

FACILITATING TRANSITION

For much of the 20th century, mainstream educators dismissed proposals for time-shortening and for reorganizing grades 11–14 as unattainable, if not undesirable. These proposals, offered amidst substantial secondary school growth between the two world wars, never took center stage because of relatively low entry rates into college. High schools had difficulty populating their senior years—as did upper-level community college transfer courses a half century later—and did not avidly support programs that might truncate their own course offerings. Some acceleration schemes took hold on the elementary and middle school levels, but except for specific situations, such as the College of the University of Chicago, grades 11–14 reform proposals languished (Lynch, 1994; Ramaswami, 1993; Tomlinson, 1994).

The 1950s saw the launching of one successful attempt to bridge secondary and postsecondary education, when high schools began to offer advanced placement (AP) college-level courses and examinations (Casserly, 1986; Keller, 1980; Peterson, 1965–1966; Rothschild, 1995; Valentine, 1987; Wilcox, 1960). AP curricula and exams—as opposed to proposals for early admission, dual enrollment, or grouping grades 11–14—permitted students to earn college credits while in high school without either "creaming" or delaying their entrance to a "real" college, and without changing school district administrative or funding mechanisms. Some critics, echoing earlier charges of college domination, termed AP's prescribed curricula constricting, even stifling, but the program showed gradual, steady growth during a time of increasing high school graduation and college enrollment rates, and gained the support of educators who praised its "high standards" (Greenberg, 1991; Hanson, 1980; Powell, 1997; Stoel, 1988).

AP was lauded more for enrichment than for acceleration. The end of the postwar baby boom and the resultant decline in the number of high school graduates, beginning in the late 1970s, led administrators at many enrollment-driven colleges with high fixed costs to conclude that time-shortening schemes would only exacerbate the attendant financial short-falls. Some colleges did reduce the number of credit hours required for graduation during the 1980s. But the accompanying reductions in upper-level or low-enrollment specialized courses suggest that the moves were motivated by a desire to cut costs, not student time.

President Clinton reinvigorated the push for universal access to at least 14 years of schooling in his 1997 State of the Union message. Clinton did not argue for merging high schools and community colleges into one ex-tended institution—the disparity in the number of high schools and com-munity colleges made such mergers unrealistic. But reformers used the re-newed attention to a 14-year educational entitlement to resurrect two interrelated issues: restructuring 8-4-4 or 6-3-3-4 sequences to secure a 16–20 age grouping, and shortening time to the high school diploma and the baccalaureate.

"16–20" (Again)

Some advocates of "16–20" picked up where Robert M. Hutchins, Leo-nard Koos, and Clarence Faust left off. Questioning the viability of the high school in its current form, Leon Botstein, a University of Chicago graduate and president of Simon's Rock and of parent Bard College, ar-gued that the clock of adult life moved too rapidly to expect today's students to accept long delays in receiving rewards for educational accom-plishments. The American high school, he wrote, "was designed for fifteen-to-eighteen-year-olds who were children only beginning their journey to adulthood. It is now filled with young adults of the same age" (Botstein, 1997b, pp. 82–83). Serious learning came too late; stale curricula and poor pedagogy infantilized most adolescents.

Educators, Botstein added, often underestimated student abilities: Most children were ready for kindergarten at age four; ending compulsory education after 10th grade would permit 16-year-olds to attend college with older students. Decorum would increase, and college studies would challenge students who by then were ready for more-demanding and spe-cialized work. Undergraduates would profit from general education, he added, so long as their studies were related to real-life problems and to self-interest, and not grounded in remote, soon-forgotten subject matter. Accepting missions defined by discipline-based graduate schools, he as-serted, made colleges co-culprits. We fear adolescents, he concluded, and take out our anger about our loss of youth on them. A more mature relationship between adults and students should begin at an earlier age (Botstein, 1997a; see also Herbst, 1996).

Botstein (1987) had favorably acknowledged MCHS at LaGuardia on an earlier visit to the high school, but his remarks were not primarily about at-risk students. Neither were those of Mihaly Csikszentimihalyi (1997), professor of human development at the University of Chicago, who agreed with Botstein's critique: "The human body," he asserted, "was not made to sit motionless all day." Education in most high schools was passive; forcing schooling on all was a recipe for disaster. Students, he added, "should have an opportunity to learn about themselves instead of dancing to the tune of a self-contained academic world about which they are indifferent" (n.p.). In a study of 100 workers, Csikszentimihalyi (1997) noted, none mentioned school as a significant part of their vocational development. The workers cited teachers, but for interactions outside the classroom—interest of a real person around a real job. Creativity occurs, he added, in the extracurriculum.

Saving Time

Perhaps more significant than these ministrations, some prominent economists saw time-shortened education as an attractive option at a time of more-demanding graduation requirements, diminished state support for higher education, increased enrollments and a forecasted enrollment crisis, and a more diversified student population (Texas Higher Education Coordinating Board, 1996). "Many if not most young people aged 16 to 18 are capable of college-level work, given the proper curriculum, standards, and teachers—and the proper motivation," wrote economist D. Bruce Johnstone. "College-bound students in most other countries," he added, "are expected to know by the time they finish secondary school what American students are expected to learn during the first year or two of college." Increasing the amount of college-level learning during the high school years, Johnstone argued, would reduce the average time to the bachelor's degree. His list of credit-granting techniques included AP, dual credit plans, and college certification of high school courses and teachers, but not a combined high school–college (Johnstone, 1993, p. 5; see also Crooks, 1996; Fincher-Ford, 1997).

Combining mature high schools and community colleges might not be in the offing, but two factors led some states to adopt more feasible time-shortening schemes. First, after bottoming out in the early 1990s, the number of students in the 18–24 age cohort increased; the proportion of this age cohort in college grew by 7% between 1990 and 1995. The National Center for Education Statistics projected a 14% growth in higher education enrollments between 1997 and 2009, from 14.4 million to 16.3 million (U.S. Department of Education, 1999).

Second, state higher education allocations declined as a percentage of state budgets, thereby limiting options for public colleges and universities to handle anticipated enrollment increases. Many colleges were reluctant to turn students away—some community colleges, for example, accepted nonfunded students during the recession of the early 1990s—but fewer colleges could invest in new plant to accommodate enrollment gains. Some observers looked to distance learning, but the ability of this technology to attract and educate *at-risk* students had not yet been demonstrated. Thus, proposals for shortening the time to the baccalaureate received a serious hearing; the alternatives were substantial capital outlays for new construction and for faculty and staff hiring. Nearly $47 million could be saved, estimated the California Higher Education Policy Center, if the proportion of first-year University of California students entering with at least a semester of advanced placement and college credit increased from the then-current 25% to 70% by 2006 (Finney, 1997).

Advanced placement grew rapidly in the 1980s and 1990s. Exams were given in 31 subjects; between 1985–86 and 1996–97 the number of candidates more than doubled to nearly 600,000, although percentages of all high school juniors and seniors taking the exams remained under 15%; the number of exams offered nearly tripled to over 900,000, and the number of high schools offering AP exams nearly doubled to over 12,000 (Reisberg, 1998; U.S. Department of Education, 1998). California high school students showed a 65% increase in AP exams attempted between 1986 and 1994, and a 17% increase in AP exams per 1,000 California 11th and 12th graders between 1994 and 1995. The top quarter of California high school graduates, the numbers suggested, commonly enrolled in AP courses, although only about 15 to 20% of the exam-takers received a score of 4 or 5 (colleges, on average, awarded credit for scores of 3.2 to 3.5). Fewer high school students may take AP exams than AP courses, noted some analysts, since high schools may try to maintain high test scores by prohibiting some enrolled students from taking the exams.

Most consortium principals did not promote AP, arguing that the courses relied on "inappropriate, traditional" teaching methods, and the prescribed curricula implied college domination, not collaboration. The $74 exam fee (in 1998) appeared prohibitive, although the federal Advanced Placement Incentive Program subsidized the fee for some low-income students. Consortium principals often counseled students to take courses in college, if necessary, rather than attempt AP courses, even when available.

Replications in states relying heavily on AP—sending high school teachers for AP training, for example—were disadvantaged by implicit comparisons, and some consortium principals fought to gain college credit for their students who neither went to the partner community college nor took the AP exams. The Los Angeles Community College District, for example, did not distinguish between college courses and AP when awarding credit. AP, the principals concluded, was one innovation devised for another group of students that *could not* be adapted to an at-risk population. Conversely, faculty members at selective colleges criticized AP for inadequately preparing students for advanced courses, although some College Board studies suggested the opposite (Burdman, 2000; Reisberg, 1998).

Some colleges organized their own outreach programs (Tinto, 1993). Project Advance, established in the mid-1970s by Syracuse University, permitted high school students to take SU freshman courses in 13 subjects at their own schools, taught by their own teachers after training from Syracuse staff. Project Advance showed substantial growth during the 1990s; about 3,900 high school students in five states participated in 1997–98 (Gaines & Wilbur, 1985; Lambert & Mercurio, 1986; Mercurio et al., 1982, 1983; Moro & Mercurio, 1988; Reisberg, 1998). Only a handful of colleges ventured into this area—perhaps fortunately, since working with the idiosyncrasies of more than one college would have bedeviled most high school staff.

State-level experiments with time-shortening, capacity-utilizing programs and with school–college collaborations began in the 1980s. No plan integrated high school and college, but a decline in the percentage of students obtaining the baccalaureate in four years and projected increases in college enrollments led state policy-makers to consider other time-saving options. As with AP, most states aimed their programs at average to above-average students (Crooks, 1998a). In 1995–96, over 200,000 students participated in dual enrollment schemes and in "credit validation" plans that allowed certified high school teachers to offer college-level courses. Desiring curricular enrichment and cost savings, 23 states offered credit validation plans in 1995; by 1998, 38 states offered dual enrollment plans (Crooks, 1998b).

Minnesota's Postsecondary Enrollment Options Program (PSEOP), the first substantial program in this genre, permitted high school juniors and seniors to take regular college courses for free. PSEOP, as first proposed in the state's 1985 Omnibus School Aids Act, reduced state K–12 funding by the amount the state paid for tuition, thereby prompting high school officials to charge "creaming." In 1986, the state legislature limited students to a maximum equivalent of two years of college credit, and prohibited students from earning both high school and college credits for college courses taken and passed. Students would pay tuition for college courses taken for college credit; the state paid tuition for college courses taken for high school credit. The primary beneficiaries, wrote Arthur Greenberg (1991), were rural students enrolled in small high schools, *if* they were located near a college (see also Urahn, 1993).

Washington State modeled its 1990 "Running Start" program after PSEOP. High school juniors and seniors could receive dual credit for taking certain community college courses, and local school districts reimbursed the colleges for high school student enrollments on a per-credit basis (Colwell, 1995; Crossland, 1998; Office of Financial Management, 1995). The number of high school students enrolled for college credit grew from 230 in 1990–91 to about 5,300 in 1994–95; by the mid-1990s all 32 public two-year colleges participated in Running Start. But success meant avoiding disincentives to secondary school cooperation in recruiting, counseling, and preparing students (Zumeta, 1996a, 1996b).

Other states adopted dual funding, hoping that dual enrollment plans would result in cooperation, not competition (Sauer, 1995). Virginia's 1988 dual enrollment plan gave considerable discretion to high school–community college pairs, including choice of site, faculty appointments, and admissions criteria (Vogt, 1991). Once admitted, high school students in about half the pairs were restricted to between one and four college courses per semester; other pairs asked students to follow the same regulations as regular college matriculants. This decentralized program produced predictably uneven enrollment patterns among the 27 participating community college campuses. Headcounts ranged from 40 to 1,841; considerable variance occurred even among pairs of similar size (Vogt, 1991). Much depended on the commitment of the program coordinator and the terms of specific plans—whether the student was responsible for tuition, textbooks, and transportation, for example. The Virginia plan, recommended an analyst of its early history, needed improved communication, especially between faculty members, and better publicity.

Idaho (in 1997) was the first state to allow high school students to attend college on a full-time basis. Heretofore largely confined to AP and college vocational courses, high school students could, after counseling, enroll in the full range of college coursework offered by Idaho colleges (Taylor, 1997). But most states proceeded cautiously; in 1993, for example, the state's principals' association opposed a Michigan plan to give 10th and 11th graders who passed a state-administered examination the option to enroll in college. "They are virtually saying," bristled an opponent, "there is nothing in high school worth learning past the sophomore year" (Schmidt, 1993, p. 32).

These innovations led states to devise policies for accepting college work completed in high schools. Uniform policies with minimal restrictions, consortium principals noted, were difficult to achieve, since intermediate-level boards, such as school and community college districts, might impose more severe restrictions. But, invoking "the power of the site," the principals favored local agreements, fearing that uniformity might come at the cost of accommodating at-risk students (Jun & Tierney, 1999). Could students, asked consortium principals, gain college credit for *double-counted* college courses taken in high school? Could students secure college credit for college work completed prior to 12th grade? And could students gain credit from nonhost colleges for college-level courses taught by high school faculty members appointed as adjuncts by the host college?

Policies governing dual credit for college courses taken by students at replications varied, even within a state. In Virginia, high school students could receive dual credit, but students and high schools were often responsible for community college tuition (Vogt, 1991). California permitted double counting college courses taken while in high school. The Richmond school district permitted dual credits, but the Los Angeles schools required students to opt for high school *or* college credit. The availability of dual credit, Myra Silverman added, helped to ensure the financial viability of MCHS at Contra Costa, since significant numbers of its students took college courses. Similarly, noted Christine Curtis, Texas officials were more lenient than their Dallas school district colleagues, who closely monitored student–faculty ratios in college classes for high school students.

Consortium principals did end runs when dual credit was restricted. High school and community college transcripts might list the same courses under different titles. Maintaining two separate transcripts minimized the possibility of discovery, especially in team-taught courses where each transcript could list a different instructor. At one site, the principal obtained college numbers for dual credit courses from the state education department, listing herself as the instructor of record.

Nor did nonhosting colleges automatically accept college credits presented by middle college students. Students enrolled at MCHS at LaGuardia could take college courses for free, earning high school credits while banking earned credits for college if they attended that community college. But administrators at other colleges might adopt more restrictive policies, since granting credit would cost their schools tuition revenues, even if they obtained state aid for the credits. Together, MCHS principals feared, the free college tuition accorded students at some replications, and the reluctance of nonpartner colleges to accept their credits, might hold students back. Elsewhere, high school students paid for college classes, although some partner community colleges, such as El Centro, provided scholarships. Principals noted another barrier: Even when tuition was free, high school students might have to pay for college textbooks. Some sites created textbook banks, but frequent new editions limited the effectiveness of this strategy.

Some colleges and states restricted credit to 12th graders, even though mid-1990s estimates of college readiness at the end of 11th grade, offered by consortium principals, varied from 5 to 60%. Students at Shelby State's MCHS took and received credit for college courses throughout their high school years. Officials at MCHS at El Centro obtained college credits for some 11th-grade work, although Texas officially accepted only college courses completed in 12th grade. Other states and colleges capped the number of college credits. California permitted 12 credits, but awarding four credits for some courses led students and guidance counselors at Contra Costa's MCHS to request waivers, which Candy Rose considered on a case-by-case basis.

Besides noting problems with policies that varied among districts and between districts and the state, consortium principals also asked whether state-level policies might damage carefully nurtured relationships with host community colleges and with school districts. Strong state participation at the outset, some analysts found, might help to overcome barriers to liberal credit policies (Hawthorne, 1991; Hawthorne & Zusman, 1992; Vogt, 1991). But states, the principals suggested, did not have at-risk students in mind when contemplating most reforms (Cooper, Paisley, & Phelps, 1998). Cullen cited one example: CUNY Chancellor Ann Reynolds tried to designate the New York City high school honors and AP classes that CUNY would accept for credit. The same CUNY initiative, Cullen added, stated that if students took courses in college that they skipped in high school, they might not receive college credit. High school principals successfully opposed the initiative, stating that they wished to retain the right to designate their college-level classes.

Extricating a replication from regulated K–12 systems, consortium principals argued, should not result in regulation by centralized postsecondary education authorities and in conflicting regulations among separate multicampus systems in some states. Systemic change—widespread adoption of an apparently salutary reform—might, the principals feared, adversely affect at-risk students thought most to benefit. What good was being a "lighthouse" if community—the trust and informality built up among local residents at great investment of time and effort—was lost?

CONCLUSION

In 1870, the University of Michigan, wishing to cement its relationship with the state's growing public high school system, and seeking an alternative to administering oral entrance exams to each applicant for admission, offered to inspect each public high school in the state and to admit graduates of schools passing muster. Few secondary school principals viewed the university's move as hostile or self-serving, and over 95% of all high schools in the state eventually gained this accreditation. This move began a quarter century of collaboration between high schools and colleges that secondary school officials often used to leverage support from parsimonious local school districts. The results included "model" high school curricula for the growing number of subjects in high school and college curricula, uniform college entrance requirements in many fields, and even uniform entrance examinations, administered after 1900 by the College Entrance Examination Board, itself a product of collaboration (Wechsler, 1977).

But by 1915, high schools embracing a comprehensive "people's college" mission routinely denounced "college domination." Meeting college entrance requirements, argued secondary school officials, often meant devoting a disproportionate share of resources to the small proportion of college-bound students. Ever since, promoters of high school–college collaboration contended with fears of college domination and with a corresponding concern (or worse) expressed by college officials over the declining quality and standards of American high schools. Reformers faced especially sharp opposition to collaborations that reduced curricular duplication, thereby shortening time to a high school diploma or a college degree, since money *and* institutional independence were at stake.

Most 1960s collaborations enriched or accelerated the education of academically able college-bound students, but a handful, including CUNY's SEEK and College Discovery, aimed to improve the preparation of minority students for college. Weak academic preparation, a lack of time and tuition, and foregone income combined to deny college access to many potential first-generation students. But before CUNY could legitimately lay claim to a partnership with the public schools, its leaders concluded, it had to open its own doors more widely.

Open Admissions at CUNY guaranteed admission to a unit of CUNY to any graduate of a New York City high school. The university's free tuition policy resulted in a major increase in the size of CUNY's 1970 entering class and in a substantial increase in minority enrollments. But access did not guarantee success in college, and between 1970 and 1976, many CUNY educators asked what lay beyond the open door for their new students. Limited to recruiting New York City residents, CUNY officials again turned to improving student preparation for college. Critics believed that guaranteed entrance to CUNY deterred students from performing at their best in high school. But Open Admissions, CUNY staff responded, only called attention to a previously ignored problem. Middle and secondary school interventions and collaborations, Joseph Shenker agreed, must replace criticism of inadequate academic preparation. SEEK and College Discovery presaged other ambitious, but mostly unrealized, plans, including a CUNY takeover of five New York City high schools. A middle college might show the way to improved academic preparation, while reducing the administrative distance between CUNY and the city's schools.

The proposed school might have supported Open Admissions by educating at-risk youth in a school that integrated grades 10–14. Picking up where Elizabeth Hall and Baird Whitlock left off at Simon's Rock, such a school would have re-ignited a century of debate over the ideal organization of elementary and secondary education, and over the desirability of separating high schools from community colleges. It also would have led educators to confront a key issue in educating at-risk students: Could a "seamless web" of American education integrate these students, or did the diversity of missions shown by schools and colleges make that goal unrealistic, if not undesirable?[4]

A middle college also could have signaled a return to a 19th-century model: a preparatory department on the college campus that ensured a flow of students prepared to institutional specifications. An increasing supply of graduates from a growing number of public high schools permitted many colleges to abolish their often-profitable preparatory departments after 1870. Some historians might consider the separation of the two-year college from the high school during the first half of the 20th century to be part of the same trend.

But LaGuardia's Middle College High School became neither a grades 10–14 school for at-risk students nor a high school-level department preparing at-risk students exclusively for one community college. Novelty was limited when the state compelled high school attendance but left postsecondary education volitional, when the need for revenue tempered collaboration, and when the age gap between community college and high school students widened. Serving as the preparatory department for a single community college might have diminished the support gained by MCHS from the public university systems, and from the Regents, as a feeder for many units of CUNY, SUNY, and the state's independent colleges.

Instead, for 25 years MCHS at LaGuardia grew with elements familiar and novel, borrowed and indigenous, successful and wanting. Its principals—not under the scrutiny accorded more radical innovators—often turned the need to modify the design into opportunities. Multiple postsecondary-level constituencies, for example, often led to desirable increases in autonomy, not to integration. Gained at the cost of novelty were feasibility of replication and usefulness as a yardstick. MCHS at LaGuardia exported the model to community colleges in other cities—one or two per major city appeared sustainable, assuming conditions were ripe (Janowitz, 1969). New schools seeking a niche among others with longer histories nearly always confronted a gap between intent and realization. But as yardsticks, the replications challenged comprehensive high schools—the dominant form of urban secondary education for a century—to defend the quality and effectiveness of the education they offered to at-risk youth.

CUNY pulled back from its commitment to Open Admissions in 1976, a year after New York City nearly fell victim to bankruptcy, by tightening admissions requirements and by imposing tuition for the first time (Lavin & Hyllegard, 1996). The middle college movement—following turn-of-the-20th-century secondary school officials—survived by gaining autonomy from the college and the school district (especially the latter).

But freedom *from* was antecedent to freedom *to*. For 25 years, faculty and staff at LaGuardia's Middle College High School pushed for the freedom not only to adopt, but also to improve the components laid out in the original plan, knowing that responsibility for educating their students—students who otherwise would have fallen by the wayside—accompanied that freedom.

Notes

Acknowledgments

1. Cunningham was known as Cecilia Cullen; for consistency, we use Cullen throughout this book.

Chapter 1

1. Not all believers in stages agreed that late adolescence was a unique stage. Gesell, Ilg, and Ames (1956) considered the ages 10–16 "a distinctive cycle of development," but considered the next age group too heterogeneous to make a similar claim.

2. The authors represented Phillips Academy, Phillips Exeter Academy, the Lawrenceville School, and the Hill School. A 1952 report, written by members of the faculties of Andover, Exeter, and Lawrenceville, and of Harvard, Princeton, and Yale, came to similar conclusions, although for academic, not social-developmental, reasons. The earlier report noted substantial overlap in high school and college courses among schools in close communication and with similar goals. "It may be argued," concluded the report, "either that this repetition shows the failure of the school, or that the school and college courses are so differently taught as to be two separate educational experiences." The latter argument, the report stated, "is wishful thinking"; students duplicated most of the work (Committee Report, 1952, pp. 12–13). The committee called for integrating general education in school and college, not necessarily for a new entity.

Chapter 2

1. "Preparing high school students for the local junior college," argued an ambivalent Edward A. Krug, a historian of the secondary school curriculum, "is not quite the same as college preparation in general." Urban community colleges, he reasoned, might provide four-year colleges some relief on increasingly overburdened physical plants, and reduce the need for rigid admission and retention policies. "Admissions policies can be worked out within local school systems with the transition from twelfth to thirteenth grade not necessarily more marked or critical than that from ninth to tenth in a 6-3-3 system." But this flexibility—Krug assumed K–12 school board jurisdiction over the junior colleges—presented "the unwel-

come possibility that the junior college may become the dumping ground for those students who cannot meet the admission requirements of other colleges" (Krug, 1960, pp. 158, 159).

   2. Tyack and Cuban (1995) discuss other attempted high school reforms with no "counterweight."

   3. Dunham requested endorsements from Shenker, CUNY, BHE, the school system's chancellor, local principals, and the local school superintendent. The words "not candid" were written next to the paragraph about these letters on the corporation's evaluation of the proposal.

   4. Designers asked whether the state would permit LaGuardia to grant a high school diploma to a middle college student who completed 12th grade. Under state law, Lieberman learned, a college student who completed 12th grade and earned 23 college credits could receive a high school diploma. "But this wasn't good enough," she added. "The kids needed the piece of paper." LaGuardia never received this permission, but opening the school as an alternative high school rendered the question moot.

   5. Hentoff (1966) discusses the work of principal Elliott Shapiro at New York's P.S. 119.

   6. Gold and Miles (1981) discuss the conflict between traditionalist parents and an innovative district superintendent.

   7. Teachers, critics argued, required more knowledge of affective development and socialization than was offered in most teacher preparation programs. Advocacy of "teacher-as-researcher," another reform gaining currency by the late 1980s, implied, some observers predicted, "add-on" tasks, rather than professional reorientation (Hollingsworth & Sockett, 1994). The often-offered answer was in-service education.

Chapter 3

   1. In 1974–75, the mean reading composite score of LaGuardia freshman-year students who took level five of the CAT was 10.4; the mean CAT math score was 8.6.

   2. A consultant estimated the "true" costs of MCHS a year into the program as $2,021 per student, assuming a 125-student enrollment—almost all of the costs covered teaching, administrative, and support staff salaries ("The estimated cost of the Middle College Program," Weintraub to Moed, May 14, 1975, MCA, "AED Report" file). BOE staff continued to debate the per-student costs at MCHS for years. The board, for example, calculated that the school ran in the mid-1980s at about $500–$600 per student *above* average costs. But the board itself contributed only the usual per-student cost ($3,200 per student; $1.6 million total), calculated on a citywide formula. BHE and in-kind contributions from LaGuardia made up the difference ($300,000 in noninstructional support, including rent) (Staff notes for June 19, 1986 officers' meeting at LaGuardia Community College, FFA, Grant file 86–585).

   3. Cecilia Cullen is now known as Cecilia Cunningham; for consistency we use Cullen throughout this book.

4. When MCHS was opened to 9th graders in 1988, students were required to take the first internship in their year of entrance. All internships were standardized at four hours per day, four days a week. Including 9th graders raised questions about student maturity. Could students learn to reconcile personal and institutional agendas? Would unchallenging, boring, and repetitive tasks discourage 9th graders, or lead them to learn coping strategies? An experimental 9th-grade seminar tested whether staff- and peer-counseling strategies could answer these questions (Gregory et al., 1989).

5. The widespread growth, beginning in the 1970s, of community colleges with Open Admissions policies, argued sociologist James Rosenbaum, implied a diminution in the selective role played by high schools and in the gatekeeper role of high school guidance counselors (Rosenbaum, Miller, & Krei, 1996).

6. In January 1993, I attended a group counseling session at the Middle College at Seattle Community College. The students had used a previous group counseling session to decide whether I should be admitted—an unprecedented event at this school. They decided to admit me on the condition that I divulge nothing of the substance of the class. The class was arranged in a tight semicircle, with the guidance counselor in the middle. The intense, personal discussion did not remain focused on any one student. The counselor watched student body language to engage students, especially to encourage participation of students who, on their own, would have said little.

7. At the time, MCHS did not accept students with limited English proficiency or special education students (Cullen, 1993; Lieberman, 1986). In 1997–98, 41 students were mandated to receive resource room services; by using half a lunch period for these activities, they lost no class time (Ort, 1998). A program for mainstreamed deaf and hard-of-hearing students also capitalized on the lengthy lunch period; crediting American Sign Language as a foreign language for hearing students encouraged informal student interaction and support.

8. This curriculum precluded course sequencing, in disfavor since Greenberg's tenure. The few exceptions included completing algebra before taking trigonometry. During the late 1990s, MCHS moved toward sequencing in core disciplines. But classes officially remained age-heterogeneous, and students could break a sequence to take an elective. Nor did MCHS maintain separate sections for course repeaters.

9. When asked to cite the most important reason for founding, 43.5% of 971 surveyed pre-existing public charter schools responded, "to realize an alternative vision"; 34.5% responded, "to gain autonomy from state or district regulation" (National Study of Charter Schools, 2000, p. 42).

10. One issue remained unresolved in early 2000. The Regents reserved the right to have its State Assessment Panel review—and the state education commissioner approve—proposed performance assessment alternatives to newly revised Regents exams, required by the state for graduation.

Chapter 4

1. Rigid state regulations, MCHS staff complained, inhibited curriculum design. At Bowen's behest, the Tennessee State Board of Education designated MCHS

a pilot school, providing maximum curricular and instructional flexibility (Bowen to Bernstein, June 14, 1988, Ford Foundation, Grant file 86–587, and Lillian Hammond to Lieberman, November 18, 1988, MCA, "Shelby State Community College" file). Bowen secured a state waiver that permitted hiring elementary and middle school teachers for MCHS faculty positions.

Chapter 5

1. Feeder schools, the evaluators noted, did not record the names and where-abouts of the "true" control group—students identified by feeders as eligible to attend MCHS, but who did not apply. The comparison group was not a true con-trol, the evaluators acknowledged; other factors may have affected its dropout rate. But, they added, both groups included "high-risk potential dropout students who fit the criteria of high absenteeism, multiple failures, and/or emotional problems" (*Middle College High School at LaGuardia Community College*, 1989, p. 21).

2. An N of 176, Clark argued, was "well-earned and as complete as possible given 1) the time elapsed since the earliest graduation classes and 2) a highly mobile population." She found only slight academic and demographic differences between the respondents and a control group of 133 nonresponding MCHS graduates (Clark, n.d., pp. 8, 11).

3. The website for the consortium is www.mcconsortium.org. The websites for MCHS at LaGuardia and the American Social History Project are www.edu-net.com/~mchs and www.ashp.cuny.edu, respectively.

4. Ernest Boyer employed the term "seamless web"—part of the epigraph to the Carnegie Commission's report *Continuity and Discontinuity: Higher Education and the Schools*—in his many writings about the postsecondary curriculum. Here is the full quotation: "Education for the individual is a seamless web of learning. Organized formal education seeks to impose a pattern on one portion of this seam-less web. This pattern will always be to some degree artificial and confining—it may, however, be either more helpful than harmful, or more harmful than helpful" (Carnegie Commission, 1973, p. iii).

References

Documents and correspondence used in this book are located in the following archives. This reference list includes archival reports and documents; correspondence is noted only in the text.

CCP: Carnegie Corporation Papers, Rare Books and Manuscripts Room, Columbia University Libraries.

FFA: Ford Foundation Archives, New York City.

IA: Institutional Archives, Fiorello H. LaGuardia Community College Archives, Room 101, 31–10 Thomson Avenue, Long Island City, New York.

MCA: Middle College Archives, Fiorello H. LaGuardia Community College Archives, Room 101, 31–10 Thomson Avenue, Long Island City, New York.

Academy for Educational Development. (1974). *First interim report on the Middle College project*, attached to Ruth G. Weintraub to Martin Moed, December 13, 1974. MCA, AED report file.

Ackerman, T. (1994, February 20). Leadership, timing fostered Dallas' first-rate system. *Houston Chronicle*, p. A20:1.

Adams, F. C., & Stephens, C. W. (1970). *College and university student work programs*. Carbondale: Southern Illinois University Press.

Agenda: Middle College Advisory Committee. (1973, June 19). Attachment 2. IA.

Aikin, W. (1942). *The story of the eight-year study*. New York: Harper & Brothers.

Allen, H. L. (1994). Workload and productivity in an accountability era. In National Education Association, *The NEA 1994 almanac of higher education* (pp. 25–38). Washington, DC: Author.

American Academy of Arts and Sciences, Assembly on University Goals and Governance. (1971). *Report*. Cambridge, MA: Author.

Anderson, M. (2001). Middle College High School in Memphis. In G. I. Maeroff, P. M. Callan, & M. Usdan (Eds.), *The learning connection: New partnerships between schools and colleges* (pp. 42–50). New York: Teachers College Press.

Angell, J. R. (1915, March 19–20). The junior college and the senior high school. In North Central Association of Colleges and Secondary Schools, *Proceedings of the twentieth annual meeting*.

Angus, D. L., & Mirel, J. E. (1999). *The failed promise of the American high school, 1890–1995.* New York: Teachers College Press.

Armor, D. J. (1971). *The American school counselor: A case study in the sociology of professions.* New York: Russell Sage Foundation.

Bangert-Drowns, R. L. (1984). The effects of school-based substance abuse education: A meta-analysis. *Journal of Drug Education, 18,* 243–264.

Barnard, F. A. P. (1872). *Causes affecting the attendance of undergraduates in the incorporated colleges of the city of New York.* New York: D. Van Nostrand.

Battersbee, N. (1992, March). [Interview]. Middle College High School, Los Angeles Southwest College.

Battersbee, N. (1993, December 4). [Interview]. Pittsburgh.

Battersbee, N., & Warren, S. T. (1991, March). *LaGuardia Middle College High School, Long Island, New York: A case study of five replications.* MCA, Ford Foundation file.

Belmont High comes back. (1986, September 28). *Los Angeles Times Magazine,* pp. 10–15.

Benware, C. A., & Deci, E. L. (1984). Quality of learning with an active versus passive motivational set. *American Educational Research Journal, 21*(4), 755–765.

Blanchard, R. E. (1971). *A national survey: Curriculum articulation between the college of liberal arts and the secondary school.* Chicago: DePaul University.

Blase J., & Blase, J. R. (1996). *Empowering teachers: What successful principals do.* Thousand Oaks, CA: Corwin Press.

Blos, P. (1966). *On adolescence: A psychoanalytic interpretation.* New York: Free Press.

Board of Higher Education in the City of New York. (1964). *1964 master plan for the City University of New York.* New York: Author.

Board of Higher Education in the City of New York. (1968). *Master plan of the Board of Higher Education for the City University of New York, 1968.* New York: Author.

Board of Higher Education in the City of New York. (1972). *1972 master plan of the Board of Higher Education for the City University of New York.* New York: Author.

Board of Higher Education in the City of New York. (1973, November 26). *Minutes,* Calendar No. 4A.

Born, T. (1991). SBM/SDM at Middle College High School: The first six months. In Center for Urban Ethnography, *An evaluation of the City University of New York and New York Board of Education collaboration programs, IV. Middle College High School.* MCA, Center for Urban Ethnography file.

Botstein, L. (1987, November). *General education and liberal arts at LaGuardia.* Attached to Fred Low et al. to College Community. MCA, Middle College Evaluation file.

Botstein, L. (1997a, March 24). *The development of talent and the reforming of secondary education: A university president's perspective.* Paper presented at the annual meeting of the American Educational Research Association, Chicago.

Botstein, L. (1997b). *Jefferson's children: Education and the promise of American culture*. New York: Doubleday.

Bowen, R. (1991, November 15). [Interview]. New York City.

Bremer, J., & von Moschzisker, M. (1971). *The school without walls: Philadelphia's parkway program*. New York: Holt, Rinehart and Winston.

Breneman, D. W., & Nelson, S. C. (1981). *Financing community colleges: An economic perspective*. Washington, DC: Brookings Institution.

Budget and funding rationale. (c. 1973). MCA, M.C. Time Table and Budget file.

Burdman, P. (2000). The new advanced placement push. *Crosstalk, 8*(3), 1, 14–16.

Bush, T. (1992). International High School: Building a new real world. *Journal of Educational Issues of Language Minority Students, 10,* 57–65.

Butler, N. M. (1939). *Across the busy years* (2 vols.). New York: Scribner's.

California Community Colleges, Office of the Chancellor. (1993, May 13–14). *The California Middle College High School program*. Agenda Item 7, meeting of the Board of Governors of the California Community Colleges, Sacramento. (ERIC Document Reproduction Service No. ED 332 747)

Callagy, A. (1989, July). *Middle College High School information*. MCA, 1980s assessments file.

Campbell, D. S. (1930). *A critical study of the purposes of the junior college*. Nashville: Peabody College for Teachers, Vanderbilt University.

Camper, D. (1986, December 5). Editorial notebook: Dramatic drop in dropouts. *New York Times*, p. A-34.

Carnegie Commission on Higher Education. (1970a). *Less time, more options*. New York: McGraw-Hill.

Carnegie Commission on Higher Education. (1970b). *The open door colleges: Policies for community colleges*. New York: McGraw-Hill.

Carnegie Commission on Higher Education. (1973). *Continuity and discontinuity: Higher education and the schools*. New York: McGraw-Hill.

Carnegie Council for Policy Studies in Higher Education. (1980). *Giving youth a better chance: Options for education, work, and service*. San Francisco: Jossey-Bass.

Casserly, P. L. (1986). *Advanced placement revisited* (College Board Report 86–6). New York: College Entrance Examination Board.

Center for New Schools. (1972). Strengthening alternative high schools. *Harvard Educational Review, 42,* 313–350.

Center for Urban Ethnography. (1990). *An evaluation of the City University of New York and New York Board of Education collaboration programs, IV. Middle College High School*. MCA, Center for Urban Ethnography file.

Center for Urban Ethnography. (1991). *An evaluation of the City University of New York and New York Board of Education collaboration programs, IV. Middle College High School*. MCA, Center for Urban Ethnography file.

Cheit, E. (1971). *The new depression in higher education*. New York: McGraw-Hill.

Cicourel A. V., & Kitsuse, J. L. (1963). *The educational decision-makers: An advanced study in sociology*. Indianapolis: Bobbs-Merrill.

City University of New York, University Senate. (1969). *Report on special admissions policy, adopted by the Senate on February 12.* New York: Author.

City U. planning "Middle College." (1973, November 27). *New York Times,* p. 7.

Clark, B. R. (1960a). The "cooling-out" function in higher education. *The American Journal of Sociology, 65*(6), 569–576.

Clark, B. R. (1960b). *The open-door college.* New York: McGraw-Hill.

Clark, B. R. (1972). The organizational saga in higher education. *Administrative Science Quarterly, 17*(2), 178–184.

Clark, B. R. (1980). The "cooling out" function revisited. In G. B. Vaughan (Ed.), *Questioning the community college role (New directions for community colleges), 32* (pp. 15–31). San Francisco: Jossey-Bass.

Clark, T. A. (n.d.). *The influence of Middle College High School on the work and postsecondary experiences of its graduating classes from 1977 to 1986.* MCA, Middle College Evaluation file.

Clift, R. T., Veal, M. L., Holland, P., Johnson, M., & McCarthy, J. (1995). *Collaborative leadership and shared decision making.* New York: Teachers College Press.

Cohen, A. M., et al. (1976). *Cooperative education: A national assessment: An annotated bibliography.* Silver Spring, MD: Applied Management Associates.

Cohen, D. K. (1972). Compensatory education. In H. Walberg & A. T. Kopan (Eds.), *Rethinking urban education* (pp. 150–164). San Francisco: Jossey-Bass.

Cohen, D. K. (1995). What is the system in systemic reform? *Educational Researcher, 24*(9), 11–17, 31.

Colwell, L. H. (1995, June/July). Two degrees for the price of one. *Community College Journal, 65,* 8–10.

Committee report by members of the faculties of Andover, Exeter, Lawrenceville, Harvard, Princeton, and Yale. (1952). *General education in school and college.* Cambridge, MA: Harvard University Press.

Community College Planning Center, Stanford University, & Center for Continuing Education, University of Chicago. (1964). *Community colleges in urban settings.* Stanford: Western Regional Center of Educational Facilities Laboratories.

Conant, J. B. (1959). *The American high school today.* New York: McGraw-Hill.

Cooke, R. L. (1931, March). The origin of the six-four-four plan. *Junior College Journal, 1,* 370–373.

Cooper, D. L., Paisley, P. O., & Phelps, R. E. (1998). Developing precollege programs for at-risk middle and high school students. *Journal of College Student Development, 39*(4), 387–388.

Cooper, W. J. (1929, May). Some advantages expected to result from administering secondary education in two units of four years each. *School Review, 37,* 335–346.

Cooperative education. (1971). In *Encyclopedia of education* (Vol. 2; pp. 438–444). New York: Crowell-Collier.

Crooks, K. A. (1996, Autumn). State enhancements to foster collegiate level learning in high school. *The Learning Productivity News, 1*(2), 4–5. Available http://www.gse.buffalo.edu/org/LPN/f96news.htm.

Crooks, K. A. (1998a). State enhancement of college-level learning for high school students: A comprehensive national policy study and case studies of progressive states (Minnesota, Utah, Virginia) (Doctoral dissertation, State University of New York at Buffalo, 1998). *Dissertation Abstracts International, 59*(05A), 1479.

Crooks, K. A. (1998b, November). State sponsored college-level learning for high school students: Selected findings from a national policy study. *The Learning Productivity News, 4*(2). Available: http://www.gse.buffalo.edu/org/LPN/news1.html.

Cross, K. P. (1971). *Beyond the open door.* San Francisco: Jossey-Bass.

Crossland, R. (1998). *Running start annual progress report, 1996–1997.* (ERIC Document Reproduction Service No. ED 416 921)

Csikszentimihalyi, M. (1997, March 24). *Response to Botstein.* Paper presented at the annual meeting of the American Educational Research Association, Chicago.

Cullen, C. L. (1991). Middle College High School: Its organization and effectiveness (Doctoral dissertation, Teachers College, Columbia University, New York, 1991). *Dissertation Abstracts International, 52*(02A), 358.

Cullen, C. L. (1993, December 5). [Interview]. Pittsburgh.

Cullen, C. L., & Moed, M. (1988). Serving high risk adolescents. In J. E. Lieberman (Ed.), *Collaborating with high schools (New directions for community colleges), 63* (pp. 37–49). San Francisco: Jossey-Bass.

Curtis, C. (1993, December 5). [Interview]. Pittsburgh.

Daly, W. T. (Ed.). (1985). *College–school collaboration: Appraising the major approaches (New directions in teaching and learning), 24.* San Francisco: Jossey-Bass.

DeLany, B. (1991, February). Allocation, choice, and stratification within high schools: How the sorting machine copes. *American Journal of Education, 99,* 181–207.

Denniston, S., Lumachi, M., & Rosenberg, B. (1984, March). *LaGuardia Community College: Middle States/State Education evaluation: Report of the subcommittee on the Middle College.* MCA, 1980s assessments file.

DeRosenroll, D. A. (1988). *Peer counseling implementation, maintenance, and research issues: Implications for the future.* Victoria, BC: University of Victoria.

Diener, T. (1986). *Growth of an American invention: A documentary history of the junior and community college movement.* New York: Greenwood Press.

Dispenzieri, A., & Giniger, S. (1969). *The college discovery program: A synthesis of research.* New York: City University of New York Research and Evaluation Unit.

Doll, R. C. (1972). Urban teachers' problems. In H. Walberg & A. T. Kopan (Eds.), *Rethinking urban education* (pp. 12–22). San Francisco: Jossey-Bass.

Doxey, W. H. (1980). An academic analysis of the articulation of early admission students with diversified academic abilities in Middle College from 1971 to 1974 (Doctoral dissertation, University of Utah, Salt Lake City, 1980). *Dissertation Abstracts International, 41*(02a), 550.

Duffus, R. L. (1936). *Democracy enters the college: A study of the rise and decline of the academic lockstep.* New York: Scribner's.

Duke, D. L. (1995). *The school that refused to die: Continuity and change at Thomas Jefferson High School.* Albany: State University of New York Press.

Dunham, E. A. (1969). *Colleges of the forgotten Americans: A profile of state colleges and regional universities.* New York: McGraw-Hill.

Dzuback, M. A. (1991). *Robert M. Hutchins: Portrait of an educator.* Chicago: University of Chicago Press.

Eaton, J. S. (1994). The fortunes of the transfer function: Community colleges and transfer, 1900–1990. In G. A. Baker, III (Ed.), *A handbook on the community college in America: Its history, mission, and management* (pp. 28–40). Westport, CT: Greenwood Press.

Eby, F. (1928). The four-year junior college and the advent of the six-four-four plan. *Educational Administration and Supervision, 14,* 536–542.

Eby, F. (1929, February). Should the junior college be united with the senior high school? *Nation's Schools, 3,* 33–38.

Eby, F. (1932, May). The four year junior college. *Junior College Journal, 2,* 471–489.

Educational Policies Commission. (1964). *Universal opportunity for education beyond the high school.* Washington, DC: Author.

Educational Research Department, Richmond Unified School District. (1986, December). *Student attrition report: High schools for school year 1985–86.* MCA, Richmond Middle College file.

Eells, W. C. (1931a). *The junior college.* Boston and New York: Houghton Mifflin.

Eells, W. C. (1931b, February). What manner of child shall this be? *Junior College Journal, 1,* 309–328.

Erickson, F. (1975). Gatekeeping and the melting pot: Interaction in counseling encounters. *Harvard Educational Review, 45*(1), 44–70.

Eriksen, A., & Gantz, J. (1974). *Partnership in urban education: An alternative school.* Midland, MI: Pendell.

Erikson, E. H. (1963). *Childhood and society* (2nd ed.). New York: Norton.

Evaluation report for FY 92. (1992). Attached to Terri Bush and Janet Lieberman to principals of the Middle Colleges, September 12, 1992. MCA, "Replications: Notes for final report" file.

Evans, I. M. (Ed.). (1995). *Staying in school: Partnerships for educational change.* Baltimore: Paul H. Brookes.

Fincher-Ford, M. (1997). *High school students earning college credit: A guide to creating dual-credit programs.* Thousand Oaks, CA: Corwin Press.

Finney, J. E. (1997). Educational collaboration: The challenge of meeting unprecedented enrollment demands. *Crosstalk, 5*(2), 3.

Fiorello H. LaGuardia Community College. (c. 1975). *9th grade absence rate of prospective Middle College students.* MCA, First year file.

Fitz-Gibbon, C. T. (1992). Peer and cross-age tutoring. In *Encyclopedia of educational research* (6th ed.; Vol. 4; pp. 980–984). New York: Macmillan.

Ford Foundation. (1962). *The new teacher.* New York: Author.

Ford Foundation. (1972). *A foundation goes to school: The Ford Foundation comprehensive school improvement program 1960–1970.* New York: Author.

Ford Foundation. (1983, March). *The education and culture program: A status report.* Report 007555, FFA.

Ford Foundation. (1984). *The education and culture program's work in higher education: An appraisal of the issues and a prospectus for action.* Report 009556, FFA.

Ford Foundation project—Replicating Middle College: Highlights of evaluators' meeting. (1988). MCA, Evaluators' meeting, January 15, 1988 file.

Four-School Study Committee. (1970). *16–20: The liberal education of an age group.* New York: College Entrance Examination Board.

Frederick, A. (1982). *Northeastern University: An emerging giant; 1959–1975.* Boston: Northeastern University.

Freedman, S. G. (1990). *Small victories: The real world of a teacher, her students, and their high school.* New York: Harper & Row.

Frey, M. W. (1973, January 29). *Feasibility study for LaGuardia Middle College, high school division.* MCA, M.C. Time Table and Budget file.

Fund for the Advancement of Education. (1953). *Bridging the gap between school and college: Progress report on four related projects supported by the fund.* New York: Author.

Fund for the Advancement of Education. (1957). *They went to college early: A report on the early admission in college program.* New York: Author.

Fund for the Advancement of Education. (1961). *Decade of experiment: The Fund for the Advancement of Education 1951–1961.* New York: Author.

Funding for the proposed Middle College. (1972). MCA, M.C. Time Table and Budget file.

Gaines, B. C., & Wilbur, F. P. (1985). Early instruction in the high school: Syracuse's project advance. In W. T. Daly (Ed.), *College–school collaboration: Appraising the major approaches (New directions for teaching and learning),* 24 (pp. 27–36). San Francisco: Jossey-Bass.

Gamson, Z. (1989). *Higher education and the real world: The story of CAEL.* Wolfeboro, NH: Longwood Academic.

Garms, W. I. (1977). *Financing community colleges.* New York: Teachers College Press.

Gaudiani, C. L. (1990). Critical connection: School–college faculty alliances. *Thought & Action,* 6(1), 47–51.

Geiger, L. G. (1970). *Voluntary accreditation: A history of the North Central Association, 1945–1970.* Menasha, WI: North Central Association of Colleges and Secondary Schools.

Gelatt, H. B. (1973). *Decisions and outcomes: A leader's guide.* Princeton, NJ: College Entrance Examination Board.

Gelatt, H. B., Varenhorst, B., Carey, R., & Miller, G. P. (1973). *Decisions and outcomes.* Princeton, NJ: College Entrance Examination Board.

Gesell, A., Ilg, F. L., & Ames, L. B. (1956). *Youth: The years from ten to sixteen.* New York: Harper & Row.

Gibbons, H. E. (1975). The historical development of the Dallas county community college district: A study of a multi-college district (Doctoral dissertation, University of Oklahoma, Norman, 1975). *Dissertation Abstracts International, 36*(08A), 5099.

Gold, B. A., & Miles, M. B. (1981). *Whose school is it anyway? Parent/teacher conflict over an innovative school.* New York: Praeger.

Goodlad, J. (1983). *A place called school: Prospects for the future.* New York: McGraw-Hill.

Gordon, L. D. (1990). *Gender and higher education in the progressive era.* New Haven, CT: Yale University Press.

Gordon, S. (1975). The transformation of the City University of New York, 1945–1970 (Doctoral dissertation, Teachers College, Columbia University, New York, 1975). *Dissertation Abstracts International, 38*(07A), 4325.

Grant, G. (1972, September). Let a hundred Antiochs bloom! *Change, 4,* 47–58.

Grant, G. (1985). The world we created at Hamilton High. *Antioch Review, 4,* 385–400.

Grant, G., & Murray, C. E. (1999). *Teaching in America: The slow revolution.* Cambridge, MA: Harvard University Press.

Grant, G., & Riesman, D. (1978). *The perpetual dream: Reform and experiment in the American college.* Chicago: University of Chicago Press.

Greenberg, A. R. (1982a). *High school/college articulated programs: Pooling resources across the abyss.* MCA, 1980s assessments file.

Greenberg, A. R. (1982b). High school/college articulated programs: Pooling resources across the abyss. *National Association of Secondary School Principals Bulletin, 66*(1), 79–86.

Greenberg, A. R. (1982c). *Middle College: The first five years.* MCA, 1980s assessments file.

Greenberg, A. R. (1987). College study in high school for low and moderate achievers (Doctoral dissertation, Teachers College, Columbia University, New York, 1987). *Dissertation Abstracts International, 48*(07A), 1724.

Greenberg, A. R. (1991). *High school–college partnerships: Conceptual models, programs, and issues* (ASHE–ERIC Higher Education Report 5). Washington, DC: George Washington University, School of Education and Human Development.

Greenberg, A. R. (1993, December 1). [Interview]. Miami.

Gregory, L. (1995). The "turnaround" process: Factors influencing the school success of urban youth. *Journal of Adolescent Research, 10*(1), 136–154.

Gregory, L., Sweeney, M., & Strong, M. (Public/Private Ventures). (1989). *An evaluation of the City University of New York/New York City Board of Education collaborative programs.* MCA, PPV evaluations file.

Gross, T. R. (1988). *Partners in education: How colleges can work with schools to improve teaching and learning.* San Francisco: Jossey-Bass.

Group for the Advancement of Psychiatry, Committee on Adolescence. (1968). *Normal adolescence: Its dynamics and impact.* New York: Scribner's.

Grunfeld, K. K. (1991). Purpose and ambiguity: The feminine world of Hunter

College, 1869–1945 (Doctoral dissertation, Teachers College, Columbia University, New York, 1991). *Dissertation Abstracts International, 52*(11A), 3842.

Haberman, M. (1971). Twenty-three reasons universities can't educate teachers. *Journal of Teacher Education, 22*(2), 133–140.

Haberman, M. (1994). Preparing teachers for the real world of urban schools. *Educational Forum, 58*(2), 162–168.

Hall, E. B. (n.d.). *The house of education needs overhaul.* Great Barrington, MA: Simon's Rock College.

Hampel, R. L. (1993, Spring/Summer). Apart-nerships. *Record in Educational Administration and Supervision, 13*(2), 27–31.

Hansen, C. (1992). Peer counseling. In *Encyclopedia of educational research* (6th ed.; Vol. 4; pp. 976–980) New York: Macmillan.

Hanson, H. P. (1980, Spring). Twenty-five years of the advanced placement program. *The College Board Review, 115,* 8–12.

Harbeson, J. W. (1928, October). The 6-4-4 plan of school organization with special reference to its application in the city of Pasadena. *California Quarterly of Secondary Education, 4,* 45–50.

Harbeson, J. W. (1931, October). The Pasadena junior college experiment. *Junior College Journal, 2*(1), 4–10.

Harbeson, J. W. (1940, December). The program of the four-year junior college: Advantages and disadvantages. *Bulletin of the National Association of Secondary School Principals, 24,* 94–104.

Hawthorne, E. M. (1991). Experiences of state departments of education in school/college collaboration: Lessons for school executives. *Journal of Research for School Executives, 1*(1), 15–21.

Hawthorne, E. M., & Zusman, A. (1992). The role of state departments in school/college collaborations. *Journal of Higher Education, 63*(4), 418–441.

Heathers, G. (1967). *The dual progress plan.* Danville, IL: Interstate.

Henderson, A. D. (1970). *Policies and practices in higher education.* New York: Harper & Brothers.

Henderson, A. D. (1971). *The innovative spirit.* San Francisco: Jossey-Bass.

Hentoff, N. (1966). *Our children are dying.* New York: Viking Press.

Herbst, J. (1996). *The once and future school: Three hundred and fifty years of American secondary education.* New York: Routledge.

Herman, D. (1979). *College and after: The Vassar experiment in women's education, 1861–1924* (Doctoral dissertation, Stanford University, 1979). *Dissertation Abstracts International, 40*(02A), 1027.

Hill, M. E. (1931, October). Advantages of separation. *Junior College Journal, 2*(1), 10.

Hollingsworth, S., & Sockett, H. (1994). *Teacher research and educational reform. Ninety-third yearbook of the National Society for the Study of Education.* Chicago: University of Chicago Press.

Horizon: A journal of the middle college, 1(2). (1975, January).

Horn, L. J., & Chen, X. (1998). *Toward resiliency: At-risk students who make it to college.* Washington, DC: U.S. Department of Education.

Houle, C. O. (1996). *The design of education* (2nd ed.). San Francisco: Jossey-Bass.

How New York City's high schools spend their money. (1996, November 24). *New York Times*, p. 42.

Hutchins, R. M. (1936). *The higher learning in America*. New Haven, CT: Yale University Press.

Hyland, J. L. (1981). Challenge and accommodation: Stratification conflict in an urban community college (Doctoral dissertation, New School for Social Research, New York, 1981). *Dissertation Abstracts International, 42*(08A), 3770.

Information for New York State. (c. 1973). MCA. Curriculum: Notes for state file.

Janowitz, M. (1969). *Institution building in urban education*. New York: Russell Sage Foundation.

Jencks, C., & Riesman, D. (1962). The viability of the American college. In N. Sanford (Ed.), *The American college: A psychological and social interpretation of the higher learning* (pp. 74–192). New York: Wiley.

Jencks, C., & Riesman, D. (1968). *The academic revolution*. Garden City, NY: Doubleday.

Johnstone, D. B. (1993, December). Enhancing the productivity of learning. *American Association for Higher Education Bulletin, 46*(4), 3–5.

Jun, A., & Tierney, W. G. (1999). At-risk urban students and college success: A framework for effective preparation. *Metropolitan Universities: An International Forum, 9*(4), 49–60.

Keller, C. P. (1980, Summer). AP: Reflections of the first director. *The College Board Review, 116*, 22–23.

Kerr, C. (1995). *The uses of the university* (4th ed.). Cambridge, MA: Harvard University Press.

Klohmann, E. L. (1987). Intergroup dynamics in a collaborative relationship: A study of an alternative high school and a sponsoring college (Doctoral dissertation, New York University, 1987). *Dissertation Abstracts International, 49*(01A), 0019.

Knowles, A. (1971). The future of cooperative education. In A. Knowles & Associates (Eds.), *The handbook of cooperative education* (pp. 324–335). San Francisco: Jossey-Bass.

Koos, L. V. (1925). *The junior college movement*. Boston: Ginn.

Koos, L. V. (1949). *Integrating high school and college: The six-four-four plan at work*. New York: Harper & Brothers.

Kopan, A. T. (1972). Robert J. Havighurst: Pursuit of excellence. In H. Walberg & A. T. Kopan (Eds.), *Rethinking urban education* (pp. 317–324). San Francisco: Jossey-Bass.

Krug, E. A. (1960). *The secondary school curriculum*. New York: Harper & Row.

Krug, E. A. (1969). *The shaping of the American high school, Volume 1: 1890–1920*. Madison: University of Wisconsin Press.

Krug, E. A. (1972). *The shaping of the American high school: Vol. 2. 1920–1941*. Madison: University of Wisconsin Press.

Kuner, C. (1984). Peer group counseling: Applied psychology in the high school. *Curriculum Review, 23*(1), 89–92.

Labaree, D. F. (1988). *The making of an American high school: The credentials market and the Central High School of Philadelphia, 1838–1939.* New Haven, CT: Yale University Press.

Lagemann, E. C. (1989). *The politics of knowledge: The Carnegie Corporation, philanthropy, and public policy.* Middletown, CT: Wesleyan University Press.

LaGuardia Community College: Profile. (1980). MCA, "1980s assessments" file.

Lambert, L. M., & Mercurio, J. A. (1986, Spring). Making decisions: College credits earned in high school. *Journal of College Admissions, 111,* 28–32.

Lavin, D. E., Alba, R. D., & Silberstein, R. A. (1981). *Right vs. privilege: The open-admissions experiment at the City University of New York.* New York: Free Press.

Lavin, D. E., & Hyllegard, D. (1996). *Changing the odds: Open admissions and the life chances of the disadvantaged.* New Haven, CT: Yale University Press.

Lawton, M. (1996, October 23). Carson City school vote puts middle-college idea on the line. *Education Week, 16,* pp. 1, 12.

Learned, W. S., & Wood, B. D. (1938). *The student and his knowledge: A report to the Carnegie Foundation on the results of the high school and college examinations of 1928, 1930, and 1932.* New York: Carnegie Foundation for the Advancement of Teaching.

LeCroy, R. J. (1984, June). Building leadership expertise through on-the-job experience. In R. L. Alfred (Ed.), *Emerging roles for community college leaders (New directions for community colleges, 46)* (pp. 109–116). San Francisco: Jossey-Bass.

Leonard, R. J. (1925, May). Professional education in junior colleges. *Teachers College Record, 26,* 729.

Levine, A. (1978). *Handbook on undergraduate curriculum.* San Francisco: Jossey-Bass.

Levine, A. (1980). *Why innovations fail.* Albany: State University of New York Press.

Levine, D. O. (1986). *The American college and the culture of aspiration, 1915–1940.* Ithaca, NY: Cornell University Press.

Lieberman, J. E. (1965). The effect of direct instruction in vocabulary concepts on reading achievement (Doctoral dissertation, New York University, 1965). *Dissertation Abstracts International, 27*(04A), 960.

Lieberman, J. E. (1971, November 19). *Student profile.* MCA.

Lieberman, J. E. (1973). *A proposal for a new substructure in education: The Middle College.* MCA, Design file.

Lieberman, J. E. (c. 1974, January). *Status report.* MCA.

Lieberman, J. E. (1975, May 14). *The Middle College High School: A new model for remediation.* MCA, Design file.

Lieberman, J. E. (1986, February). *Middle College: A ten year study.* MCA, 1980s assessments file.

Lieberman, J. E. (1987a, May). *Ford Foundation: Interim report—Calendar of activities completed.* MCA, Old replication material file.

Lieberman, J. E. (1987b, September). *Ford Foundation: Replicating Middle College grant—Year end report.* MCA, Old replication material file.

Lieberman, J. E. (1990, July 12). *Final report*. MCA.

Lieberman, J. E. (1991, November 14). [Interview]. New York City.

Lieberman, J. E. (1992, December 15). *A final report to the Ford Foundation on Middle College replication*. MCA, Ford Foundation final report file.

Lieberman, J. E. (1995, July 24). [Interview]. New York City.

Lieberman, J. E., & Callagy, A. K. (1990). Reach them and teach them: The International High School program. *Urban Education, 24,* 376–390.

Lieberman, J. E., & Hungar, J. Y. (1998). *Transforming students' lives: How exploring transfer works, and why*. Washington, DC: American Association for Higher Education.

Lieberman, J. E., Nadelstern, E., & Berman, D. (1988). *After three years: A status report on the International High School at LaGuardia Community College*. Long Island City, NY: International High School.

Light, P., & Glachan, M. (1985). Facilitation of individual problem solving through peer interaction. *Educational Psychology, 5*(3,4), 217–225.

Lillard, J. B. (1930, August 23). The 6-3-3-2 versus the 6-4-4 plan of organization for the public junior college. *School and Society, 32,* 262–264.

Lowell, A. L. (1934). *At war with academic traditions in America*. Cambridge, MA: Harvard University Press.

Lynch, S. J. (1994, June). Should gifted students be grade-advanced? Reston, VA: Council for Exceptional Children. (ERIC Document Reproduction Service No. ED 370 295)

Maeroff, G. I. (1981, January 20). Experiment to join high school and college is lonely effort. *New York Times,* p. C4.

Maeroff, G. I. (1985, December 8). Faculty defends academic custom. *New York Times,* p. I-2:63.

Maeroff, G. I., Callan, P. M., & Usdan, M. (Eds.). (2001). *The learning connection: New partnerships between schools and colleges*. New York: Teachers College Press.

Marczely, B. (1996). *Personalizing professional growth: Staff development that works*. Thousand Oaks, CA: Corwin Press.

Martorana, S. V., & Kuhns, E. (1975). *Managing academic change: Interactive forces and leadership in higher education*. San Francisco: Jossey-Bass.

McCabe, H. M. (1980). Cooperative education in the community college: A critical analysis (Doctoral dissertation, Columbia University, New York, 1980). *Dissertation Abstracts International, 41*(09A), 4089.

McLane, C. L. (1913, March). The junior college, or upward extension of the high school. *School Review, 21,* 166–167.

Meier, D. (1995). *The power of their ideas: Lessons for America from a small school in Harlem*. Boston: Beacon Press.

Mercurio, J., et al. (1982). College courses in the high school: A four-year followup of the Syracuse University project advance class of 1977. *College and University, 58*(1), 5–18.

Mercurio, J., et al. (1983). College credit earned in high school: Comparing student performance in project advance and advanced placement. *College and University, 59*(1), 74–86.

Middle College Charter High School. (1999). *The academic program at Middle College Charter High School: An overview of curriculum and assessment.* Long Island City, NY: Author.

Middle College High School. (c. 1977). *Career education personal and career development curriculum guide, Tom Sena, developer.* MCA, Curriculum-career file.

Middle College High School. (c. 1998). *From dream to reality.* Long Island City, NY: Author.

Middle College High School. (1999, September 1). *Middle College High School charter proposal* (rev. ed.). Long Island City, NY: Author.

Middle College High School at LaGuardia Community College. (1989, Spring). MCA, 1980s assessments file.

Middle College High School, Contra Costa College. (1988). Attached to Santiago Wood to Janet Lieberman, October 29, 1988. MCA, Richmond Middle College file.

Middle College High School [Shelby State Community College]. (1987). Attachment 1 to "Survey questions." MCA, Shelby State Community College file.

Middle College High Schools established for at-risk students. (1989, July 6). *Los Angeles Sentinel*, p. A-10:1.

Middle College hoping for success. (1987, August 27). *The Commercial Appeal*, pp. B:1–2.

Middle College proposal. (n.d.). Draft. MCA, Curriculum file.

Middle College proposal. (1973, June). MCA, Design file.

Middle College proposal. (1988, May 9). Attached to Board of Education agenda item, May 26, 1988. MCA, Dallas County Community College file.

Middle College II: An integrated multi-cultural Middle College. (c. 1984). MCA, Middle College II file.

Mission [Middle College High School at Shelby State Community College]. (1987). MCA, Shelby State Community College file.

Mitchell, J. (1993, December 5). [Interview]. Pittsburgh.

Morison, S. E. (1936). *Three centuries of Harvard.* Cambridge, MA: Harvard University Press.

Morisseau, J. J. (1975). *The mini-school experiment: Restructuring your school: A handbook.* New York: New York Urban Coalition.

Moro, S. M., & Mercurio, J. A. (1988). Eliminating senioritis. *Gifted Child Today, 11*(4), 28–30.

National Commission on Excellence in Education. (1983). *A nation at risk: The imperative for educational reform: A report to the nation and the secretary of education, United States Department of Education.* Washington, DC: Author.

National Education Association. (1893). *Report of the committee on secondary school studies appointed at the meeting of the National Education Association, July 9, 1892.* Washington, DC: U.S. Government Printing Office.

National Education Association. (1929). *The articulation of the units of American education. Seventh yearbook of the department of superintendence.* Washington, DC: Author.

National Education Association. (1938). *The structure and administration of education in American democracy.* Washington, DC: Author.

National Education Association, Commission on the Reorganization of Secondary Education. (1918). *Cardinal principles of secondary education: A report of the commission on the reorganization of secondary education.* Washington, DC: U.S. Government Printing Office.

National Study of Charter Schools. (2000). *The state of charter schools, 2000.* Washington, DC: U.S. Department of Education, Office of Educational Research and Improvement.

New York State requirements: Curriculum requirements. (c. 1974). MCA, Notes for state-curriculum file.

Newman, F. (Chair). (1971). *Report on higher education.* Washington, DC: U.S. Department of Health, Education, and Welfare.

Newman, G. C. (1987). *Leadership and the politics of innovative change: Antioch under Arthur E. Morgan.* Toledo, OH: Center for the Study of Higher Education.

Newmann, F. (1981). Reducing student alienation in high schools: Implications of theory. *Harvard Educational Review, 51,* 546–564.

North Central Association of Colleges and Secondary Schools. (1915). Report of the committee on the revision of the definition of the unit. In North Central Association of Colleges and Secondary Schools, *Proceedings, 20,* 27–30.

Notes on Visitors from Cuyahoga Community College. (1989, November 16). MCA, Ford replication—Statistics file.

Office of Financial Management, State of Washington. (1995, October 4). *Running start program summary.* Seattle: Author.

Orlans, H. (1990). Changing conditions: Minority education at Oakes College. *Thought & Action, 6*(1), 21–34.

Ort, S. W. (1998). *Middle College High School: A case study of a school on the move.* Unpublished paper, Teachers College, Columbia University, National Center for Restructuring Education, Schools and Teaching.

Overacker, I. (1994, Summer). School reform in Rochester, N.Y., 1965–1980: The challenge of desegregation and integration. *Alliance: Publication of the National Center for Urban Partnerships, 2*(1), 26–29.

Palmer, J. C. (1994). Faculty practices and attitudes as teachers and scholars: A review of research. In G. A. Baker, III (Ed.), *A handbook on the community college in America: Its history, mission, and management* (pp. 423–435). Westport, CT: Greenwood Press.

Pascarella, E. T. (1985). Racial differences in the factors associated with bachelor's degree completion: A nine-year follow-up. *Research in Higher Education, 23,* 351–373.

Pedersen, R. P. (1993). Value conflict on the community college campus: An examination of its historical origins. In A. M. Hoffman & D. J. Julius (Eds.), *Managing community and junior colleges: Perspective for the next century* (pp. 17–31). Washington, DC: College and University Personnel Association.

Pedersen, R. P. (1994). Challenges facing the urban community college: A literature review. In G. A. Baker, III (Ed.), *A handbook on the community college in America: Its history, mission, and management* (pp. 176–189). Westport, CT: Greenwood Press.

Pedersen, R. P. (2000). The origins and development of the early public junior college (Doctoral dissertation, Teachers College, Columbia University, New York, 2000). *Dissertation Abstracts International, 60*(12A), 4348.

Peltz, F. K. (1974, August–October). *Middle College progress report.* MCA, Progress report file.

Peterson, R. E. (1965–1966, Winter). What's really happening in advanced placement. *The College Board Review, 58,* 12–17.

Phelps, D. G. (1992–1993, December–January). Kindling hope in the ashes: LACCD and Los Angeles after the riots. *Community College Journal, 63*(3), 14–17.

Pianelli, M. A. (1995, February 8–11). *Technology middle college.* Unpublished paper presented at Workforce 2000, the annual conference on workforce training of the League for Innovation in the Community College, San Diego, CA. (ERIC Document Reproduction Service No. ED 380 177)

Poteat, C. (1975a, January 31). *Middle College progress report.* MCA, Progress report file.

Poteat, C. (1975b, April). *A comparison of the Middle College plan with Middle College High School.* MCA, Middle College history—1973 file.

Powell, A. G. (1997). *Lessons from privilege: The American prep school tradition.* Cambridge, MA: Harvard University Press.

Powell, A. G., Farrar, E., & Cohen, D. K. (1985). *The shopping mall high school: Winners and losers in the educational market place.* Boston: Houghton Mifflin.

President's Commission on Higher Education. (1947). *Higher education for American democracy* (6 vols.). New York: Harper & Brothers.

President's Science Advisory Committee, Panel on Youth. (1974). *Youth, transition to adulthood; Report.* Chicago: University of Chicago Press.

Proposal for Innovative Partnership Activities. (1988). Attached to Ray Bowen to Alison Bernstein, October 13, 1988. MCA, Shelby State Community College file.

Proposal Narrative. (1989, September 29). Attached to *Middle College High School project.* MCA, Richmond Middle College file.

Ramaswami, S. (1993, May). *Accelerating the learning of at-risk students: An evaluation of Project ACCEL.* Newark, NJ: Newark School System. (ERIC Document Reproduction Service No. ED 364 640)

Rating sheet. (1988). MCA, Ford evaluators' meeting, January 15, 1988 file.

Ray, M. (1987, September). Making the grade? *Memphis, 12*(6), 60–62.

Recommendation for grant/FAP action—supplement 86-585. (1987, July 16). FFA, Grant file 86-585.

Record of interview, EAD, KP, Joseph Shenker, Dean Lieberman, faculty and students. (1972, June 26). CCP, "New York City University—LaGuardia Middle College" file.

Record of interview: Janet Lieberman, EAD, and KP. (1972, February 10). CCP, "New York City University—LaGuardia Middle College" file.

Reel, G. (1990, July 2). Rescue plan offers hope to school. *The [Memphis] Commercial Appeal,* pp. A1, A5.

Reese, W. J. (1995). *The origins of the American high school.* New Haven, CT: Yale University Press.

Reisberg, L. (1998, June 26). Some professors question programs that allow high-school students to earn college credits. *Chronicle of Higher Education*, p. A40.

Reynolds, J. W. (1965). *The junior college.* New York: Center for Applied Research in Education.

Rhoads, R. A., & Valadez, J. R. (1996). *Democracy, multiculturalism, and the community college: A critical perspective.* New York: Garland.

Riesman, D. (1980). *On higher education: The academic enterprise in an era of rising student consumerism.* San Francisco: Jossey-Bass.

Rippey, D. (1987). *Some called it Camelot: The El Centro story.* Dallas: El Centro College.

Rogers, D. (1968). *100 Livingston street: Politics and bureaucracy in the New York City school system.* New York: Random House.

Rosenbaum, J. E. (1976). *Making inequality.* New York: Academic Press.

Rosenbaum, J. E., Miller, S. R., & Krei, M. S. (1996). Gatekeeping in an era of more open gates: High school counselors' views of their influence on students' college plans. *American Journal of Education, 104*(4), 257–279.

Rossman, J. E., Astin, H. S., Astin, A. W., & El-Khawas, E. (1975). *Open admissions at City University of New York: An analysis of the first year.* Englewood Cliffs, NJ: Prentice-Hall.

Rothschild, E. (1995). Aspiration, performance, reward: The advanced placement program at 40. *The College Board Review, 176/177*, 24–32.

Roundtree, G. D. (1995). The evaluation of the Vassar College exploring transfer program (Doctoral dissertation, Teachers College, Columbia University, New York, 1995). *Dissertation Abstracts International, 56*(11A), 4260.

Ryder, K. G. (1987). Social and educational roots. In K. G. Ryder & J. W. Wilson et al. *Cooperative education in a new era: Understanding and strengthening the links between college and the workplace* (pp. 1–12). San Francisco: Jossey-Bass.

Ryder, K. G., Wilson, J. W., et al. (1987). *Cooperative education in a new era: Understanding and strengthening the links between college and the workplace.* San Francisco: Jossey-Bass.

Sanford, N. (1962). Developmental status of the entering freshman. In N. Sanford (Ed.), *The American college: A psychological and social interpretation of the higher learning* (pp. 253–282). New York: Wiley.

Sauer, K. R. (1995, February). *Secondary students who earn postsecondary credit through instruction taken at their high school: A working paper.* (ERIC Document Reproduction Service No. ED 390 339)

Schafer, W. E., & Olexa, C. (1971). *Tracking and opportunity: The locking-out process and beyond.* Scranton, PA: Chandler.

Schmidt, P. (1993, January 13). Michigan board's proposal would provide high school youths a shortcut to college. *Education Week*, p. 32.

Schreiber, V., & Haberman, M. (1995). Building a gentler school. *Educational Leadership, 52*(5), 69–71.

Scott, C. W., & Hill, C. M. (1954). *Public education under criticism.* New York: Prentice-Hall.

Scribner, H. B. (1972). Leadership for change: My first year in New York City as chancellor of the public schools. *Journal of Research and Development in Education, 5*(3), 18–28.

Sealander, J. (1988). "Forcing them to be free": Antioch College and progressive education in the 1920s. *History of Higher Education Annual, 8*, 59–78.

Semel, S. F. (1992). *The Dalton school: The transformation of a progressive school.* New York: Peter Lang.

Semel, S. F., & Sadovnik, A. R. (Eds.). (1999). *Schools of tomorrow; schools of today: What happened to progressive education?* New York: Peter Lang.

Sexton, J. A., & Harbeson, J. W. (1946). *The new American college: The four-year junior college.* New York: Harper & Brothers.

Shapiro, B. C. (1986, December). Two plus two: The high school/community college connection. *National Association of Secondary School Principals Bulletin, 70*, 90–96.

Shapiro, H. (Chair). (1987). *The Ford Foundation program on education and culture.* New York: Ford Foundation.

Shenker, J. (1992, May 30). [Interview]. New York City.

Silverman, M. (1992, April 21). [Interview]. Richmond, CA.

Silverman, M., & Carlton, B. (1993, December 5). [Interview]. Pittsburgh.

Sirotnik, K., & Goodlad, J. (Eds.). (1988). *School–university partnerships in action: Concepts, cases, and concerns.* New York: Teachers College Press.

Sizer, T. (1984). *Horace's compromise: The dilemma of the American high school.* Boston: Houghton Mifflin.

Sizer, T. (1996). *Horace's hope: What works for the American high school.* Boston: Houghton Mifflin.

State of New Jersey, Department of Higher Education. (1984). *Going to college in New Jersey.* Trenton, NJ: Department of Higher Education.

Stocking, W. R. Jr., (1926). The Detroit house plan. In *National Association of Secondary School Principals tenth yearbook* (pp. 83–90).

Stoel, C. F. (1987). *Report on May 15, 1987 visit to Union County College.* MCA, New Jersey Department of Higher Education file.

Stoel, C. F. (1988). History of the high school connection. In J. E. Lieberman (Ed.), *Collaborating with high schools (New directions for community colleges, 63)* (pp. 13–23). San Francisco: Jossey-Bass.

Stone, E. (1992). *The Hunter College campus schools for the gifted: The challenge of equity and excellence.* New York: Teachers College Press.

Summary and clarification of Middle College plan. (3rd revision). (1973, July 26). MCA, Board of Education file.

Summary of activity on Middle College proposal. (1972). MCA, Middle College evaluation file.

Summary of Middle College activity. (1974, July). MCA, Proposals and letters file.

Summary of Middle College grant activity. (n.d.). MCA, Carnegie file.

Summary of 1987 evaluations. (1988). MCA, Ford evaluators' meeting, January 15, 1988 file.

Summer training. (1987). Attached to Janet Lieberman to Alison Bernstein, June 1, 1987, Ford Foundation Archives, Grant file 86–587.

Survey. (1988). Attached to Eugene Campbell to Janet Lieberman, January 7, 1988. MCA, New Jersey Department of Higher Education file.

Survey of desired college courses. (1987). MCA, Los Angeles City College file.

Survey questions. (1987, November). Attached to Toni Forsyth to Janet Lieberman, November 30, 1987. MCA, Evaluators' meeting, January 15, 1988 file.

Survey questions [Cuyahoga Community College]. (1988a, January 8). Attached to Alfred D. Tutela to Lieberman, January 8, 1988. MCA, Evaluators' meeting—January 15, 1988 file.

Survey questions [Contra Costa College]. (1988b, September 23). Attached to *Proposal for Middle College High School*, MCA, Richmond Middle College file.

Task Force on School Cultivation, Edgar F. Beckham (Chair). (1987, June 15). *The recruitment and retention of minority students in liberal arts colleges.* Ford Foundation Archives. Record Group ACC 91/5.

Taylor, I. K. (1997, April 2). Idaho to allow high schoolers to attend college full time. *Education Week*, p. 18.

Texas Higher Education Coordinating Board. (1996). *Ten strategies and their financial implications for reducing time-to-degree in Texas universities.* Austin: Author. (ERIC Document Reproduction Service No. ED 401 799)

Tinto, V. (1993). *Leaving college: Rethinking the causes and cures of student attrition* (2nd ed.). Chicago: University of Chicago Press.

Tomlinson, C. A. (1994). Middle school and acceleration: Guidance from research and the kids. *Journal of Secondary Gifted Education*, 5(4), 42–51.

Trickett, E. J. (1991). *Living an idea: Empowerment and the evolution of an alternative high school.* Cambridge, MA: Brookline Books.

Trump, J. L., & Georgiades, W. (1972, May). The NASSP model schools action program. *The Bulletin of the National Association of Secondary School Principals*, 56(364), 116–126.

Turner, R. (1960). Modes of social ascent through education: Sponsored and contest mobility. *American Journal of Sociology*, 25, 855–867.

Tussman, J. (1969). *Experiment at Berkeley.* New York: Oxford University Press.

Tyack, D., & Cuban, L. (1995). *Tinkering toward utopia: A century of public school reform.* Cambridge, MA: Harvard University Press.

Tyler, J. L., Gruber, D., & McMullan, B. J. (Public/Private Ventures). (1987, July). *An evaluation of the City University of New York and New York Board of Education collaboration programs, IV. Middle College, 81–103.* MCA, PPV evaluations file.

Tyler, R. W. (1961). Introduction to the study: Conclusions and recommendations. In J. W. Wilson & E. H. Lyons (Eds.), *Work–study college programs: Appraisal and report of the study of cooperative education* (pp. 1–14). New York, NY: Harper and Brothers.

Tyler, R. W., & Mills, A. I. (1961). *Report on cooperative education: Summary of the two-year national study of cooperative education.* New York: Thomas Alva Edison Foundation.

Unique community college collaboration. (1993, Summer). *Educational Record*, 74(3), 32.

Urahn, S. (1993, February). *The postsecondary enrollment options program: A research report.* St Paul: Minnesota House of Representatives Research Department. (ERIC Document Reproduction Service No. ED 369 312)

U. S. Department of Education, National Center for Education Statistics. (1998). *The condition of education, 1998*, NCES 98-013. Washington, DC: U.S. Government Printing Office.

U. S. Department of Education, National Center for Education Statistics. (1999). *Projections of education statistics to 2009*. Washington, DC: Author.

U. S. Department of Labor, Office of Policy Planning and Research. (1965). *The Negro family: The case for national action*. Washington, DC: Author.

Valentine, J. A. (1987). *The College Board and the school curriculum*. New York: College Entrance Examination Board.

Vandenberg, V. (1996, September). Washtenaw Technical Middle College: High school for the high tech. *Tech Directions, 56*, 14–15.

Varenhorst, B. B. (1984a). Peer counseling: Past promises, current status, and future directions. In S. D. Brown & R. W. Lent (Eds.), *Handbook of counseling psychology* (pp. 716–750). New York: Wiley.

Varenhorst, B. B. (1984b). Training adolescents as peer counselors. *Personnel and Guidance Journal, 53*, 271–275.

Veysey, L. (1973). Stability and experiment in the American undergraduate curriculum. In C. Kaysen (Ed.), *Content and context: Essays on college education* (pp. 1–63). New York: McGraw-Hill.

Vogt, J. W. (1991). Dual enrollment articulation practices between Virginia's community colleges and public schools. (1989–1990). (Doctoral dissertation, University of Virginia, Charlottesville, 1991). *Dissertation Abstracts International, 53*(03A), 0737.

Wasmund v. LaGuardia, 287 N.Y. 417 (1942).

Waters, D. (1990a, June 30). Regent says high school can be saved. *The [Memphis] Commercial Appeal*, p. B1.

Waters, D. (1990b, July 4). Middle college stirs ill feelings. *The [Memphis] Commercial Appeal*, pp. B1–2.

Wechsler, H. S. (1977). *The qualified student: A history of selective college admission in America*. New York: Wiley–Interscience.

Wechsler, H. S. (1989). *The transfer challenge: Removing barriers, maintaining commitment*. Washington, DC: Association of American Colleges.

Wehlage, G. (1983). The marginal high school student: Defining the problem and searching for policy. *Children and Youth Services Review, 5*, 321–342.

Wehlage, G., & Rutter, R. A. (1986, Spring). Dropping out: How do schools contribute to the problem? *Teachers College Record, 87*, 374–392.

Wehlage, G., Rutter, R. A., Smith, G., Lesko, N., & Fernandez, R. (1989). *Reducing the risk: Schools as communities of support*. New York: Falmer Press.

Whitlock, B. W. (1978). *Don't hold them back: A critique and guide to new school–college articulation models*. New York: College Entrance Examination Board.

Wilbur, F. P. (1990). *National directory of school–college partnerships.* Washington, DC: American Association for Higher Education.

Wilcox, E. T. (1960, Spring). Advanced placement at Harvard. *The College Board Review, 41,* 17–20.

Williams, B. (1987, November 29). School once going to seed now sprouting new hope. *Los Angeles Times,* p. 2:1.

Williams, D. E. (1979). Descriptive-analytic survey of experiential/career education at LaGuardia Community College. (Doctoral dissertation, Teachers College, Columbia University, New York, 1979). *Dissertation Abstracts International, 40*(09A), 4867.

Wilson, C. L. (1971). *The open-access curriculum.* Boston: Allyn & Bacon.

Wilson, J. W. (Ed.). (1978). *Developing and expanding cooperative education.* San Francisco: Jossey-Bass.

Wilson, J. W., & Lyons, E. H. (1961). *Work–study college programs: Appraisal and report of the study of cooperative education.* New York: Harper & Brothers.

Wilson, T. H. (1939, April). The first four-year junior college. *Junior College Journal, 9,* 361–365.

Woodring, P. (1970). *Investment in innovation: An historical appraisal of the Fund for the Advancement of Education.* Boston: Little, Brown.

Yount, R., & Magrun. N. (1989). *School/college collaboration: Teaching at-risk youth.* Washington, DC: Council of Chief State School Officers.

Zumeta, W. (1996a). A case study: Where can we put all the students? *Thought & Action, 12*(2), 34–35.

Zumeta, W. (1996b, January). *Where to put all the students? Dilemmas of higher education access and finance in the state of Washington* (Working Paper 95-10). Seattle: University of Washington, Graduate School of Public Affairs.

Index

Absenteeism, 100, 172
  and Cullen years at MCHS, 79
  and first years of MCHS, 59–61
  and Greenberg years at MCHS, 66–68
  MCHS success and, 140–141
  and replications of MCHS, 96, 112, 129
Academic engagement, academic reform, 66–89
Academy for Educational Development (AED), 36, 44, 56, 61–62, 65, 170
Ackerman, T., 128
Adams, F. C., 24
Advanced placement (AP), 16, 149
  and high school to college transitions, 158, 160–163, 165
  and replications of MCHS, 100–101
African-Americans, xiii, 20, 42
  cooperative education and, 24
  and Cullen years at MCHS, 82–83
  CUNY admissions policy and, 26
  dropout rates among, x
  high school-college integration and, 2
  and replications of MCHS, 97, 109–110, 113, 130, 134
Agenda: Middle College Advisory Committee, 34, 55–56, 153
Aikin, W., 3
Alba, R. D., 19, 26
Allen, H. L., 150
American Academy of Arts and Sciences, 24
American Jewish Congress, 49
Ames, L. B., 169
Anderson, Connie, 122
Anderson, M., 108

Angell, James Rowland, 9, 11
Angus, D. L., 143
Anker, Irving, 49
Antioch College, 23
Armor, D. J., 74
Arrick, Charlotte, 121
Asian-Americans, 95
Associate of arts degrees, 16, 34
Astin, A. W., 19
Astin, H. S., 19
Atlantic Community College (ACC), 133–134
Atlantic County Alternative High School, 133–134
At-risk students, xiv–xv, 139–140, 167–168
  adapting educational practices to needs of, 140, 142–149
  and Cullen years at MCHS, 78–79, 81, 89
  and first years of MCHS, 55, 61–62, 64
  and Greenberg years at MCHS, 67, 69–70, 74, 77
  high school-college collaborations and, 142–144, 146, 148–149, 151–152, 154–156
  and high school to college transitions, 160–162, 164–165
  Lieberman's background and, 28
  MCHS administration and, 46–47
  as MCHS clientele, x, xiv, 1, 19, 27, 29, 31, 33, 36, 41–42, 51, 53
  MCHS components and, 33, 36, 41–44
  MCHS success and, 140, 142
  and replications of MCHS, 94, 96, 100–101, 104–105, 107, 111–113, 116–117, 119, 122–123,

At-risk students (*continued*)
  128–129, 133, 135–136, 145–
  149, 152, 154, 168
Attendance. *See* Absenteeism

Baccalaureate degrees, 14, 17, 34
Bangert-Drowns, R. L., 79
Bank Street College of Education, 91
Bard College, 17, 159
Barnard, Frederick A. P., 21
Barnard College, 27–28, 143
Barton, Laurel, 123
Baruch College, 76
Battersbee, Natalie, 108, 118–121, 138
"Belmont High Comes Back," 117
Benware C. A., 81
Berger, Ken, 61–62
Berkeley Institute, 27
Berman, D., 96
Bernstein, A., 115, 128, 131, 172
Blanchard, R. E., 7
Blase, J., 85
Blase, J. R., 85
Blaustein, Lee, 133
Blos, P., 10
Board of Higher Education (BHE) in the
  City of New York, 22, 24–27, 29,
  36, 45–50, 55, 65, 170
Bongo Theater Travelling Herd, 69–70
Born, T., 87–88, 110
Borough of Manhattan Community Col-
  lege, 23
Botstein, Leon, 17, 159–160
Bowen, Raymond, 31, 81, 91, 108–115,
  171–172
Bowker, Albert H., 22, 26, 149
Boyer, Ernest L., 50, 94, 172
Brawley, Tawana, 82
Bremer, J., 40
Breneman, D. W., 15
Britton, Leonard, 106
Bronx Community College (BCC), 95,
  97–98, 147
Brookdale Community College, 133
Brooklyn College, 95–96
Brooklyn College Academy (BCA), 95–
  96, 98
Budget and Funding Rationale, 43, 48

Burdman, P., 162
Bush, T., 96
Butler, Nicholas Murray, 9, 14

California, University of, 161
California Community Colleges, 128
Callagy, A. K., 75, 95
Campbell, D. S., 11
Camper, D., 157
Cardinal Principles of Education, 3
Carey, R., 72
Carlton, B., 122
Carnegie Commission on Higher Educa-
  tion, 14, 17–18, 24–25, 29, 32–33,
  47, 149, 172
Carnegie Corporation, 17, 20, 29, 32, 44
Carnegie Council for Policy Studies in
  Higher Education, 77
Carnegie Foundation for the Advance-
  ment of Teaching (CFAT), 3, 29,
  94
Casserly, P. L., 158
Center for New Schools, 44, 61
Center for Urban Ethnography, 77, 79,
  82–83, 86–87, 89–90
Chaffey Junior College, 15
Charton, Harry, 50
Cheit, E., 149
Chelius, Thomas V., 133
Chen, X., 142–143
Cicourel, A. V., 74
Cincinnati Technical College, 107–108
City College of New York (CCNY), 28,
  146, 152
  admissions policy of, 21–22, 26
  MCHS administration and, 45–46
  sit-in at, xiii
  Townsend Harris High School of, 21,
    46
City University of New York (CUNY),
  22–29, 77, 149, 155, 165–168
  admissions policy of, x, xiii–xiv, 19–
    20, 22, 25–26, 29, 54
  Center for the Advanced Study of Edu-
    cation at, 82
  cooperative education and, 24–25
  and Cullen years at MCHS, 82
  Faculty Senate of, 85

and high school to college transitions, 165–166
Lieberman's background and, 28–29
MCHS administration and, 44–47
MCHS approval and, 49
MCHS components and, 33–34, 39, 44
MCHS design and, 29–30, 32–33
MCHS success and, 141
and replications of MCHS, 97–98, 120, 133
Clark, Burton R., 55, 74, 104, 136
Clark, T. A., 141–42, 172
Clark University, 9
Clift, R. T., 150–151
Clinton, Bill, 159
Cohen, A. M., 24
Cohen, D. K., 1, 78, 135
College, colleges. *See also* High school-college integration, high school-college cooperation
    access to, in New York City, 21–22
    atmosphere of, 15
    entrance requirements of, 2–4, 6, 13
    facilitating transition from high school to, 158–166
    finances of, 14–15
    house model and, 40–41
    preparatory departments of, 2, 4, 167
College classes, 4, 169
    and adapting to at-risk students' needs, 148
    and Cullen years at MCHS, 85
    and first years of MCHS, 58–60
    and Greenberg years at MCHS, 71, 76
    and high school to college transitions, 160–165
    MCHS success and, 141
    and replications of MCHS, 98, 110, 114–115, 118, 121, 124–126, 130–131
College Discovery, 26, 149, 166–167
Colleges of the Forgotten Americans: A Profile of State Colleges and Regional Universities (Dunham), 29, 32
Columbia University, 14, 21

Colwell, L. H., 163
Committee of Ten, 3, 14, 53
Committee Report, 169
Community College Planning Center, 22
Community colleges, 15–17, 139, 169–171
    and adapting to at-risk students' needs, 142–149
    admissions policies of, 15–16, 21–22, 26
    commitments from, 144–145
    cooperative education and, 24–25
    growth of, x, 16–17, 23
    high school-college collaborations and, 152–158
    high school-college integration and, 4–7, 13–17, 19, 29–30
    and high school to college transitions, 159–164
    MCHS administration and, 45, 49
    MCHS approval and, 49–50
    MCHS components and, 35–36, 42
    of New York City, 21–26
    and replications of MCHS, 95, 97–98, 101–137, 146–149, 153–154, 158, 167
Comprehensive design, 145–146
Comprehensive School Improvement Program (CSIP), 101
Conant, James B., 29, 40
Concord Academy, 16
Continuity and Discontinuity: Higher Education and the Schools, 17–18, 172
Contra Costa College (CCC), 103, 107–108, 153–154, 164–165
    success of replication at, 122–128, 136
Cooke, R. L., 8
Cooper, D. L., 165
Cooper, William J., 8, 10
Cooperative education, 30–34, 51, 70–78, 171
    and adapting to at-risk students' needs, 145, 147–148
    and Cullen years at MCHS, 77–78, 92, 142
    and first years of MCHS, 63–64

Cooperative education (*Continued*)
    and Greenberg years at MCHS, 68,
        70–77, 145
    at LaGuardia Community College, 23–
        25, 27, 30
    MCHS components and, 33–34, 38–
        39, 41
    MCHS design and, 30–32
    MCHS success and, 141–142
    and replications of MCHS, 98,
        103, 105–107, 114, 116, 118,
        120–121, 126, 131, 134, 147–148
Course duplication, 4, 7, 9, 14, 17, 166
Crooks, K. A., 160, 162
Cross, K. P., 147
Crossland, R., 163
Csikszentimihalyi, M., 160
Cuban, L., 3, 41, 170
Cullen, Cecilia L., 140–142, 144, 146–
        47, 154–157, 165, 169–171
    MCHS under, 70–71, 77–93, 142, 155
    and replications of MCHS, 94–95,
        106, 108, 111, 115, 123, 129–
        130, 138
Curriculum, curricula, 48, 54–55, 169,
        171–172
    and adapting to at-risk students' needs,
        143, 146, 148–149
    of CCNY, 21
    and Cullen years at MCHS, 70, 77, 80,
        82–86, 91–92, 142
    duplication of, 4, 7, 9, 14, 17, 166
    and first years of MCHS, 55–56, 58–
        59, 62–64
    and Greenberg years at MCHS, 69–75
    high school-college collaborations and,
        149–150, 153, 166
    and high school to college transitions,
        158–162, 166
    and history of high school-college inte-
        gration, 3, 5–14, 16–17
    house model and, 40–41
    of LaGuardia Community College,
        23–25
    MCHS components and, 33–34, 37–
        39, 42
    MCHS design and, 31–32
    MCHS success and, 142

    and replications of MCHS, 96–98,
        101–102, 106, 111, 113–116,
        119–120, 126, 130, 132, 134–
        136, 146, 149
Curtis, Christine, 128–131, 164
Cuyahoga Community College, 107–108,
        132, 153

Dallas Independent School District
        (DISD), 128–131, 164
Dalton School, 28, 41, 143
Daly, W. T., 150
Daytop Village, 79
Dearing, Bruce, 50
Deci, E. L., 81
DeLany, B., 74
Denniston, S., 60, 71, 76, 81, 140
DeRosenroll, D. A., 80
Developmental stages, developmental
        theory
    and Greenberg years at MCHS, 74
    and history of high school-college inte-
        gration, 9–12, 14
Dickens, Alice, 133
Diener, T., 13
Discipline
    and first years of MCHS, 59–61
    and Greenberg years at MCHS, 68, 70,
        76
    and replications of MCHS, 96, 113,
        119–120, 123–125, 131
Dispenzieri, A., 26
Doll, R. C., 64
Downey, Martha, 50
Doxey, W. H., 19
Dropouts, dropout rates, x, 139–141,
        172. *See also* At-risk students
    high school-college collaborations and,
        150
    and history of high school-college inte-
        gration, 8, 14, 19
    MCHS components and, 36
    MCHS design and, 29, 32
    MCHS success and, 140–141
    and replications of MCHS, 109, 125
Duffus, R. L., 3
Dugan, John, 133
Duke, D. L., 40

Dunham, E. Alden, 20, 29–32, 47, 170
Dzuback, M. A., 8

Eaton, J. S., 26
Eby, F., 5, 10, 15
Economic Opportunities Act, 23
Economics, 17, 32–34, 46–51, 164, 170
    and adapting to at-risk students' needs,
        142, 144, 146–147
    cooperative education and, 23–25
    and first years of MCHS, 55–56,
        59, 65
    and Greenberg years at MCHS, 68,
        71–73, 76
    of high school-college collaborations,
        7, 14–19, 149–150, 153–155, 166
    and high school to college transitions,
        159, 161–163
    and history of high school-college inte-
        gration, 7, 9, 14–19
    MCHS administration and, 46–49
    MCHS approval and, 50
    MCHS components and, 34, 36–37, 39
    MCHS design and, 29–30, 32
    and replications of MCHS, 96, 101–
        103, 105–123, 125–138, 146–
        147, 153–154
Educational Policies Commission, 16
Educational Research Department, 122
Education Department, U.S., 139,
    160–161
Eells, Walter Crosby, 11, 14–15
Ehrlich, Dan J., 61–62
8-4 plan, 7
Eight-Year Study, 3, 18
El Centro College (ECC), 103, 107–108,
    164–165
    success of replication at, 128–131
Elementary and Secondary Education
    Act, 101
11–14 plans, 5–8, 10, 92
    and high school to college transitions,
        158–159
    in practice, 12–16
Eliot, Charles W., 14
El-Khawas, E., 19
Erickson, F., 74
Eriksen, A., 40

Erikson, Erik H., 10–11
Essex County Community College, 133
Evaluation Report, 117
Evaluations, 170–171
    and Cullen years at MCHS, 79–80, 83,
        86–89
    and first years of MCHS, 55, 61
    and Greenberg years at MCHS, 76–77
    and high school to college transitions,
        158, 161–162
    MCHS components and, 44
    MCHS success and, 140–142
    and replications of MCHS, 98, 100–
        101, 107–108, 111, 126, 134–135
Evans, I. M., 138
Evanston Township High School, 41
Exploring Transfer program, 102
Extracurricular activities, 160
    and first years of MCHS, 59, 63
    and Greenberg years at MCHS, 69–70

Faculties, xiv–xv, 168, 170. *See also*
    Teacher-counselors
    and adapting to at-risk students' needs,
        143, 145–146, 148
    and Cullen years at MCHS, 78–89, 91
    and first years of MCHS, 55–56,
        58–66
    and Greenberg years at MCHS, 67–69,
        71–73, 75–76, 89
    high school-college collaborations and,
        150–157
    and high school to college transitions,
        160–162, 164
    and history of high school-college inte-
        gration, 13, 15, 18
    MCHS administration and, 47–49
    MCHS components and, 34, 42–43
    MCHS design and, 30–31
    MCHS success and, 141–142
    in New York City, 22
    recruitment of, 51, 55–56, 97, 111,
        119, 123, 130, 136
    and replications of MCHS, 95–98,
        100, 103–121, 123–128, 130–
        132, 135–137, 146, 148, 154–155
Faculty governance, 43–44, 70
    and Cullen years at MCHS, 85–89

Farrar, E., 78
Faust, Clarence, 9, 159
Fernandez, Joseph, 85
Fernandez, R., 78
Fincher-Ford, M., 160
Finney, J. E., 161
Fiorello H. LaGuardia Community Col-
    lege, xiii–xv, 23–31, 60
  administration of, 151
  admissions policy of, 26–27
  cooperative education at, 23–25,
    27, 30
  finances of, 72–73
  location of, xiii, 1, 16, 23–24, 27, 30,
    35–36, 47, 58–59, 63–64, 66–67
  Middle College High School of. *See*
    Middle College High School
  mission statement of, 25
  Office of College Security of, 60
  origins of, xiv
  secondary education provided at, 26
  Sony Annex of, 36–37
Fitz-Gibbon, C. T., 81
Ford Foundation, 9, 23, 37, 93–94, 155,
    172
  and replications of MCHS, 98–107,
    115, 123, 135, 146–147
Ford Foundation Project, 107, 118,
    133
Forsyth, Toni, 117–118
Four-School Study Committee, The, 1,
    10–11, 29, 32, 40–41
Frederick, A., 23–24
Free Academy, 21
Freedman, S. G., 41
Frey, M. W., 47–48
Friedman, Martin S., 133–134
Fund for the Advancement of Education
    (FAE), 9, 99–100
Fund for the Improvement for Postsecond-
    ary Education (FIPSE), 32
*Funding for the Proposed Middle Col-
    lege*, 47

Gaines, B. C., 162
Gaither Report, 99
Gamson, Z., 105
Gantz, J., 40

Garland, Thomas J., 109
Garms, W. I., 15
Gaudiani, C. L., 92
Gear-Up program, 150
Geiger, L. G., 13, 100, 149
Gelatt, H. B., 72
General education, 148, 159
  and history of high school-college inte-
    gration, 7–11, 13, 17–19
Georgiades, W., 42
Gesell, A., 169
Gibbons, H. E., 128
Giniger, S., 26
Glachan, M., 81
Glassboro State College, 133
Gold, B. A., 170
Goodlad, J., 78, 150
Gordon, L. D., 28
Gordon, S., 19
Gordon, Sheila, 31–32
Grant, G., 24, 78, 87, 143, 157–
    158
Great Cities-Gray Areas (GCGA),
    100–101
Greenberg, Arthur R., 19, 53, 140, 143–
    145, 147, 153–155, 158, 163,
    171
  MCHS under, 58–61, 64, 66–77, 79,
    85, 89–92, 145, 155
Gregory, L., 73, 75–76, 82–83, 90–92,
    142, 148, 171
Griffen, Richard L., 122
Gross, T. R., 150
Group counseling, 79, 81, 117, 145,
    171
Group for the Advancement of Psychia-
    try, 10
Gruber, D., 96–98
Grunfeld, K. K., 21
Guidance counselors, 165, 171
  and adapting to at-risk students' needs,
    143–145
  and Cullen years at MCHS, 79–80
  and first years of MCHS, 56, 64
  and Greenberg years at MCHS, 70
  and history of high school-college inte-
    gration, 5, 13
  MCHS administration and, 47

MCHS components and, 35,
42–43
and replications of MCHS, 106, 112,
119, 124, 130, 132, 134

Haberman, Martin, 80, 151–152
Hall, Elizabeth B., 16–17, 33, 167
Hall, G. Stanley, 9, 11, 29
Hammond, Lillian, 172
Hampel, R. L., 2
Hansen, C., 80
Hanson, H. P., 158
Harbeson, J. W., 5
Harvard University, 2, 13–14, 29, 40–41,
169
Havighurst, Robert, 20
Hawthorne, E. M., 165
Healy, Timothy, 28–29, 50
Heathers, G., 151
Henderson, A. D., 24
Hentoff, N., 170
Herbst, J., 143, 160
Herenton, Willie, 109, 112
Herman, D., 28
Higher Education Act, 24
Higher Education Amendments, 24, 32,
54
High school, high schools
college-level courses at, 4
efficiency of, 139
facilitating transition to college from,
158–166
house model of, 40–41
of New York City, 26–27
High school-college collaboration, 53–54,
90–93, 162–167, 169
at-risk students' and, 142–144,
146, 148–149, 151–152, 154–
156
cooperative education and, 148–
158
and Cullen years at MCHS, 80–87,
91–92
developmental justifications for, 9–12,
14
economics of, 7, 9, 14–19, 149–150,
153–155, 166
and 11–14 idea in practice, 12–16

and first years of MCHS, 57–66
and Greenberg years at MCHS, 66–69,
71–73, 76
and high school to college transitions,
162–166
history of, 1–19
institutional autonomy and, 155–156
MCHS administration and, 47–49
MCHS approval and, 50
MCHS components and, 35–36, 38
MCHS design and, 29–32
normative congruence and, 151–152,
154, 156–157
rationales for, 4–12
and replications of MCHS, 94, 96–
110, 113–116, 118–120, 122–
127, 129–133, 135–137, 148–
149, 152–155
structural justifications for, 6–8
Hill, C. M., 100
Hill, M. E., 15
Hill School, 169
Hispanics, x, xiii, 20, 90, 139
and replications of MCHS, 95, 97,
102, 118, 130, 134
Holland, P., 150–151
Hollander, Theodore Edward, 46, 50,
133, 135
Hollingsworth, S., 170
Horizon, 61
Horn, L. J., 142–143
Hostos Community College, 95, 97
Houle, C. O., 33
Hungar, J. Y., 102
Hunter College, 21, 28, 46, 76, 143
Hunter College High School, 21, 46,
48–49
Hutchins, Robert M., 8–10, 13, 17, 33,
99, 159
Hyland, J. L., 23
Hyllegard, D., 19, 168

Ilg, F. L., 169
Illinois Central College (ICC), 106, 108
success of replication at, 115–117
Information for New York State, 41
Interactive Mathematics Program (IMP),
84

International High School (IHS), 93, 95–96, 151

J. Sargeant Reynolds Community College, 107
Jane Addams Business Careers Center, 132
Janowitz, Morris, 43, 139, 143, 167
Jencks, C., 11
Johnson, Coltun, 102
Johnson, Lyndon, 23
Johnson, M., 150–151
Johnson, Rosa, 129
Johnstone, D. Bruce, 160
Jun, A., 164
Junior colleges. *See* Community colleges
Junior high schools, 36, 95
    and history of high school-college integration, 7, 13

Kahn, Arthur, 46
Keller, C. P., 158
Kerr, C., 53
Kibbee, Robert, 50
Kingsborough Community College, 24
Kitsuse, J. L., 74
Klohmann, E. L., 49, 106, 156–157
Knowles, A., 24
Koos, Leonard V., 4, 6–8, 10, 13, 15, 17, 29, 33, 159
Kopan, A. T., 20
Krei, M. S., 171
Kreisman, Leonard T., 133
Krug, Edward A., 2–3, 13, 41, 53, 169–170
Kuhns, E., 16
Kuner, C., 80

Labaree, D. F., 40
Labor Department, U.S., 42
Lagemann, E. C., 29
LaGuardia Community College: Profile, 25
LaGuardia Community College. *See* Fiorello H. LaGuardia Community College
Lakin, Thomas G., 118–120

Lambert, L. M., 162
Late adolescents, 35, 60, 169
    and history of high school-college integration, 4–6, 10–12
Lavin, D. E., 19, 26, 168
Lawrenceville School, 169
Lawton, M., 135
Leadership, 103
Learned, W. S., 3
LeCroy, R. Jan, 128
Leonard, R. J., 8
Lesko, N., 78
Less Time, More Options (Carnegie Commission on Higher Education), 149
Levine, A., 16–17, 53, 143, 157
Levine, D. O., 40
Lieberman, Janet E., 1, 19, 23, 27–34, 41–51, 81, 90–91, 93–96, 139–140, 170–172
    and adapting to at-risk students' needs, 142–147
    background of, 27–29
    and first years of MCHS, 55–65
    and Greenberg years at MCHS, 68, 70–74, 77
    high school-college collaborations and, 152–153, 155, 157
    MCHS administration and, 44–49
    MCHS approval and, 50
    MCHS components and, 33–34, 41–44
    MCHS design and, 27, 29–32
    MCHS success and, 140
    and replications of MCHS, 94–96, 98, 102, 105–110, 113–114, 116–119, 121, 123–124, 126, 128–129, 131–137, 146–147, 152
Light, P., 81
Lighthouse projects, 101, 105
Lillard, J. B., 12–13, 15
Lincoln Academy of Science (LAS), 95, 97
Livingston School for Girls, 28
Los Angeles City College (LACC), 117–118, 120, 162
Los Angeles Sentinel, 119
Los Angeles Southwest College (LASC), 103, 107–108, 138
    success of replication at, 117–121, 138

Los Angeles Trade–Technical College, 118
Lowell, Abbott Lawrence, 40
Lumachi, M., 60, 71, 76, 81, 140
Lynch, S. J., 158
Lyons, E. H., 23

Maeroff, Gene I., 77, 85
Magrun, N., 151
Malcolm X, 82
Malloy, Joseph C., 119, 123
Marczely, B., 85
Marland, Sidney, 25, 30
Martorana, S. V., 16
Marx, Walter, 122
Maslow, Abraham, 75
McCabe, H. M., 23
McCabe, Robert H., 106
McCarthy, J., 150–151
McCrary, 129, 131
McGrath, James J., 30, 50
McLane, C. L., 7, 15
McMullan, B. J., 96–98
McVeigh, Bob, 50
Meier, D., 40
Mercurio, J. A., 162
Merrill, George A., 8
Miami-Dade Community College, 106
Middle adolescence, 9–10
Middle College Charter High School, 76
Middle College High School (MCHS), xiv–xv, 25, 72–76, 93, 109, 141
  academic reform at, 66–77
  administration of, 44–49, 54–55, 57–93, 104, 142–145, 151, 155–157
  admissions policy of, x, xiv, 1, 19, 27, 29, 31, 33, 35–36, 41–42, 51, 53, 55–56, 70, 81, 112
  advantages of, 136
  Advisory Committee of, 63
  approval of, 49–51, 54
  at-risk students as clientele of, 140, 142–148, 160, 167
  charter school status of, 76, 93
  components of, 33–44
  designing of, 18–19, 27, 29–33, 51
  faculty governance at, 43–44, 70, 85–89

  finances of, 17, 29–30, 32–34, 36–37, 39, 46–51, 55–56, 59, 65, 68, 71–73, 76, 164, 170
  first years of, 54–66, 68, 70–71
  getting through a day at, 61–66
  goals of, 74–75
  house model of, 39–42, 62, 65, 68, 79–80, 84
  institute for redesign of, 69–76
  location of, 1, 58–59, 63–64, 67, 90, 92, 147
  plant for, 36–37
  recruitment of students for, 35–36
  replications of, 94–138, 145–149, 151–155, 157–158, 167–168
  16–20 age grouping at, 33–35
  student governance at, 43–44, 70
  success of, x–xi, 77, 81, 89–90, 93, 140–142, 157
  teacher-counselors at. *See* Teacher-counselors
  total enrollments of, 89–90
Middle College High School (Shelby State Community College), 109
Middle College High School at LaGuardia Community College, 70, 140–141, 147, 172
Middle College High School Consortium, 142–143, 148–149, 153–156, 158, 161–165
Middle College Proposals, 25, 34–39, 41, 43, 129, 147
Middle College II, 95
Middle schools, 112
Miles, M. B., 170
Miller, G. P., 72
Miller, S. R., 171
Millonzi, Joel, 61–62
Mills, 23
Mirel, J. E., 143
Mission (Middle College High School at Shelby State Community College), 109
Mitchell, Joyce Colbert, 110–115, 119
Moed, Martin, 61–62, 68, 81, 91, 157, 170
Moore, Jimmie, 116
Morgan, Arthur, 23

Morison, S. E., 40
Morisseau, J. J., 41
Moro, S. M., 162
Mott Community College, 135
Moynihan Report, 42
Murray, C. E., 87

Nadelstern, E., 96
National Center for Education Statistics, 139, 160–61
National Commission on Excellence in Education, ix
National Council of Teachers of Mathematics, 84
National Education Association (NEA), 3, 8, 13
National Institute of Education, 30
National Society for the Study of Education, 10
National Study of Charter Schools, 171
Nation at Risk, A, ix
Nelson, S. C., 15
New Jersey, failure of replication in, 132–135
Newman, F., 24
Newman, G. C., 23
Newmann, F., 78
New York City, 21–27
  access to public higher education in, 21–22
  replications of MCHS in, 94–98, 105, 132–133, 151
New York City High School Principals' Association, 81
New York City Technical College, 21–22
New York Community College, 21–22
New York State Education Department (NYSED), 44–45, 50, 133
New York State Requirements, 63
New York State Textbook Law, 47
New York Times, The 39, 45, 49, 50, 77
New York University, 28, 45
Nixon, Richard, 25
Normative congruence, 151–152, 154, 156–157

North Central Association (NCA) of Colleges and Secondary Schools, 13, 100, 149
Northeastern University, 24
Notes on Visitors, 132
Nyquist, Ewald, 50

Office of Financial Management, 163
Olexa, C., 74
Omnibus School Aids Act, 162
Open Admissions, x, xiii–xiv, 44, 133, 166–168
  CUNY on, 20, 25–26, 29
  high school preparation and, 26
  MCHS design and, 29, 31
  and replications of MCHS, 109
Open-Door College, The (Clark), 136
Orlans, H., 157
Ort, S. W., 85, 90, 171
Overacker, I., 18, 151

Paisley, P. O., 165
Palmer, J. C., 104, 152
Pasadena Junior College (PJC), 5, 13
Pascarella, E. T., 44
Pedersen, R. P., 4, 14, 26, 152
Peer counseling, 132, 171
  and adapting to at-risk students' needs, 143, 145
Peer teaching, 82
Peltz, Fillmore K., 55–57, 62, 71
Peterson, Karen, 30–32, 47
Peterson, R. E., 158
Phelps, D. G., 121
Phelps, R. E., 165
Phillips Academy, 169
Phillips Exeter Academy, 169
Pianelli, M. A., 135
Planning, 103
Postsecondary Enrollment Options Program (PSEOP), 162–163
Poteat, Carol M., 53, 55–66, 68, 70–71, 155
Poverty
  cooperative education and, 23
  culture of, ix–x

CUNY admissions policy and, 26
Lieberman's background and, 28
and replications of MCHS, 96, 116,
    121–122
Powell, A. G., 78, 142, 158
President's Commission on Higher Educa-
    tion, 6–7, 13, 16–17, 19, 44
President's Science Advisory Committee,
    23, 35
Princeton University, 29, 169
Principals, 81, 170
    and adapting to at-risk students' needs,
        142–149
    and first years of MCHS, 55, 65–66
    high school-college collaborations and,
        153–156, 158
    and high school to college transitions,
        161–165
    and history of high school-college inte-
        gration, 2–3, 5, 15
    MCHS administration and, 48
    MCHS components and, 35, 43
    MCHS success and, 140, 142, 157
    recruitment of, 51
    and replications of MCHS, 97, 100,
        103–105, 110–121, 123–132,
        134–138, 145–149, 153–155
Project Advance, 162
*Proposal for Innovative Partnership Activ-
    ities*, 115
Proposal Narrative, 124

Qualified Student, The (Wechsler), xiii
Queensborough Community College, 23,
    25

Ramaswami, S., 158
Rating Sheet, 106
Ray, M., 109, 113
Reagan, Ronald, ix
*Recommendation for Grant/FAP Ac-
    tion—Supplement 86-585*, 107
Records of Interviews, 30-32, 47
Reel, G., 115
Reese, William J., xi, 2
Reisberg, L, 161–162
Remediation, remedial courses, 2–5, 167
    and Cullen years at MCHS, 85

and first years of MCHS, 56, 64
and Greenberg years at MCHS,
    73, 76
and history of high school-college inte-
    gration, 3, 5
MCHS administration and, 47
MCHS components and, 34, 36
MCHS design and, 32
and replications of MCHS, 108–109
Resistance, 103–104, 107, 111–116,
    119, 137–138
Reynolds, Ann, 165
Reynolds, J. W., 16
Rhoads, R. A., 108
Richmond Unified School District
    (RUSD), 122–128, 164
Riesman, D., 11, 16, 23, 53, 143,
    157–158
Rippey, D., 128
Rogers, David, 18, 45–46
Rose, Candy, 122–123, 125, 127, 165
Rosenbaum, James E., 74, 171
Rosenberg, Burt, 60, 71, 76, 81, 135,
    140
Rosenberg, Gustave, 22
Rossman, J. E., 19
Rothschild, E., 158
Roundtree, G. D., 102
Rowan College, 133
Running Start program, 163
Rutter, R. A., 78
Ryder, K. G., 24

Sadovnik, A. R., 41, 142
St. Hill, Winston, 68–69
San Diego Community College, 107
Sanford, Nevitt, 10–12
San Jose Community College, 136
Sauer, K. R., 163
Schafer, W. E., 74
Schmidt, P., 16, 163
School membership, 78–89
Schreiber, V., 80
Scott, C. W., 100
Scribner, Harvey B., 45, 47
Sealander, J., 23
Seattle Community College, 135, 171
SEEK, 26, 149, 166–167

Semel, S. F., 41, 142
Sena, Tom, 68–69, 71–74, 76, 148
Sexton, J. A., 5
Shapiro, B. C., 150
Shapiro, Elliott, 170
Shapiro, H., 102
Shelby State Community College, 91,
    103, 106, 165, 172
  success of replication at, 108–115
Shenker, Joseph, 1, 19, 24–27, 44–51,
    91–93, 138, 147, 157, 166, 170
  cooperative education and, 24–25
  and Cullen years at MCHS, 79,
    85, 89
  and first years of MCHS, 55, 63–64
  and Greenberg years at MCHS, 68
  MCHS administration and, 44–49
  MCHS approval and, 49–51
  MCHS components and, 33, 37
  MCHS design and, 27, 29–33
  MCHS success and, 140
  and replications of MCHS, 96, 98,
    104, 155
Shoehorn, Operation, 22
Silberstein, R. A., 19, 26
Silverman, Myra, 122–128, 154, 164
Simon's Rock Early College, 16–17, 33,
    66–67, 159, 167
Sirotnik, K., 150
6-4-4 plans, 5–8, 10, 13, 15–16
*16–20: The Liberal Education of an Age
    Group*, 11, 32, 41
16–20 age grouping
  and high school to college transitions,
    159–160
  MCHS components and, 33–35
Sizer, T., 78, 143
Smith, G., 78
Sockett, H., 170
South Mountain Community College,
    107–108
Spielman, Lise S., 121
Stanford University, 7, 11
State University of New York (SUNY),
    40, 44–45, 50, 77, 167
Stephens, C. W., 24
Stocking, W. R., Jr., 41
Stoel, C. F., 134–135, 158

Stone, E., 46
Strong, M., 73, 75–76, 82–83, 90–92,
    148, 171
Students
  at-risk. *See* At-risk students
  governance by, 43–44, 70
  profiles of, 23
  recruitment of, 35–36, 55–56, 81, 86,
    90, 97, 100, 112, 117, 119–120,
    122–124, 128–130, 132–136, 166
  terminal, 2, 6, 25, 135
*Summary and Clarification of Middle Col-
    lege Plan*, 32, 36–37, 43, 55
*Summary of Activity on Middle College
    Proposal*, 29
Summary of Middle College Activity, 49
*Summary of Middle College Grant Activ-
    ity*, 52, 55
Summary of 1987 Evaluations, 106
Sweeney, M., 73, 75–76, 82–83, 90–92,
    148, 171
Syracuse University (SU), 162

Task Force on School Cultivation,
    102
Taylor, I. K., 163
Taylor, Karl, 116
Teacher-counselors
  and Cullen years at MCHS, 78–80
  and first years of MCHS, 55, 64–65
  and Greenberg years at MCHS, 70–71,
    79
  MCHS components and, 42–43
Teacher education, 101, 151
Teachers. *See* Faculties
Tech Prep Middle College (TPMC), 135
Testing. *See* Evaluations
Texas Higher Education Coordinating
    Board, 160
They Went to College Early (report),
    100
Thorndike, E. L., 11
Tierney, W. G., 164
Tinto, V., 44, 162
Tomlinson, C. A., 158
Transfer Opportunity Program, 117
Trickett, E. J., 40
Trump, J. L., 42

Turner, R., 74
Tussman, J., 53, 143
Tutoring programs, 64
12-2 configuration, 13
Tyack, D., 3, 41, 170
Tyler, J. L., 96–98
Tyler, Ralph W., 10–11, 23, 29

Union County Community College, 106, 108
  failure of replication at, 134–135
Union County Middle College (UCMC), 134–135
Union County Technical Institute, 134
United Federation of Teachers, 88
University Heights High School (UHHS), 95, 97–98, 147
University of Chicago, 20
  College of, 8, 33, 99, 158
  and high school to college transitions, 158–160
  and history of high school-college integration, 6, 8–10, 17
University of Michigan, 40, 165–166
University of Washington, 146
Urahn, S., 163
Urban Community College Transfer Opportunity Program (UCCTOP), 102, 106, 108, 117

Valadez, J. R., 108
Valentine, J. A., 158
Vandenberg, V., 135
Varenhorst, B. B., 72, 80
Vassar College, 27–28, 102, 142–143
Veal, M. L., 150–151
Veysey, L., 11
Vista Community College, 122
Vocational courses, 163
  cooperative education and, 24–25

and history of high school-college integration, 3, 5, 8
  MCHS components and, 36
  MCHS design and, 32
  and replications of MCHS, 102, 112, 117, 135
Vogt, J. W., 163–165
von Moschzisker, M., 40

Ward, F. Champion, 9
Warren, S. T., 108, 121
Washtenaw Technical Middle College (WTMC), 135
Wasmund v. LaGuardia, 46
Waters, D., 111–113
Wayne State University, 40, 108, 146
Wechsler, Harold S., xiii, 2–4, 8, 14, 19, 144, 166
Wehlage, Gary, 78
Weintraub, Ruth G., 61–62, 170
Whitlock, Baird W., 16–17, 66–68, 142, 167
Wilbur, F. P., 150, 162
Wilcox, E. T., 158
Williams, B., 118
Williams, D. E., 23
Wilson, C. L., 64
Wilson, J. W., 23–24
Wilson, Malcolm, 50, 95
Wilson, T. H., 5
Women, 2, 16, 28
Wood, B. D., 3
Wood, Santiago, 122–123
Woodring, P., 23, 100

Yale University, 9, 40–41, 169
Yount, R., 151

Zumeta, W., 163
Zusman, A., 165

About the Author

Harold S. Wechsler is professor of education at the Margaret S. Warner Graduate School of Education and Human Development, University of Rochester. He previously chaired the programs in higher education at Northwestern University and the University of Chicago, and edited the higher education publications of the National Education Association.

A frequent writer on the history of access to higher education, Wechsler is the author of *The Qualified Student: A History of Selective College Admission in America* (1977) and *The Transfer Challenge: Removing Barriers, Maintaining Commitment* (1989). He co-authored *Jewish Learning in American Universities: The First Century* (1994) and *The New Look: The Ford Foundation and the Revolution in Business Education* (1988), and co-edited *The History of Higher Education*, Second Edition (1997), an anthology. He serves on the academic council of the American Jewish Historical Society and the board of directors of Hillel: The Foundation for Jewish Campus Life, and previously served on the boards of the Pew Center for At-Risk Students and the Rochester Educational Access Coalition.

Wechsler edits the *NEA Almanac of Higher Education*, is an associate editor of *Urban Education*, and serves on the editorial board of *Liberal Education*. He previously edited *Thought and Action: The NEA Higher Education Journal*, co-edited the *History of Higher Education Annual*, and was associate editor and book review editor of the *American Journal of Education*.

Harold Wechsler holds an A.B. (1967) from Columbia College, and an M.A. (1969) and Ph.D. (1974) from the Department of History, Columbia University. In 1969, he was chosen one of the Greatest Mets Fans. He, his wife, Lynn Dorothy Gordon, and his children, Abigail Gordon Wechsler and Samuel Benjamin Wechsler, live in the Town of Brighton, near Rochester, New York.